W9-CZZ-795

What is Genocide?

For Annabel, always and forever

What is Genocide?

Martin Shaw

polity

Copyright © Martin Shaw 2007

The right of Martin Shaw to be identified as Author of this Work has been
asserted in accordance with the UK Copyright, Designs and Patents Act 1988.

First published in 2007 by Polity Press

Polity Press
65 Bridge Street
Cambridge CB2 1UR, UK

Polity Press
350 Main Street
Malden, MA 02148, USA

All rights reserved. Except for the quotation of short passages for the purpose of
criticism and review, no part of this publication may be reproduced, stored in a
retrieval system, or transmitted, in any form or by any means, electronic,
mechanical, photocopying, recording or otherwise, without the prior permission
of the publisher.

ISBN-10: 0-7456-3182-7
ISBN-13: 978-07456-3182-0
ISBN-10: 0-7456-3183-5 (pb)
ISBN-13: 978-07456-3183-7 (pb)

A catalogue record for this book is available from the British Library.

Typeset in 10.5 on 13 pt Monotype Times
by Servis Filmsetting Ltd, Manchester
Printed and bound in Great Britain by MPG Books Ltd, Bodmin, Cornwall

The publisher has used its best endeavours to ensure that the URLs for external
websites referred to in this book are correct and active at the time of going to
press. However, the publisher has no responsibility for the websites and can make
no guarantee that a site will remain live or that the content is or will remain
appropriate.

Every effort has been made to trace all copyright holders, but if any have been
inadvertently overlooked the publishers will be pleased to include the necessary
credits in any subsequent reprint or edition.

For further information on Polity, visit our website: www.polity.co.uk

HV
6322.7
.S53
2007

Contents

Preface and
Acknowledgements

This book grew out of my critical introduction to the study of organized violence in modern society, *War and Genocide*, which Polity published in 2003. Even while writing that study, the first extension of my longstanding interest in war into the topic of genocide, I felt that I had proposed a radical revision of the terms of genocide debate without – because of the volume's textbook format – fully addressing the debate itself. I began work on an article that would remedy this deficiency. This began to look as though it would need to be rather longer than any journal would tolerate, so instead I proposed a short book – still conceived as a long essay – and Polity agreed to publish this too. But still the project continued to grow and I applied to the Economic and Social Research Council for time to make the book more substantial. The Research Fellowship that I was granted in 2004 and 2005 enabled me to write this book, as well as to finish *The New Western Way of War* which discusses violence against civilians in a different context. I am very grateful to the council for this most generous award, as well as for the encouraging and thought-provoking comments of its anonymous reviewers. I want to express my appreciation for the patience and understanding of all at Polity who dealt with the changing plans and timescales of the book project, the support of my editor, Emma Longstaff, and the useful comments of the reviewers. Intellectually, I have many debts that will be obvious from the text. My Sussex colleagues, John Holmwood and William Outhwaite, gave valuable advice on reading. Participation in the founding conference of the European (now International) Network of Genocide Studies, in Berlin in 2005, enabled me to put faces to many names that I had come across in my reading; I should like to thank all those who welcomed me into the field. Presentations to the Historical Sociology working group of the British International Studies Association, the Sociology Department at Cambridge University and the Justice and Violence Research Centre at Sussex, as well as exchanges with my Master's students on Genocide in World Politics, also helped me to clarify my ideas. As usual, however, they remain my sole responsibility.

Martin Shaw
Brighton, 2006

Introduction

1

The Sociological Crime

Social classification and genocide

This book addresses the question: how should we understand the idea of genocide? Genocide has been a central topic of current politics several times in the last two decades, especially over Bosnia and Rwanda. Its history has also been a topic of controversy, in countries such as Germany, Japan and Turkey over murderous violence in the two world wars, and in North America and Australia over earlier violence against indigenous peoples. The spectre of the archetypal genocide, the Nazi Holocaust, stalks twenty-first-century relations between Israelis and Palestinians. In many other places in today's world, allegations of genocide are made and, almost invariably, disputed. Few ideas are as important, but in few cases are the meaning and relevance of a key idea less clearly agreed.

From the point of view of politics, therefore, it is very important that the idea of genocide should be clarified, and one would expect that scholarship would have something to offer. Genocide studies have indeed made important advances in contemporary academia, and should have a considerable amount to contribute to public debate. However, scholarship has mostly been legal and historical – the new international tribunals established for the Yugoslav and Rwandan cases have produced important cases that have been analysed, and historical research has fanned out from the Holocaust to many other episodes. Yet amidst the array of often impressive case and comparative studies, the debate on what genocide means has hardly advanced since the beginning of the 1990s. Many scholars (not just lawyers) even uncritically use the

1948 Genocide Convention as their benchmark, despite some generally admitted inadequacies in its framework. This situation means that, despite many insights, scholarship has inadequate answers to the vexed question of the meaning of genocide. When new challenges arise (for example, over the crisis in Darfur, Sudan, to which I return in my final chapter) the same confused debate takes place over whether attacks on civilians constitute 'genocide', 'ethnic cleansing' or just the excesses of a dirty 'civil war', almost as though similar arguments had not already raged over Bosnia and Rwanda a decade earlier. Academic arguments often seem as unclear as their political counterparts. The social sciences, in which one would expect conceptual clarification to occur, have had relatively little to contribute to the growth of genocide studies.

This book therefore takes an unremittingly – and unapologetically – conceptual look at genocide, although I try hard to show how conceptual arguments are related to historical cases and contemporary disputes. The book argues that genocide studies have lost some of the central insights of their founding thinker, Raphael Lemkin, and that the Genocide Convention (despite some real strengths) started a process of narrowing his core idea that many subsequent academic writers (despite some important advances) have unfortunately continued. The book criticizes some of the 'new' concepts introduced in recent decades – especially 'ethnic cleansing' – and argues that 'genocide' still offers a better overall framework for understanding violence against civilians. Indeed the book highlights how the fact that the victims are generally 'civilians' is, strangely, missing from how genocide is understood, and that introducing this idea helps clarify some of the confusion surrounding the concept. Above all, this book argues that genocide studies are stuck at the preliminary stage of concept formation, defining genocide primarily in terms of the 'intentions' of the 'perpetrators', rather than looking at the *structure of conflict* within which attempts to destroy populations and groups are played out. I aim, therefore, to construct a more sociologically adequate concept of genocide, the foundations for which are laid through the second half of the book. My concept is summarized in 'definitional' form at the beginning of the final chapter, to which impatient readers may turn before, hopefully, returning to the justification in the intervening chapters.

Studying genocide?

In this introductory chapter, before I launch into detailed argument about the origins, development and future of the genocide idea, I aim to provide fuller justification for the approach outlined above. I am aware that, to many, 'definitional' discussion over horrendous experiences of violence can seem beside the point. Indeed to ask *how* we should study genocide merely seems to beg other questions: should we *study* genocide, and do we *need* concepts? On this subject, normal academic assumptions cannot be taken for granted. The Auschwitz survivor Charlotte Delbo spoke of 'useless knowledge' when she referred to experiences that were 'so dark as to be unforgettable but also so overpowering that the more one encounters their stark realities – even in reading about them, let alone in the flesh or in personal memory – the more likely we are to be disoriented and overwhelmed by them.'[1] Study could help to overcome disorientation – but it might also compound it. Genocide has often been seen as involving murderous tendencies so horrible and irrational as to be both utterly exceptional and virtually inexplicable. It can seem devaluing to discuss them within the explanatory frameworks that scholars adopt. This crime of crimes demands more than a normal commitment to scholarship and truth. Study of the Holocaust and genocide, John Roth argued, 'presupposes values that are not contained in historical study alone. . . . Any debate . . . is worthwhile just to the extent that it never loses sight of the fact that *ethical reasons* are the most important ones for studying these dark chapters in history.'[2] Here scholars must bear witness, show solidarity with victims, and stand unequivocally on one side of the historical process.

And yet there are many different victims, in many different political circumstances. Sometimes one group of victims – or rather people of the same identity, speaking in their name – become perpetrators of new crimes, making new victims. Sometimes powerful governments, adopting a victim group's cause, expose other civilian populations to violence. Shockingly, genocidal regimes themselves appropriate the genocide critique: in Serbia, 'genocide was a favorite rhetorical device for the nationalist policy-makers and hatred-mongers. . . . *genocide* was the most overused word in . . . [Yugoslav and Serbian President] Slobodan Milošević's vocabulary.'[3] Studying genocide, we can move quickly from straightforward good and evil into murky political waters.

Precisely because scholars come to the study of genocide with moral commitments, they are not immune to these problems. Israel Charny has even claimed that 'jingoistic/ideological wars (above and beyond a healthy diversity of ideas and emphases) . . . are going on in Holocaust and genocide studies', with 'a nasty lack of reverence for the victims'.[4] We do not think of scholars as practitioners of denial, and they rarely engage in its most basic form, literal, factual or blatant denying of 'the fact or knowledge of the fact'. However, they are much more open to interpretative denial, in which 'the raw facts (something happened) are not being denied. Rather, they are given a different meaning from what seems apparent to others.'[5] They may also be involved in rationalization or implicatory denial, in which 'there is no attempt to deny either the facts or their conventional interpretation. What are denied or minimized are the psychological, political or moral implications that conventionally follow.'[6] Thus while we may be clear that in principle *all* victims of genocide should be treated with respect, this does not free us from the complex political questions that often arise in studying what is at first sight the simplest moral issue.

Disciplining the study of genocide

Of course, academic study is about complexity, so the discovery that genocide is no exception seems to offer reassurance for students. Yet the morally overriding nature of victims' claims continues to gnaw away at scholarship. How can we define, describe or explain genocide if we are not contributing to exposing, punishing or preventing it? Since 'genocide studies' examine what is so abnormal, can they form a normal scholarly field? Each writer and discipline engages with these questions in their own way, bringing the strengths, constraints and histories – whether of witness or neglect, commitment or denial – of their standpoints. I shall briefly review some principal approaches before I explain my own starting points and why I believe they can contribute to clarifying genocide.

As I describe in chapter 2, 'genocide' was only invented in the 1940s and, like the international law to which it gave rise, was hardly pre-eminent in public debate during the Cold War. Only in the last quarter-century, beginning with Leo Kuper's pathbreaking *Genocide* (1981), have the founding texts of genocide studies appeared. Only in the 1990s, with the appalling new stimuli of Yugoslavia and Rwanda, was there a rapid expansion of scholarly work. Then a number of pioneering writers published important works, creating a new debate on genocide's meaning and scope. Yet even then, general and comparative studies remained poor relations of Holocaust research. Setting up a genocide course in 2001, I found my university library had roughly ten books on the Holocaust for every one on other genocides and general questions. The main academic journal was *Holocaust and Genocide Studies* – note the order of words. Holocaust studies had many upsides: the concentration of research meant that many dimensions were carefully explored and a mature historical debate developed through several phases of argument. Issues relevant to other genocides were painstakingly uncovered. Yet another effect was to unbalance genocide studies, with uneasy comparisons of the Holocaust with other episodes which gave rise to the ideological 'wars' (I discuss the issues raised in chapter 3). Meanwhile new experiences of violence against civilians in Yugoslavia led to the rapid spread of an alternative concept, 'ethnic cleansing'. Although these horrors reminded many of Nazi persecutions, there was a feeling that they fell short and deserved a different label. Genocide's scope remained confused when Rwanda erupted in 1994. At the beginning of the crisis world leaders obfuscated its genocidal character in order to avoid their responsibilities. Afterwards, few continued to deny it *was* genocide: the extreme murderousness of the attacks on Tutsis even made comparisons with Nazism unavoidable. But overall, the scope of the concept was ever more contested. 'Ethnic cleansing' still seemed – to scholars too – an easier concept to apply to many situations, with less complicated baggage. I disagree with this view, yet it highlighted real issues in the understanding of genocide. I explain in chapter 4 how genocide should be rethought to make 'cleansing' terminology redundant.

If there were still big disagreements about genocide's meaning and scope, it is not surprising that general *explanations* were even less clear. As genocide studies emerged as a general interdisciplinary field, their distinguishing feature appeared to be an agreement on the limitations of individual case studies and the need for *comparative* research.[7] Yet the call for comparative history left on one side the aim of systematic, general theoretical explanation that arises from a social-scientific approach. It threatened to brush unresolved conceptual issues under a carpet of empirical advance, yet comparison without theory was a fundamentally limited basis for progress.

Certainly, lines of enquiry developed in disciplines other than history. The most important was, not surprisingly, international law: it was in law that genocide had first been defined (by Lemkin and the Genocide Convention) and it was in the legal field that the most urgent challenges of new episodes were felt. The United Nations' establishment of the International Criminal Tribunals for Former Yugoslavia and Rwanda was a crucial stimulus. These saw the first international prosecutions and convictions for genocide (as well as war crimes and crimes against humanity) since the 1940s. Reviving the law of genocide, the tribunals clarified its scope – for example, defining 'ethnic cleansing' not as a separate crime but as a form of genocide – and made some interesting refinements of other concepts – for example, whether particular target groups had to fit into the ethnic, racial, national and religious categories of 'group' laid down by the Convention (see chapter 7). Yet the courts were adjudicating complex sociological issues that had hardly been addressed by social scientists themselves. The legal concern with *individual* responsibility of perpetrators meant that legal means were an indirect way of getting at the more fundamental issues involved. The constraints of legal standards of proof meant that law was hardly the most satisfactory discipline in which to come to balanced judgements about historical episodes, let alone creative theoretical interpretations. And yet political, historical and sociological issues were being addressed not only because cases before the courts demanded answers, but also because there was insufficient non-legal work available. So international law found itself on the front line of the world's interrogation of the concepts as well as the realities of genocide, and the disciplines of legal practice and scholarship became surrogate arenas for larger debates. Yet the limitations of legal means were often obvious: for example, the long-running trial of Milošević became bogged down in technicalities and his own use of them to achieve delays, before foundering on his death in custody. Even in an exceptional case where law provided judgement *on* historical scholarship – a British court's dismissal of a libel suit launched by the Holocaust-denying historian David Irving – the judgement clarified only a modest range of issues.[8]

Moreover, law's focus on individual crimes meant that the broad general charge of genocide was the most difficult to bring and convict on. Prosecutors often preferred easier charges whose success rates were higher. This situation led the legal scholar William Schabas to argue for a narrow interpretation of genocide's remit:

> For decades, the Genocide Convention has been asked to bear a burden for which it was never intended, essentially because of the relatively underdeveloped state of international law dealing with accountability for human rights violations. In cases of mass killing and other atrocities, attention turned inexorably to the Genocide Convention because there was little else to invoke. This . . . has changed in recent years. The law applicable to atrocities that may not meet the strict definition of genocide but that cry out for punishment has been significantly strengthened. Such offences usually fit within the definition of 'crimes against humanity', a broader concept that might be viewed as the second tier of the pyramid.[9]

Although this is too narrow an interpretation of the legal possibilities, 'genocide' probably has a more promising future as a *sociological* and *political* than as a legal concept.

Yet the mainstream social sciences are coming very slowly to the subject. Some of the most creative engagements have come from social anthropologists, but they have had to overcome the historical entanglements of their discipline with lines of thought that led, in the worst cases, to active participation in the Holocaust. Gretchen E. Schafft has claimed that

> it is not a single branch of European anthropology or only a few anthropologists who were engaged in creating or supporting events that were tied to the Holocaust's horrors. Physical anthropologists, eugenicists, ethnographers, and social anthropologists were equally busy during the first half of the 1940s in 'racial' studies, in Mendelian genetics, in ethnographic studies of prisoners of war, and in sorting people by psychological and physical characteristics. In these and in so many different ways they helped to determine the outcomes of the lives of their subjects.[10]

After the deportation of Polish academics to concentration camps in 1940, the Institut für Deutsche Ostarbeit took over university buildings in Cracow.[11] Anthropological researchers carried out ethnographic research 'in conjunction with the SS, who provided protection for the scientists and ensured the compliance of the subjects. People were taken at gunpoint to collection places where they were measured, interviewed, and sometimes fingerprinted.'[12] The infamous Auschwitz doctor Josef Mengele had qualified in anthropology as well as in medicine, and described his investigations as 'anthropological'.[13] And anthropology's involvement in genocide was not an unfortunate aberration. In the business of racial classification, 'one could move so easily from a study of differences to the conviction that differences could be gradated into a hierarchical value system.'[14] As Alexander Hinton argued, there was something inherent in the discipline's concept of social classification that lent itself: 'Diverse ways of life were compressed into relatively stable categories, a homogenizing tendency that was paralleled by the anthropological typologies of race. If later anthropologists moved towards a more pluralistic conception of cultural diversity . . . the discipline nevertheless continued to employ a concept of culture that was frequently reified.'[15] Thomas Cushman argued that, in Yugoslavia, relativistic arguments put forward by anthropologists masked and elided central historical realities, often mirroring and offering legitimation to perpetrators' accounts.[16]

Sociology and the sociological crime

Sociology's history has not revealed quite the same depths. The early twentieth-century German sociologist Max Weber – although not immune to nationalism – dismissed race as a social category, pointing out that 'the possession of a common biological inheritance by virtue

of which persons are classified as belonging to the same "race", naturally implies no sort of communal social relationship between them.'[17]
According to Wolfgang Glatzer's history, 'just about all reputable
sociologists emigrated, especially those of Jewish origin', while some
'attempted to struggle through the years of the Third Reich without
giving in to the Nazis'; only 'a third group adhered more or less openly
to Nazi ideology, defining themselves as Volkish sociologists.'[18] Yet classification was a sociological problem: not for nothing did the journalist
William L. Shirer describe the Nazis, whom he observed first-hand,
as themselves 'sociologists'.[19] Genocide was a crime of social classification, a *sociological crime*, in which racial pseudo-science perverted
the everyday activity of social science. Yet it was not sociologists who
invented the terminology for this crime, nor were they particularly open
to it. When Lemkin first outlined his idea of genocide in *Axis Rule in
Occupied Europe*, it was the *American Journal of Sociology* that printed
'the harshest review'. The reviewer, Melchior Palyi, astonishingly
'blamed Lemkin for his failure to explore the "extenuating circumstances" of Nazi behaviour.'[20]

Mostly the discipline passed over both phenomenon and idea: genocide 'was largely overlooked or suppressed by social scientists until
the 1970s.'[21] As Irving Louis Horowitz suggested, 'Many sociologists
exhibit a studied embarrassment about these issues, a feeling that intellectual issues posed in such a manner are melodramatic and unfit for
scientific discourse.'[22] They might as well join Michael Mann, who con-
fessed his work 'had neglected the extremes of human behaviour': he
'had not thought much about good and evil'.[23] For a long time text-
books neglected genocide, and most continue to ignore or marginalize
it even today. Zygmunt Bauman claimed: 'When measured against the
work done by historians or theologians, the bulk of academic sociology
looks more like a collective exercise in forgetting and eye-closing.'[24] Not
surprisingly, he concluded that 'the Holocaust has more to say about
the state of sociology than sociology in its present shape is able to add
to our knowledge of the Holocaust.'[25] His attack was fundamental:

> The nature and style of sociology has been attuned to the selfsame
> modern society it theorized and investigated; sociology has been engaged
> since its birth in a mimetic relationship with its object – or, rather, with
> the imagery of that object which it constructed and accepted as the frame
> for its own discourse. And so sociology promoted, as its own criteria of
> propriety, the same principles of rational action it visualized as constitu-
> tive of its object. It also promoted, as binding rules of [its] own discourse,
> the inadmissibility of ethical problematics in any other form but that of a
> communally-sustained ideology and thus heterogenous to sociological

(scientific, rational) discourse. *Phrases like 'the sanctity of human life' or 'moral duty' sound as alien in a sociology seminar as they do in the smoke-free, sanitized rooms of a bureaucratic office.*[26]

He concluded that we should embrace 'the task of bringing the socio-logical, psychological and political lessons of the Holocaust episode to bear on the self-awareness and practice of the institutions and the members of contemporary society.'[27] Recognizing that the Holocaust was not 'an interruption in the normal flow of history, a cancerous growth on the body of civilized society, a momentary madness among sanity',[28] we needed to see the light it cast on the underlying nature of our society and our methods of understanding.

The historian Herbert Hirsch saw some of these limitations as intrin-sic to social science: 'It is unfortunate that Holocaust and genocide studies are being pressured into a phase of social science rationality . . . only to become bogged down in the elusive variable and definition, as everyday life becomes almost entirely eliminated from their concern.'[29] Nevertheless Bauman's work proved a starting point for sociological research, informed by the very humane values that Hirsch advocated, without abandoning his discipline's generalizing concerns. Bauman's agenda, 'to open up the findings of the specialists to the general use of social science, to interpret them in a way that shows their relevance to the main themes of sociological inquiry, to feed them back into the mainstream of our discipline',[30] has guided some significant scholars. Mann, especially, showed that sociology can fruitfully reinterpret his-torical material without excluding 'ethical problematics'.[31] Weber's 'principles of rational action' could be utilized in critical analysis, explaining contextually the development of murderous intentions and violent means and their realization in political conflict. Nevertheless Mann's sociology had, as I explain later, one major problem. It adopted a very narrowed-down meaning of 'genocide' – neither that which Lemkin proposed nor the version that the UN embedded in inter-national law. Mann's focus was not genocide but 'murderous ethnic cleansing', his adaptation of this alternative term.

Revisiting concepts and classification

Of course some say we can have too much 'definitionalism', and that – whatever we call things – the important thing is concrete understanding. Nevertheless, words matter. As Weber put it: 'The apparently gratuitous tediousness involved in the elaborate definition of . . . concepts is an example of the fact that we often neglect to think out clearly what seems to be "obvious", because it is intuitively familiar.'[32] Lemkin invented 'genocide' because he wanted to describe – and highlight for counter-vailing action – a general class of violent actions. We do not have to adopt his terminology or definitions; indeed we cannot avoid modifying them. Yet if it was important that Lemkin introduced 'genocide', it is also important we are aware of how we change its meaning. If we use it in new ways, or introduce new terms to describe some of the phenomena it originally designated, we need to explain why. In any case, all serious concepts must be used coherently – with internal coherence of meaning as well as valid reference – and must be capable of explanation. For sociology to make a lasting contribution to genocide studies, it must forge adequate concepts.

The answer to the misuse of classification is not, therefore, to abandon classification. We simply cannot do this: classification is an inescapable part of human cognition and social life. Social scientists' classifications – like those of genocidists – are particular versions of this general human activity. Classification's danger is always, as Nigel Eltringham suggested, that 'we "misplace concreteness" and set out to "prove" that our abstract concepts . . . really do *correspond* to reality, rather than being contingent approximations.'[33] Genocidists go a big step further in trying to *enforce* their social classifications, making reality correspond at the cost of lives. Physical violence backs up the conceptual violence in their representations. But victims, especially resisters, also advance their own categories. They assert *their* understandings of the groups to which they belong, their versions of identity. They assert their status as *victims*, and as *civilians*, refuting genocidists' beliefs that unarmed people can be treated as combatants. And at the same time, resisters impose classifications on those who would classify *them*. They describe their persecutors' actions as *genocide* and classify them as *crimes*; they call those who attack them *perpetrators*, *criminals* and *génocidaires*. Social scientists cannot avoid referring to categories developed by these active participants, whether perpetrators, victims or bystanders. These influence our own classifications: social science is a part of society and mostly develops existing meanings rather than inventing new terms. As 'bystanders' ourselves, but committed against genocide, we need to develop these classifications. We cannot avoid trying to make sense of perpetrators' intentions, but I shall argue that ultimately we should reject their absolutist and euphemistic categories – 'ethnic cleansing' is a case in point – and refine those of resisters and fellow committed bystanders.

In picking its way through the conceptual minefield of genocide studies, this book aims to contribute not just to intellectual clarification but also to anti-genocidal action. Genocide studies need to recognize the variety of social collectivities and attacks on them. Yet we need also to remember the concept's founding rationale: violent, destructive and murderous actions against civilian groups and populations constitute *a general class* of social actions and conflict, whose commonalities are definitive. We need to remember that classification is the beginning, not the end, of analysis. We need to use the concepts we develop to produce coherent accounts that will aid both historical understanding and action to prevent, halt and punish genocide.

This book adopts a critical theoretical approach to its subject. It is not a history of ideas, but an interrogation of the concepts we use to understand violence, informed by arguments about how these have developed. These are guided, in turn, by how changing contexts – from the Second World War to the post-Cold War – have influenced changes in ideas. This historical approach guides the presentation, especially in the book's first half. In the second half, although the approach remains critical and historical, I adopt a different way of presenting the argument. The book now turns to how we should understand the main terms of genocide debates in the light of sociological theory; how we should develop social theory itself to take account of genocide's challenges; and how we should begin the task of explanation. In conclusion I return to the core of my conceptual clarification and to its relevance for anti-genocidal action.

Part I: Contradictions of Genocide Theory

2

Neglected Foundations

Genocide as social destruction and its connections with war

Only a few major ideas can be traced unequivocally to a single person. Yet one man, Raphael Lemkin, developed the terminology and basis for understanding genocide that we use today. Even more remarkably, he succeeded in getting his 'crime of crimes' defined by the United Nations in an international convention to which most states have become parties. Surprisingly, while accounts of his life and work are available,[1] there is as yet no full biography of Lemkin. Every account pays lip-service to his achievements, yet there is little appreciation of how significant his distinctive understanding remains. The debate has moved considerably beyond Lemkin's formulations – indeed this study will extend it further. He was a lawyer and campaigner, and his ideas reflected his legal orientation and the political contexts in which he worked. In the half-century since Lemkin died new genocides have occurred, the understanding of the past has changed (in his day the name 'Holocaust' was not yet applied to the Nazi genocide) and political and legal responses have developed. The appreciation of Lemkin's work has suffered, however, from his success. It is to the Convention, rather than Lemkin himself, that most refer in defining genocide. This tendency is unfortunate because, although Lemkin's was far from the last word, he offered a more adequate understanding. Moreover many authors, trying to improve on the Convention, have actually moved even further from Lemkin in ways that militate against understanding. We should approach his contribution with more than the ritual piety of commentators who discard his key ideas. Recovering the meaning of genocide for Lemkin is a necessary beginning for serious study.

Lemkin's sociological framework

Lemkin first formulated his ideas in 1933, when he proposed a draft law banning 'barbarity' – 'the premeditated destruction of national, racial, religious and social collectivities' – and 'vandalism' – 'destruction of works of art and culture, being the expression of the particular genius of these collectivities'.[2] Barbarity included

> first and foremost, acts of extermination directed against ethnic, religious or social collectivities whatever the motive (political, religious, etc.); for example massacres, pogroms, actions undertaken to ruin the economic existence of the members of a collectivity, etc. Also belonging in this category are all sorts of brutalities which attack the dignity of the individual in cases where these acts of humiliation have their source in a campaign of extermination directed against the collectivity in which the victim is a member.[3]

Lemkin aimed to define a *general* crime that was more than the individual types of violent or repressive action and subsumed these:

> Taken as a whole, all the acts of this character constitute an offence against the law of nations which we will call by the name 'barbarity.' Taken separately all these acts are punishable in the respective codes; considered together, however, they should constitute offences against the law of nations by reason of their common feature which is to endanger both the existence of the collectivity concerned and the entire social order.

He argued that barbarity and vandalism were international crimes: 'It is not particularly a question of public danger, but of a broader concept, general danger, that we want to call international danger.'[4]

'Barbarity' is usually noted as the forerunner of 'genocide'. Lemkin was looking for a term and a law that brought together a whole *class* of violent and humiliating actions against members of collectivities. Genocide was not a specific type of violence, but a general charge that highlighted the common elements of many acts that, 'taken separately', constituted specific crimes. In contrast to subsequent interpreters who narrowed genocide too down to a specific crime, Lemkin saw it as including not only organized violence but also economic destruction and persecution. What concerned him was precisely the 'common feature' of these types of action: their threat to the existence of a collectivity and thus to 'the social order' itself. As Samantha Power recorded, Lemkin's concern with such threats became, during the Second World War, a campaign against the atrocities of the Nazi occupations in Europe and for recognition of their singular destructiveness. He was particularly galvanized by Winston Churchill's statement 'We are in the presence of a crime without a name.'[5] 'Suddenly', Power described, 'Lemkin's crusade took on a specific objective: the search for a new word.'[6]

His well-known solution was introduced in *Axis Rule in Occupied Europe* (1944): 'By "genocide" we mean the destruction of a nation or of an ethnic group. This new word . . . is made from the Greek word *genos* (race, tribe) and the Latin *cide* (killing).'[7] A footnote noted that another term, 'ethnocide', could be used for the same idea, combining 'cide' with the Greek word *ethnos* (which Lemkin translated as 'nation', although it is also the root for 'ethnicity').[8] Lemkin warned against a narrow interpretation: 'Generally speaking, genocide does not necessarily mean the immediate destruction of a nation, except when accomplished by mass killings of all members of a nation. It is intended rather to signify a coordinated plan of different actions aiming at the destruction of essential foundations of the life of national groups, with the aim of annihilating the groups themselves.'[9] The nuances of the key word, 'destruction', were indicated here by the difference between 'immediate destruction' of a nation and 'destruction of essential foundations' of its life. Lemkin was clear that genocide refers *generally* to the latter; 'immediate' destruction in the sense of 'mass killings of all members of a nation' was a specific type but did *not* define genocide.

Lemkin's definition was exemplified in the substance of his book. 'The Nazi genocide was effected', he wrote,

through a synchronized attack on different aspects of life of the captive peoples: in the political field (by destroying institutions of self-government and imposing a German pattern of administration, and through colonization by Germans); in the social field (by disrupting the social cohesion of the nation involved and killing or removing elements such as the intelligentsia . . .); in the cultural field (by prohibiting or destroying cultural institutions and cultural activities; by substituting vocational education for education in the liberal arts, in order to prevent humanistic thinking); in the economic field (by shifting wealth to Germans and by prohibiting the exercise of trades and occupations by people who do not promote Germanism 'without reservations'); in the biological field (by a policy of depopulation and by promoting procreation by Germans in the occupied countries); and in the field of physical existence (by introducing a starvation rationing system for non-Germans and by mass killings, mainly of Jews, Poles, Slovenes and Russians); in the religious field (by interfering with the activities of the Church, which in many countries provides not only spiritual but also national leadership); in the field of morality (by attempts to create an atmosphere of moral debasement through promoting pornographic publications and motion pictures, and the excessive consumption of alcohol).[10]

This full explanation is important. It shows that genocide, for the term's inventor, was a comprehensive process in which a power 'attacked' and 'destroyed' the way of life and institutions of peoples.[11] By the standards of later debates, Schabas pointed out, Lemkin's definition was both narrow, because it addressed crimes directed against 'national groups' rather than against 'groups' in general, and broad, because it contemplated not only physical genocide but also acts aimed at destroying the group's culture and livelihood.[12] 'Physical' genocide – mass killing – was only one dimension of the comprehensive 'attack'.

Lemkin's was clearly different from many later definitions, as some of their proposers acknowledged. Steven Katz, for example, redefined genocide as happening '*only* where there is an actualized intention, however successfully carried out, to physically destroy an *entire* group (as such group is defined by the perpetrators).'[13] This narrowed down Nazi genocide to the Jews, yet Katz recognized that 'Lemkin's own use of the term *genocide* . . . did not, in his own understanding, apply only to Nazi anti-Jewish policy. He appears to have held that Nazi behaviour vis-à-vis a number of other groups approached, if not actually replicated, Nazi anti-Jewish activity and, therefore, should also be identified as genocide.'[14] Katz stated: 'The reason I give primacy to physical genocide is directly and unambiguously due to the fact that this is what one means, first and foremost, when one characterizes the Holocaust as an instance of genocide.'[15] He added: 'I make bold to suggest that Raphael Lemkin may well have formulated a definition closer to (if not exactly like) mine had he been writing after the end of World War II when it became clear what Hitler's Judeocidal intentions were. Working in 1942–43, Lemkin was still unable to see the entire uncompromising, totalistic assault for what it was.'[16] Yet since Lemkin (who lived until 1959) campaigned against the Nazis to the end of the war and beyond, lobbying for genocide charges in the Nuremberg trials and for the Convention, it seems that if he had wished to revise his definition he would have done so. The reason he did not is clear when we examine the short chapter on the idea of genocide in the context of *Axis Rule* as a whole. For Lemkin (although himself Jewish and absolutely concerned about the horrors inflicted on the Jews), Nazi genocide was never exclusively or primarily an anti-Jewish campaign; that was not the standard against which other Nazi persecutions were measured. On the contrary, his book aimed to demonstrate (by placing on record translations of Nazi laws in the occupied countries) how comprehensively, against a range of subject peoples, the Nazis had attempted to destroy the existence of nations, their well-being, institutions and ways of life. Genocide's 'two phases: one, destruction of the national pattern of the oppressed group; the other, the imposition of the national pattern of the oppressor',[17] could be seen across the continent. Genocide, like barbarity, was *a comprehensive concept of the social destruction of national groups*, and Lemkin believed that it had very wide applicability.

All this is indisputable from how Lemkin presented genocide. The reasoning of the German occupiers appeared to be that the conquered 'enemy nation' should be destroyed, disintegrated or weakened in different degrees for decades to come. Thus the German people in the post-war period would be in a position to deal with other European peoples from the standpoint of 'biological superiority'. Because the imposition of the policy of genocide was more destructive for a people than injuries suffered in actual fighting, the German people would be stronger than the subjugated peoples after the war even if the German army was defeated. Thus genocide was a new occupation technique that could win the peace even though the war itself was lost.[18] Lemkin was hardly unaware of the huge differences in the severity of Nazi policies towards different peoples, but he still saw them all under the same rubric:

> The plan of genocide . . . varies according to subject, modalities, and degree of intensity in each occupied country. Some groups – such as the Jews – are to be destroyed completely. A distinction is made between peoples considered to be related by blood to the German people (such as Dutchmen, Norwegians, Flemings, Luxemburgers) and peoples not thus related by blood (such as Poles, Slovenes, Serbs). The populations of the first group are deemed worthy of being Germanized.[19]

Thus Lemkin clearly recognized that only 'some groups', the Jews were foremost among them, were 'to be destroyed completely'. However, in all cases, the techniques of genocide 'represented a concentrated and coordinated attack upon all the elements of nationhood.'[20]

It may be the case, as Power argued, that 'the link between Hitler's Final Solution and Lemkin's hybrid term would cause endless confusion for policymakers and ordinary people who assumed that genocide occurred only where the perpetrator of atrocity could be shown, like Hitler, to possess an intent to exterminate every last member of an ethnic, national, or religious group.'[21] However, Lemkin's approach was coherent, plausible as an overall account of Nazi occupations, and took account of variation in the experiences of occupied peoples. Moreover it was this concept that largely informed public debate in the aftermath of the Second World War, although some narrowing had already set in. The third count of the 1945 Nuremberg indictment stated that all twenty-four defendants 'conducted deliberate and systematic genocide, viz. the extermination of racial and national groups, against the civilian populations of certain occupied territories in order to destroy particular races and classes of people, and national, racial or religious groups, particularly Jews, Poles and Gypsies.'[22] Here 'extermination' was still understood in a broad sense, as the destruction of ways of life as well as of lives. Since the indictment included the Poles, it clearly did not narrow genocide to the intention to kill every last member of a group, which is how 'extermination' has come to be understood since.[23]

Likewise the Convention on the Prevention and Punishment of the Crime of Genocide, by defining genocide as a *range* of 'acts committed with intent to destroy, in whole or in part, a national, ethnical, racial or religious group, as such', maintained the core of Lemkin's broad approach. However, its list of acts constituting the crime – '(a) Killing members of the group; (b) Causing serious bodily or mental harm to members of the group; (c) Deliberately inflicting on the group conditions of life calculated to bring about its physical destruction in whole or in part; (d) Imposing measures intended to prevent births within the group; (e) Forcibly transferring children of the group to another group'[24] – laid greater emphasis on physical destruction. This was particularly evident in (c), where 'inflicting on the group conditions of life' was genocidal only in so far as it was 'calculated to bring about its physical destruction'. For Lemkin, in contrast, it was quite clear that 'a synchronized attack on different aspects of life' was genocidal *in itself*. Both Nuremberg and the Convention laid stronger emphasis than Lemkin on *physical and biological destruction*, and less on broader *social destruction*. This difference is largely explicable because the former were designed to apply and define genocide law: killing and physical harm were the sharpest ends of the destructive processes and thus obvious legal foci.

In contrast Lemkin – however much he wished to establish and enforce genocide law – offered a historical and sociological account. He was surely right that, in order to understand genocide, we should see killing and physical harm as elements of the broader process of social destruction. The Nazis did not aim simply to kill subject peoples, even the Jews: they aimed to destroy their ways of life and social institutions. It is implausible to reduce this aim to a 'means' of physical destruction, as the Convention section (c) would imply. It was the other way round: when physical destruction came to be a distinct, eventually overriding end, this was an extreme development of pre-existing Nazi policies of social destruction. Lemkin was correct to stress the integrated, multidimensional, nature of the attack, and not to fall (as later writers have) into the trap of separating physical violence from social destruction. In this sense his work, rather than the Convention, remains the essential starting point for sociological understanding and hence for political and international responses.

Nevertheless Lemkin had not presented, in *Axis Rule*, a fully plausible account of the relations of socially destructive ends and violent or murderous means. His listing of 'the field of physical existence' as one aspect of Nazism's coordinated attack was too mechanical. It failed to clarify that, while genocide involved much more than killing, violence and its threat lay behind all genocidal policies. *Although genocide could not be defined by a specific violent method like killing, the idea of social destruction necessarily entailed generally violent methods.* What else could social 'destruction' mean? The deficiency of Lemkin's listing approach meant that this relationship between violence and social destruction remained to be fully grasped.

Genocide and the laws of war

While Lemkin offered a socio-historical conception of genocide, his conceptualization was heavily influenced by the legal tradition. He drew on two major sources: the international laws of minorities and of war, especially those relating to the role of occupiers and the treatment of civilians. I shall therefore examine the relationship between these sources in the evolution of the concept of genocide.

The existence of minorities with different beliefs from the ruler had been an issue in interstate politics at least since medieval conflicts between Muslims and Christians, and a central issue in the European interstate system since the splits in Christianity in the sixteenth century. Various treaties, from Augsburg (1555) to Westphalia (1648), attempted to regulate this relationship and consolidated the rule, *cuius regio, eius religio*, by which rulers defined their states' religions.[25] However, these treaties also respected subjects' rights to practise their religion and to seek the protection of a ruler of their own faith, beginning the process of defining 'minority rights'. From the nineteenth century, states were increasingly defined by nations rather than faiths, so that these rights came to be conceived in national rather than (or as well as) religious terms. This tendency reached its peak after the First World War when national and religious groups were put under a special protection by the Treaty of Versailles and by specific minority treaties, when it became obvious that national minorities were compelled to live within the boundaries of states ruled by governments representing majority groups. Lemkin noted this, [26] assuming – like most thinkers of his time – the centrality of national groups to social life: 'The trend is quite natural, when we conceive that nations are essential elements of the world community. The world represents only so much culture and intellectual vigour as are created by its component national groups. . . . The destruction of a nation, therefore, results in the loss of its future contributions to the world.'[27] Yet he was at pains to emphasize that the idea of a nation should not be confused with that of nationalism.[28] *Against* the prevalent nationalism, his view of nations as contributors to world culture was strikingly universalist. This belief inspired his determination to establish the crime of genocide in international law.

Although the First World War had seen destruction of national communities, notoriously the Armenians, minority issues were seen generally under the rubrics of persecution and rights.[29] Lemkin's efforts to enlarge the legal framework to recognize genocide were successful after the Second World War mainly because they linked minority protection to another tradition, the law of war. Lemkin's concern remained the recognition of a general crime of the destruction of national groups, but he framed his case in terms of inadequacies in the laws of war. He argued that Nazi 'techniques of genocide represent an elaborate, almost scientific, system developed to an extent never before achieved by any nation.'[30] There was an urgent need to review international law, since genocide had greatly surpassed any destructive procedures or methods imagined several decades earlier by the framers of the Hague Regulations. It was necessary, therefore, to see to it that the regulations were amended so as *expressly* to prohibit genocide in any future war.[31] Lemkin's case was (yet again) that the laws of war needed to address the destruction of groups *as a general problem*: 'Genocide is . . . a composite of different acts of persecution or destruction. Many of these acts . . . are prohibited by [various articles of] . . . the Hague Regulations. But other acts falling within the purview of genocide . . . are not prohibited by the Hague Regulations. The entire problem of genocide needs to be dealt with as a whole.'[32] It was almost as an afterthought that he extended his case beyond the war context, mentioning that 'genocide is a problem not only of war but also of peace.' An international treaty should provide, he argued, for the introduction of provisions protecting minority groups from oppression, because of their nationhood, religion, or race, in both the constitutions and the criminal code of different countries.[33]

The tension with which Lemkin grappled was that genocide was clearly not 'normal' warfare, or merely an excess of war, but a criminal enterprise that went beyond it. As he later said, 'Genocide is not war! It is more dangerous than war!'[34] And yet genocide *had* developed, in the Nazi case and in others such as Armenia, in the context of general war, as an illegitimate extension of warfare. Lemkin demarcated genocide *in relation to* legitimate warfare:

> Genocide is the antithesis of the Rousseau–Portalis Doctrine,[35] which may be regarded as implicit in the Hague Regulations. This doctrine holds that war is directed against sovereigns and armies, not against subjects and civilians. In its modern application in civilized society, the doctrine means that war is conducted against states and armed forces and not against populations. It required a long period of evolution to mark the way from wars of extermination, which occurred in ancient times and in the Middle Ages, to the conception of wars as being essentially limited to activities against armies and states.[36]

This seminal statement pinpointed the fact that identifying genocide as criminality distinct from war still *depended* on the modern distinction between 'civilized' and 'uncivilized' warfare. Only by distinguishing 'sovereigns and armies' from 'subjects and civilians' could genocide be delimited from war. Although genocide was a crime *sui generis*, which might occur at least exceptionally in 'peacetime' outside more conventional warfare, it was a modern form of the historic 'wars of extermination'. As Mark Levene put it: 'The whole thrust of Lemkin's conceptualization . . . suggests a phenomenon which does not simply take place within a war context but is itself a form of warfare.'[37]

Lemkin's prescriptions followed from this definition of the problem and were primarily concerned, at this stage, with the laws of war. His starting point was the inadequacies of the 1907 Regulations concerning occupation: he urged their revision to incorporate a definition of genocide. He also urged 'an international controlling agency vested with specific powers, such as visiting the occupied countries and making inquiries as to the manner in which the occupant treats natives in prison.'[38] If, as Schabas argued, 'he also signalled the great shortcoming of the Hague Regulations: their limited application to circumstances of international armed conflict',[39] he was clearly very concerned to improve them to ensure that genocide did not occur in wartime.

It was also through the law of war that the crime of genocide was first established. Schabas, on whose careful legal history the following relies considerably (although I have many disagreements with his position), pointed out that the Allied powers also first considered genocide in the context of war crimes. Their United Nations War Crimes Commission was originally concerned with offences against the laws and customs of war, but from an early stage it aimed to extend its jurisdiction to civilian atrocities committed against ethnic groups not only in occupied countries but also within Germany itself.[40] However the four Allied powers 'insisted upon a nexus between the war itself and the atrocities committed by the Nazis against their own Jewish populations. It was on this basis, and this basis alone, that they considered themselves entitled to contemplate prosecution.'[41] Thus as the Allies developed their plans to prosecute Nazi leaders in 1945, Robert Jackson, head of the United States delegation, argued: 'The reason that this extermination of Jews and destruction of the rights of minorities becomes an international concern is this: it was part of a plan for making an illegal war.'[42] Other delegates questioned the tightness of this connection, but it was in this context that Nazi leaders were tried at Nuremberg. As we saw above, the International Military Tribunal arraigned the defendants for genocide 'against the civilian populations of certain occupied territories'.[43] The tribunal's judgement documented the emergence of genocidal policies before as well as during the war, but noted the prosecution's central contention concerning their connections with aggressive war.

Separation of genocide from war

It was clear from this application that recognition of the crime of genocide developed primarily in the context of war and war-preparation; genocide's initial illegality was an extension of the laws of war. However, as Lemkin pinpointed, the crime's distinctiveness lay in the *fundamental* nature of its departure from the legitimate conduct of war. There was something novel in the systematic character of contemporary violence against civilian groups, going beyond the excesses termed 'war crimes' or even 'crimes against humanity'. The formulation of what became the Genocide Convention began with the first session of the United Nations General Assembly in late 1946, shortly after the conclusion of the Nuremberg trials. In the drafting process, genocide emerged as a concept in its own right, increasingly independent of its origins in the history and laws of minority rights and war. Thus Resolution 96(I) of the General Assembly, adopted unanimously on 11 December 1946, defined genocide as 'a denial of the right of existence of entire human groups, as homicide is the denial of the right to live of individual human beings.'[44] This formulation expressed a central, but theoretically difficult, idea of genocide, the comparison of group and individual harms. But, as Schabas noted, it also eliminated 'any nexus between genocide and armed conflict'.[45] I shall question whether connecting genocide with war was really the 'unfortunate legacy of the Nuremberg jurisprudence' that Schabas contended. However, it is important to note that separation was taking place.

The drafting process lasted two years until the Convention's adoption on 9 December 1948 – the day before that of the Universal Declaration of Human Rights. Its debates – of which Schabas's comprehensive analysis[46] supersedes Kuper's account[47] – resulted in an international political and legal document of fundamental importance. Not only has it remained the unamended basis of policy and law; it has also informed public debate and scholarly discussion in all disciplines. While law often informs as well as reflects social debate, it is highly unusual for a major concept to be so strongly defined by a legal document. Thus moving out of the restrictive legal framework is a major issue for the sociology of genocide.

Although the laws of war may have effectively prohibited genocide before the Convention, Article I now designated it a crime 'whether committed in time of peace or in time of war'. The contracting parties confirmed that it was a crime that 'they undertake to prevent and to punish'. Article II enumerated genocide's modalities or acts, but actually began by delimiting the crime's intentional element.[48] According to the convention, 'genocide means any of the following acts committed with intent to destroy, in whole or in part, a national, ethnical, racial or religious group, as such.' Discussion of this article has focused on the omission of 'political' groups from the list and the ambiguity of the 'in whole or in part' provision. Schabas also considered 'enigmatic'[49] the words 'as such', but they provided a useful clarification of the fact that genocide involves the aim of destroying a group *in itself* – rather than group destruction as a means of defeating a state in war.

The list of acts constituting the crime was given above. As we have noted, however, here genocide had a much narrower scope than indicated by *Axis Rule*. The emphasis was on killing, bodily harm and indirectly caused physical destruction, together with measures concerning group reproduction. The wider issue of the destruction of the social, economic, political and cultural life and institutions of groups had largely disappeared, even if there have been indications in legal discussions that 'the list of acts of genocide is non-exhaustive'.[50] Article III of the Convention dealt with acts which 'shall be punishable': conspiracy, incitement, attempting and complicity in genocide, as well genocide itself. This was significant in more than a legal sense, since it exhibited the understanding of genocide as a process, not just a result. Article IV specified that 'persons committing genocide . . . shall be punished, whether they are constitutionally responsible rulers, public officials or private individuals.' This was also important, indicating that rulers and officials were likely to be the main perpetrators. The remaining articles, V to XIX, dealt with issues such as legislation to give effect to the Convention, trials, extradition, the UN's responsibilities, resolution of issues of interpretation, signature and ratification, coming into and periods of force, revisions, etc., which were less significant for general understanding.

An important argument in the drafting process concerned genocide's relation to crimes against humanity. It was argued that the Nuremberg Tribunal had defined the latter in relation to international armed conflict, whereas genocide could be committed in war or peace.[51] This was, as we have seen, a misunderstanding of Nuremberg, which had actually dealt with crimes against humanity committed in peacetime. However, whether genocide constitutes a crime against humanity (which in non-legal terms is self-evident) remains contentious, and connected to the issue of genocide's relationship to war. The latter question remains essential for the subsequent social-scientific debates. The most striking fact about the process that produced the Convention was its separation of genocide from war. In one sense, this was entirely valid: clearly genocide was not ordinary warfare and it was conceivable that it could occur outside pre-existing contexts of warfare. However, the major, commonly recognized instances of genocide – not only the Holocaust, but also Armenia and Rwanda – have been clearly connected with war contexts, and this is an overwhelming empirical trend.[52] Thus the legal separation of genocide from war left unresolved the more general conceptual questions: what are the connections of war and genocide in terms of their *meanings*, and in terms of *causation*? These are fundamental issues for understanding genocide, which I have dealt with elsewhere[53] and return to later in this book.

Narrowing genocide to physical destruction

Criticizing the Convention has been a major industry in genocide studies, and I shall not be able to avoid joining in. At this point, however, let us summarize its strengths. These lie first and foremost in its political and legal resonance: we should almost certainly not discuss 'genocide' so much if the idea had not been embedded in this document. Conceptually, however, it also helped consolidate the basis for subsequent discussion. The idea of genocide as the *intentional destruction of social groups* remains foundational, and although none of the terms (intention, destruction, groups) is straightforward these can be elaborated. The *list of protected groups* as 'national, ethnical, racial and religious' identified some of the most important types threatened by genocide; although it is unjustifiably restricted, it can be added to or (better) replaced by a generic definition. The idea that *killing and physical harm* are the prime acts through which genocide is carried out is seminal; it is hardly possible to conceive genocide without physical violence, even if its role needs broader contextualization. The idea of the *imposition of conditions of life that led to the destruction of groups* was a reflection, albeit inadequate, of Lemkin's idea of genocide as 'a synchronized attack on different aspects of life of . . . peoples'. The relationship between 'physical' and broader 'social' destruction goes to the heart of genocide, even if here it is poorly specified. The specification of control of births and children, even if the wording resonates with the eugenics of the early twentieth century, foreshadowed the emphasis on *sexual and gendered violence* that has become important in recent accounts. Although drafted by diplomats and lawyers rather than social scientists, and approved by governments as a result of political debate and compromise, the Convention laid out an intellectually powerful concept. While it is flawed in important respects, its influence reflects real internal strengths as well as political and legal weight.

Academic commentators have simultaneously improved on and regressed from the Convention's understanding. Let us take a preliminary look at the developments they have proposed. Helen Fein, an early exponent of sociological genocide theory, has been perhaps the closest follower of the Convention. Her definition, 'Genocide is sustained purposeful action by a perpetrator to physically destroy a collectivity directly or through interdiction of the biological and social reproduction of group members, sustained regardless of the surrender or lack of threat offered by the victim',[54] was very close to its idea. 'Sustained purposeful action' resumed the Convention idea of intentional destruction. The idea that physical destruction of a group could either be 'direct' or be carried out through interdiction of reproduction faithfully reflected the Convention's specification of means. However, Fein modified the Convention concept in three respects. First, she referred only to collectivities and groups in general, and did not reproduce the Convention's restriction to 'national, ethnical, racial and religious groups'. She saw the protected groups as 'basic kinds, classes, or sub-families of humanity, persisting units of society', and argued cogently that 'the specification of groups should be consistent with our sociological knowledge of both the persistence and construction of group identities in society' and 'should conform to the implicit universalistic norm and a sense of justice, embracing the right of all non-violent groups to co-exist.'[55] Second, by inserting the word 'physically' in her definition, she went even further than the Convention in narrowing the scope of the crime from Lemkin's original idea that genocide is 'a synchronized attack on different aspects of life of (captive) peoples' towards an exclusive emphasis on killing and other measures of 'biological' rather than social destruction. Third, Fein's phrase 'sustained regardless of the surrender or lack of threat offered by the victim' emphasized genocide's separation from war: victims are destroyed even if they are not military threats.

Frank Chalk and Kurt Jonassohn offered a more distinctive refinement in their widely quoted definition: 'Genocide is a form of one-sided mass killing in which a state or other authority intends to destroy a group, as that group and members in it are defined by the perpetrators.'[56] In defining genocide simply as 'mass killing', Chalk and Jonassohn departed more radically from the Convention, identifying genocide with physical destruction even more narrowly than Fein, and moved still further from Lemkin's broad concept. Fein criticized them for failing to allow for 'other forms of intentional biological destruction' and pointed out that specifying states as perpetrators was unnecessarily restrictive.[57] Even if states are commonly organizing centres, parties, settlers, paramilitaries and others have also been responsible; thus it seems perverse to define genocide by the state (even with the let-out of 'or other authority'). However, it was Chalk and Jonassohn's description of the victim group and its members as being defined by the perpetrators that was their most distinctive contribution. This was important for emphasizing that perpetrators work according to their own, often fantastical, ideas of 'enemy' groups. This idea brought into question the assumption that groups necessarily exist 'objectively' or are defined by their own consciousness of their identity, and this is what genocidists aim to destroy. This assumption had been made by Lemkin, the Convention and Fein, and was later supported by Schabas: however, it cannot be sustained, as I explain more fully later. Since all agree that the genocidists' intention to destroy a group is central, it follows that *their* idea of that group counts in the process. We know that genocidists such as the Nazis (with their Nuremberg laws defining who was Jewish) or the Rwandan Hutu nationalists (with their ideas of who was a Tutsi) have often followed definitions of their target groups that are different from those held by the victims: thus they often appeared arbitrary in theory as well as in practice. Extending this point, we cannot rule out from the scope of genocide groups such as the *kulaks* ('rich peasants') attacked by Stalin, simply because the population did not recognize itself as belonging to this group, or because this category could not be 'objectively' defined. In cases like this, the ideological representation still refers to a real population and often a definite group (in the Soviet Union, the peasantry in general) who are subjected to genocide just as much as if they had been named in a manner they recognized. Clearly, as Fein suggested, Chalk and Jonassohn's definition involved the opposite danger of according too much significance to the ideas of the perpetrators,[58] and it needs to be corrected to acknowledge the role of victims' self-perceptions. However, by recognizing the role of ideas in genocide, Chalk and Jonassohn opened up an important, indeed an unavoidable dimension.

They also gave new emphasis to the general separation of genocide from war. Their idea of 'one-sidedness' could be taken as meaning that genocide is something one party does to another without conflict or resistance. Clearly there is a fundamental sense in which one-sidedness *is* what genocide is about: everyone understands that its violence is targeted by an organized, armed power against a largely unarmed, civilian population. However, such violence has often been imposed in the context of conflict between organized forces (war) and often provokes resistance, and hence new conflict, so that the genocidal element of one-sided killing is often part of a situation of two- or many-sided conflict and violence. Genocide's definition as 'one-sided' killing is potentially misleading if as a result we miss these connections.

These trends were taken to their logical conclusion by Israel W. Charny: 'Genocide in a generic sense is the mass killing of substantial numbers of human beings, when not in the course of military action against the military forces of an avowed enemy, under conditions of the essential defencelessness and helplessness of the victims.'[59] The 'generic' description echoed Lemkin's view of genocide as a broad category of destructive activity against groups. However, Charny went even further than Fein and Chalk and Jonassohn in reducing genocide to physical violence. He made genocide a general term for any kind of mass killing, and took any sort of social content out of the definition. He completely lost the 'group' element that was so essential to Lemkin's original account and the Convention, and which the two more sociological definitions addressed. Yet his approach had the virtue of directly addressing the issue of genocide and military action, and it is illuminating to separate its valid and invalid elements. Clearly he rightly wished to indicate that the killing of civilians in genocide was in principle *different from* the killing of civilians in war. But when he defined the difference as that genocide occurs 'not in the course of military action against the military forces of an avowed enemy', he was misleading. In the classic Holocaust case, how else did the Nazis come to control their Jewish and other victims, except through war and conquest, as Lemkin recognized? And how else did they come to practise their genocidal violence, except 'in the course of military action against the military forces of an avowed enemy'? It was during the course of the German invasion and occupation of Poland that Jews were brutally uprooted, concentrated in ghettoes, starved and overworked. The German armies that invaded the Soviet Union and Yugoslavia, and the *Einzatzgruppen* or special action groups that accompanied them, slaughtered Jews alongside Soviet prisoners of war, communists and other citizens. *To define genocide as outside the context of war is manifestly misleading and mystifying when the connections have often been so strong.*

Moreover Charny's approach mistook the meaning of genocide as well as its context. If genocidal slaughter of civilians takes place in the course of military action, what is its relationship with the 'normal' killing of soldiers or the unintended, 'collateral' killing of civilians that is going on at the same time? Charny implied no relationship. Yet it seems more plausible to propose that for the Nazis the Jews were also an 'avowed enemy', against whom (although they largely lacked military forces) a course of 'military action' was also undertaken. Thus, as Lucy Davidowicz suggested, there was a 'war against the Jews':[60] a special branch of the general Nazi war effort. Not only was genocide committed in the context of war, but it also was *a particular kind of war* that involved a new kind of enemy – an essentially civilian population – alongside more conventional ones. However 'essentially defenceless and helpless' unarmed civilians were, Charny's formulation, like Chalk and Jonassohn's, appeared to *define away the possibility of resistance*, or of a relationship of the victims to armed allies who might eventually defeat the genocidists. Many European Jews, after all, joined the war against the Nazis, either in resistance groups or in Allied armies.

To add to the confusion, Charny proceeded to develop a typology of genocide in which 'genocide in the course of an aggressive ("unjust") war' was one variety. This he defined as genocide 'that is undertaken or even allowed in the course of military actions by a known aggressive power, e.g. Germany and Japan in World War II, for the purpose of or incidental to a goal of aggressive war, such as massive destruction of civilian centers in order to vanquish an enemy in war.'[61] Even more confusingly, he proposed that 'war crimes against humanity' (an amalgam of the legal categories of 'war crimes' and 'crimes against humanity') should be considered in the 'definitional matrix for crimes of genocide'. Therefore, although genocide was defined as 'mass killing . . . not in the course of military action against the military forces of an avowed enemy', mass killing *in* the course of such action was considered a sub-type!

Perhaps it is not surprising that Charny also argued against an excess of 'definitionalism'. He was right that extended debate on definition could lead to the point 'where the reality of the subject under discussion is "lost", that is, no longer experienced emotionally by the scholars conducting the enquiry.'[62] But this was hardly a justification for adopting loose definitions that made it difficult to distinguish types of violence in a coherent way. If we are to do justice to the victims, and help understand the enormities of violence, we cannot but engage with these issues abstractly as well as in concrete ways. The point is certainly to 'prevent and punish' genocide; but to do this, we must understand the beast. The issues of definition cannot be avoided in this task.

Conclusion

I have argued in this chapter that, in the international legal and political discussions of the 1940s, genocide began to lose two key elements of Lemkin's early formulations. One was its broad sociological meaning as social destruction, of a people and their way of life, and the second was the understanding of how genocide was related to war. Despite the Genocide Convention's many strengths, its drafting assisted both losses. Moreover, the debate at the end of the twentieth century consolidated them. Although later writers reformulated 'genocide' in more generic ways – including the destruction of any social collectivity or group or even any mass killing – none restored Lemkin's broader sociological understanding, and most aided both the narrowing of the understanding of genocide to killing and its more comprehensive separation from war.

My argument is that these tendencies have been very unhelpful to the understanding of what genocide is, why it happens and how it can be prevented. To define genocide as 'physical destruction' begs the sociological question as to *why* genocidists engage in physically destroying their victims. However much they may despise the very bodies of their victims – labelling them 'vermin', 'cockroaches', and other terms indicating their fitness only to be killed – is killing itself a sufficient definition of their 'intention to destroy'? Or, as Lemkin contended, is killing one way in which groups as such are 'destroyed', as part of a more comprehensive 'attack' on their social existence? In this case, we can see the role of killing of its individual members as a *means* of destroying a social group. Killing, along with other forms of physical harm and cruelty, is the ultimate destructive means, which in the end trumps all others. But it is not the primary *meaning* of group destruction: that lies in the end of annihilating the way of life, social networks, institutions and values of the attacked community. This amounts to *destroying the (real or putative) social power* of the target groups, which is embodied in their ownership of land, houses and other property, their schools, religious institutions, cultural and political organization, and all the other ways in which their presence in given social spaces and territories is manifested.

Certainly violence and killing mark all genocidal processes. The intention to destroy a social group is always pregnant with violence, threatening the grossest violation of individual and collective lives. However, extents of killing and physical harm depend on the particular ways that genocidists frame their destructive aims, as well as on instrumental decisions about the utility of different kinds of violence and on contingent factors deriving from contexts of war and resistance. Genocide is, as Lemkin recognized from his earliest formulations of 'barbarity' and 'vandalism', about social and cultural destruction. It involves batteries of coercive powers – legal, administrative, political, ideological and economic as well as armed, violent and military. Genocide always involves physical violence but it involves many other things as well. Defining genocide by killing misses the social aims that lie behind it. *Genocide involves mass killing but it is much more than mass killing*.

Inverting the question may help the reader grasp this point. Is all mass killing genocidal? Nearly all those quoted would disagree: mass killing is genocidal only when it is carried out with the intention of 'destroying' a social group. But how do we know that there is such an intention? There has been much discussion of this issue, since such intentions are rarely clearly stated and must be inferred from patterns of action and euphemistic policy statements. However, we can circumvent the question by asking instead, in what circumstances would deliberate, organized mass killing *not* be genocidal? Charny, as we have seen, provided an answer, which can be paraphrased as 'when mass killing is warfare'. The element of truth is that most mass killing other than for war must indeed be genocidal in virtually all circumstances. This is not because it is killing, hence Charny's positive definition is wrong. It is because it is difficult to conceive of reasons (outside war) for which collective actors would plan to kill a large number of people, *other than* to destroy that group of people or a larger social group of which the victims are considered members. Although individual killers and mobs sometimes slaughter fairly randomly, apparently with little or no reason, organized killing by collective actors is invariably purposeful, informed by conceptions of group enemies to be socially destroyed – even if this too fades into arbitrary, random violence in practice. Paradoxically, although genocide *is*

not reducible to mass killing, organized mass killing *is* generally understandable as genocide. 'Can there be any case of mass murder which is
not genocide?' asks Charny. He answers, 'I do not believe so',[63] and this
is almost correct: only relatively spontaneous killings by civilians, for
example in ethnic riots and pogroms, might not be fully genocidal. But
understanding killing as genocide involves filling out the larger social
context of destruction – why the genocidists regard a group as an enemy,
what is their larger plan to destroy the group, what role killing plays, and
how they attempt to carry out their plan in the concrete social, political,
military and other circumstances that they face, including the probable
resistance of the target group and/or of armed actors allied to the group.

This understanding brings us back to war. War, supposed to be
directed (in Lemkin's terms) 'against states and armed forces', accounts
for the largest part of organized killing in modern society and is its
only generally legitimate form. Genocide, directed 'against subjects and
civilians' or 'populations', and hence by definition illegitimate, accounts
for most of the remainder. The distinction is clear, but questions remain
about the connections. Why does most genocide occur in contexts of
general war, and why is even 'peacetime' genocide committed by militarized regimes? Why does war, under certain circumstances, develop
into genocide? Are these connections causal? Or do they reflect basic
similarities in the two types of action, how practitioners understand
their aims, and how violent means fit? That is to say, are the connections
internal to the character of the two modes of action, connected to what
these *mean* to the actors themselves, and how therefore these actions
should be *understood*?[64]

I have suggested that the commonality is that, in both war and genocide, organized actors aim to 'destroy' the power of the enemy through
means that are pre-eminently violent. The idea of 'destroying' the
enemy's power, as the end of war and the reason for the violence of its
means, is fundamental to Carl von Clausewitz's *On War*.[65] Lemkin had
a closely parallel understanding of genocide, with 'destroying' a group
as its end and the reason for its use of physical violence. The key
difference lies in the nature of the enemy: in war, another state or armed
force; in genocide, a civilian social group. Yet recovering Lemkin's
broader sense enables us to see how genocide involves three elements
borrowed from the older, more legitimate social practice of war:

1 the *identification of a social group as an enemy in an essentially military* (rather than political, economic or cultural) *sense*, i.e. against
whom it is justified to use violence in a comprehensive and systematic way;

2 the *intention to destroy the real or imputed power of the enemy group*,
   including its economic, political, cultural and ideological power,
   together with its ability to resist this destruction;
3 *the deployment and threat of violence to destroy the power of the enemy
   group* through killing and physically harming a significant number of
   its members, as well as economic, political and ideological coercion.[66]

Seeing genocide in this way enables us to see it as a destructive *process*
and escape from the trap of defining it by physical destruction alone.
War, as a social activity, involves identifying the enemy, formulating the
goal of destruction, and developing its means; so too genocide. War
involves the development of strategies, and also many different moments
of preparation, organization, supply and deployment; so too genocide.
War involves political, economic and ideological as well as military
power; so too genocide. Physical destruction is the ultimate manifestation of the destructive process of war, but it is not what is going on most
of the time in most wars; so too in genocides. Thus genocide, like war,
involves much more than the mass killing through which we most easily
recognize its destructiveness. Just as war can occur without large-scale
killing, genocide too can occur where this element is not extensively
carried out.

In the remaining chapters of part I, I critically examine some of the
broader intellectual tendencies that have surrounded and followed
from the narrowing of the concept of genocide. I shall return to my new
definition, reformulating Lemkin's 'broad' concept, in the concluding
chapter of this book.

3

The Maximal Standard

The significance of the Holocaust

Discussion about political violence today is marked above all by considerable avoidance of the word 'genocide'. This is partly for political reasons: when states and international organizations acknowledge genocide, it implies legal and political action. However, the tendency also derives from the theoretical confusion surrounding the concept. This confusion and the corresponding 'genocide'-avoidance come from three apparently diverse but really complementary sources. The first is the erection of 'the Holocaust' as a maximal standard that other episodes must reach if they are to be recognized: not surprisingly, they mostly fail. The second is the deployment of 'ethnic cleansing' as a concept of sub-genocidal violence, to which the rejected cases are accommodated. 'Ethnic cleansing' comes without genocide's definite legal prohibition, but it also offers less of a theoretical challenge: it is a minimal, euphemistic term, often adopted for reasons of intellectual as well as political avoidance. The third reason is the proliferation of '-cide' terms in official, popular and scholarly discourse, so that many forms of genocide are recognized by different names. In this and the succeeding chapters, I shall examine each of these tendencies in turn, proposing how the issues they involve – principally variation in genocides, and the relationships between killing and other forms of coercion – can be understood better within the framework of genocide theory.

Holocaust 'uniqueness'

The understanding of genocide, born of the Nazi era and defined in its aftermath, remains in the shadow of what has come to be called the Holocaust. As we saw, scholarly attention is overwhelmingly dominated by this topic. Even so it is still less unbalanced than public debate and high school education, in which the Holocaust has assumed a position of overriding importance, universally commemorated and increasingly the dominant theme of the Second World War. In this debate, recognition of other cases – historical, like Armenia, and contemporary, such as Rwanda – often depends on establishing a connection to the Holocaust. Debate about them is regularly conducted in terms of their similarity. The result of this bias is considerable distortion of the Holocaust's meaning, which has affected academic genocide studies in often polemical debates about its 'uniqueness' and comparability. These debates have gone so far that protagonists have accused each other of 'denial', on one side of the Holocaust – the significance of which is diminished without 'uniqueness' – and on the other in relation to other cases – of less significance if the Holocaust is uniquely murderous. Hence in the 'jingoistic/ideological wars' in genocide studies, to which Charny referred,

> there is a disquieting pattern of claims of the 'incomparable uniqueness' of the Holocaust and a good deal of political power used in many places in academia, museums, and communities to back up these claims by pushing down and out nonadherents. No less disturbing, many of the counterclaims – however justified in epistemological and moral intent to place the genocides of *all* peoples on the same level of tragedy and evil – go on to minimize the horror of the Holocaust and display a nasty lack of reverence for the victims.[1]

While there is no denying the damaging moral and political effects of 'wars' about genocides, it is their implications for understanding that concern this chapter. As Dirk Moses pointed out, 'the primacy of the victims' point of view' reflects group traumas that 'block conceptual development' as well as mutual recognition.[2] And Holocaust studies have often taken academic understanding further from the generic concept of genocide as a crime towards an ever more refined grasp of the Nazi case. That is to say, while Lemkin advanced a general concept that was legal in purpose and sociological in character, Holocaust studies have for the most part remained relentlessly historical in a narrow sense. Of course, the richness of Holocaust research can be used to illuminate the general understanding of genocide. But when no adequate conceptual framework informs research, it either remains simply particularistic or leads to *ad hoc* comparisons between cases in which one becomes the standard for others.

Thus protagonists in the 'uniqueness' debates have tended to trade case-to-case comparisons without advancing a general framework that could explain them all. A prime exemplar is Katz, whose work makes explicit the negative idealization involved in claims of Holocaust 'uniqueness'. In order to render the Holocaust the *sole* historical case of genocide, Katz not only departed from Lemkin, as we saw he acknowledged, but also grossly misinterpreted him. Quoting Lemkin's definition of the Nazi genocide as a 'coordinated plan of different actions aimed at the destruction of the essential foundations of life of national groups, with the aim of annihilating the groups themselves', he commented: 'This and this alone, understood as the complete biological extinction of the Jewish people, defines what one today calls the Holocaust. Thus, to define the term in a way other than that which applied particularly to the Holocaust (i.e. that relativizes or loses sight of the distinctiveness of the Holocaust context) seems not only arbitrary but perverse, both logically and phenomenologically.'[3] However, what is genuinely perverse is to take Lemkin's manifestly universal concept of the destruction of national groups and reduce it to the *biological* extinction of the *Jewish* people – as though the general concept no longer held meaning.

In his argument for the uniqueness of the Jewish Holocaust experience, Katz conceded arguments based on the numbers of victims or the proportion of the Jewish population murdered by the Nazis – in these terms, evidently, the experience *was* matched by other awful cases – but drew a line concerning the uniqueness of the Nazis' intention to murder every Jew in the world. This in turn was the cue for critics to argue not only that more, or a greater proportion, of other populations have been killed, but also that murdering every last Jew was not the Nazis' intention, or that the Nazis also attacked groups such as Gypsies with similar aims, or that other perpetrators also had comparable intentions.[4] The problem is not only that, as Charny suggested, this debate sometimes exceeded morally appropriate bounds. It is also that it misplaced the real question about killing in genocide. Whether or not the Nazis actually aimed to kill every single Jew, even in occupied Europe, let alone the world, their generally genocidal policies involved the sharply distinctive attitudes that Lemkin noted towards the different occupied peoples. So how should we characterize these differences? At one end of the Nazi policy spectrum, there was relatively little direct killing of peoples 'related by blood' to Germans and hence 'deemed capable of being Germanized'; in the middle range, the 'peoples not thus related by blood' were condemned to servile status and liable to extensive killing; while at the furthest extreme, Jews, Gypsies and the disabled had no place in the Nazi order and became, finally, the objects of systematic mass murder. If we can draw a significant line through these patterns, it should surely be between killing as a *means* of the general social destruction of groups, and killing as an *end* of policy in itself – when systematic physical extermination became a policy goal. In this sense, Nazi policies towards disabled people, Polish elites, Jews, Soviet prisoners of war and Gypsies all *became* simply murderous – exterminatory – at various stages of the Second World War. However, policies towards these groups were not equally murderous in all stages of Nazi rule, warfare and occupation. If the proposed line is drawn, it divides the Final Solution phase of Nazi anti-Jewish policy from earlier phases in which this goal was not adopted. We cannot teleologically re-read the earlier phases under the rubric of the final phase, since policy development was incremental, contextual and reactive.[5]

Certainly, the shift towards attempted physical extermination – through the simple murder of as many individuals defined as belonging to the categories as possible – was a striking development. No wonder that much historical effort has gone in the case of the Jews (but surprisingly not other groups) into defining the point at which a decision was made, if indeed there was a single decision, and how far Hitler conceived this policy in the years before he implemented it. But whatever the outcomes of these investigations, it is surely valid to examine the course of anti-Jewish policy, over the whole period of Nazism's existence and rule, as a single developing process. The definition of Jewry as an enemy and the aim of destroying its real and imputed social power were consistent throughout the history of the Nazi Party. In this sense it always had genocidal aims towards the Jews, manifested in many policies, although the policy of physical extermination was concretely adopted only in 1941. So while it is important to signal the development of extermination policies, this was the final phase of a longer genocidal history. Likewise, Jewish extermination was only one thrust among several of this kind. As Christopher Browning put it:

> If the Nazi regime had suddenly ceased to exist in the first half of 1941, its most notorious achievements in human destruction would have been the so-called euthanasia killing of seventy to eighty thousand German mentally ill and the systematic murder of the Polish intelligentsia. If the regime had disappeared in the spring of 1942, its historical infamy would

have rested on the 'war of destruction' against the Soviet Union. The mass
death of some two million prisoners of war in the first nine months of that
period would have stood out even more prominently than the killing of
approximately one-half million Jews in that same period.[6]

Eventually the intensity of Nazi anti-Semitism, the industrialized nature
of the later mass killing and the greater final total of Jewish victims combined to leave Jews pre-eminent in the historical memory – and scholarly
assessments – of Nazi murderousness. Yet this murderousness had many
targets, intertwined in practice and in the experience of victims. If Nazi
murder policies require distinctive concepts to represent them, then
extermination policies should be seen as intensifications of generally
genocidal policies, conceived in the 1920s and implemented after 1933,
and manifestations of genocidal war waged from 1939.

Thus the meaning of 'the Holocaust' can only be grasped in the light
of genocidal policies and war which were *multi-targeted* at a range of
victim groups, among which the Jews were ideologically and in the end
statistically pre-eminent. Katz's approach typifies, David Stannard suggested, a tautological strand of scholarly argument: 'Uniqueness advocates *begin* by defining genocide (or the Holocaust or the Shoah) in
terms of what they already believe to be experiences undergone only
by Jews. After much research it is then "discovered" – *mirabile dictu* –
that the Jewish experience was unique.'[7] Or, if other genocides are
admitted, such criteria are used to distinguish the Jewish case as qualitatively worse. For example, Daniel Goldhagen argued that, unlike
other genocides which 'occurred in the context of some pre-existing
realistic conflict (territorial, class, ethnic, or religious)', the Holocaust
was motivated by 'an absolutely fantastical' German hatred of the Jews
without a basis in reality: 'demonizing German racial anti-Semitism . . .
because of its *fantastical* construction of Jewry, demanded, unlike in
other genocides, the *total* extermination of the Jews.'[8] He was seemingly
unaware that fantastical ideas of the enemy-victim group are common
in genocides; moreover they do not always lead to total extermination,
although they have in other cases too, such as Rwanda.

The name 'Holocaust' was, as we have seen, a later invention. 'When
I was growing up', Phillip Lopate noted,

we never spoke of a Holocaust; we said 'concentration camps', 'the gas
chambers', 'six million Jews', 'what the Nazis did'. It might seem an
improvement over these awkward phrases to use a single, streamlined term.
And yet to put any label on that phenomenal range of suffering serves to
restrict, to conventionalize, to tame. As soon as the term 'Holocaust' entered
common circulation, around the mid-sixties, it made me uncomfortable. It

had a self-important, strutting air – a vulgarly neologistic ring, combined with a self-conscious archaic sound, straining as it did for a Miltonic biblical solemnity that brought to mind such quaint cousins as Armageddon, Behemoth, and Leviathan.[9]

'What disturbs me finally', he commented, 'is the exclusivity of the singular usage, *the* Holocaust, which seems to cut the event off from all others and to diminish, if not demean, the mass slaughters of other people – or, for that matter, previous tragedies in Jewish history. . . . The image of the Holocaust is too overbearing, too hot to tolerate subtle distinctions. In its life as a rhetorical figure, the Holocaust is a bully.'[10] The fact remains, however, that the name 'Holocaust' is now so thoroughly established that it is very difficult to dispense with. In the light of its comprehensive, multi-targeted nature, perhaps *the Nazi Holocaust* would be an appropriate modification of the term. This proposal will, however, meet strong resistance from those for whom the Holocaust's Jewish character defines it. Yet, as Irving Louis Horowitz argued, 'To emphasise distinctions between peoples by arguing for the uniqueness of anti-Semitism is a profound mistake; it reduces any possibility of a unified political and human posture on the meaning of genocide or the Holocaust.'[11]

The Holocaust standard in comparative study

Gavriel Rosenfeld, in an attempt to reconcile the debate, argued sympathetically that 'uniqueness' was a response to the historicization and politicization of the Holocaust: 'the widespread adoption of uniqueness by scholars is best understood as part of a self-consciously *defensive* response to the perceived attempts by others to diminish the event for apologetic or revisionist purposes.'[12] He nevertheless concluded that

the debate has raised important questions concerning the utility of the uniqueness concept. In many ways, controversy has resulted from the concept's very ambiguity. 'Uniqueness' not only suffers from a lack of linguistic clarity – it suggests both 'unprecedented' and 'unrepeatable' – but yields very different conclusions depending on the analytical perspective: historical, philosophical, theological, and so on. . . . Furthermore, 'uniqueness' is a concept of questionable utility given the misunderstanding it has provoked as a qualitative concept carrying a moral judgement. . . . Given the drawbacks of uniqueness, might the concept not be replaced by a less attention-grabbing but more precise term, such as 'distinctiveness' or 'particularity'?[13]

This might seem no more than an agreement with Charny's uncontroversial maxim: 'all cases of genocide are similar and different, special and unique, and appropriately subject to comparative analysis.'[14] However, it is clear that Rosenfeld's kind of Holocaust distinctiveness continued to render it immune to generalization – or what he called 'historicization', namely 'turning it into a comprehensible event that could be subjected to rational historical analysis, often with the help of generalizing theories.'[15] But what was the problem with this approach, to which every other historical event would be subjected? It appeared this was an objection in principle: the mystical, 'incomprehensible' core of the Holocaust could not, even should not, be explained. Rosenfeld claimed that none of the five main concepts used to 'historicize' – totalitarianism, fascism, functionalism, modernity and genocide – 'have succeeded in integrating the Holocaust into a general explanatory framework without substantially marginalizing its significance.'[16] I shall restrict my comments to his critique of genocide scholars' 'goal of "contextualizing the Holocaust into Genocide Studies" by subjecting it to rigorous comparative analysis'. These scholars argued, according to Rosenfeld, 'that the Holocaust was not qualitatively different from other episodes of mass murder in human history . . . . These scholars also focused attention upon the similarities between the Nazis' persecution of the Jews and other "inferior" groups.'[17] Rosenfeld acknowledged that '[s]uch efforts to analyze the Holocaust as an example of genocide have contributed greatly to the broader cause of historical understanding.'[18] Yet he concluded that, '[o]verall, however, the project has been hampered by the absence of a widely accepted definition of the term "genocide" itself. The inability of scholars to agree upon which groups should be regarded as the perpetrators and which the victims has made it difficult to see how the Holocaust relates to other episodes of mass murder that may or may not be similar in character. As a result, the Holocaust continues to resist historicization as an example of genocide.'[19]

This critique was curious: if comparing the Holocaust with other genocides had contributed to the cause of historical understanding, what was its problem? And, granted obviously that there were divergent definitions and debates, were any of the differences so severe as to prevent any informed comparison of the Holocaust with other genocides? Actually, as we have seen, definitions have tended to converge towards a relatively narrow concept, recognizing mass killing against any kind of group as genocide. Whatever the problems of this concept, comparisons in its terms are perfectly feasible. There may be continuing debate about the Holocaust as a case of genocide, but it is hardly the case that it 'continues to resist historicization'.

There was, however, a paradoxical element of truth in Rosenfeld's observations. Comparison has misled precisely because it has substituted a *Holocaust standard* for a coherent conception of genocide. The problem is not too much but too little generalization. *Ad hoc* comparisons have often focused on secondary differences of limited significance, reinforcing an overall incoherence in genocide studies. A collection of 'comparative' essays on Holocaust 'uniqueness' included many examples of this flawed approach.[20] Thus Robert F. Melson analysed three dimensions on which 'the Armenian case differed from the Holocaust':

> First, the Young Turks were largely motivated by an ideology of nationalism, whereas the Nazis were moved by an ideology heavily influenced by social Darwinism and racism. Second, the Armenians were a territorial group concentrated in the eastern *vilayets* of the empire, and they had historical claims to the land. In contrast, the Jews were not a territorial group. To destroy the Jews, the Nazis had to formulate a policy of genocide that transcended Germany and even Europe. Lastly, the method of destruction of the Armenians centred on their exportation, shooting and starvation, whereas in the Holocaust the majority of Nazi victims perished in death camps. This is not to deny that a large percentage of Nazi victims also perished by shooting and starvation in the manner of their Armenian predecessors.[21]

It is striking that all three points were misleading. Clearly social Darwinism and racism were important in Nazi ideology – but the *National* Socialist German Workers Party was hardly uninfluenced by nationalism! The idea that 'the Jews were not a territorial group' is belied by their centuries of residence in certain countries, regions and localities of Eastern Europe and the attachment of Jewish village-dwellers to their land. The significance of this 'territoriality' for Nazi anti-Jewish policy is demonstrated by their determination to remove the Jews from their homelands. Melson conceded that many Nazi victims also perished by the 'exportation, shooting and starvation' that Turkish victims had suffered.[22] And while the new methodology of the extermination camps was shocking, the end of destruction was the same. This flawed point underlined the fact that, unguided by a developed general concept of genocide, discussion was focusing on historically secondary issues, the differences over which were overstated. Moreover, another Armenian scholar, Vahakn Dadrian, produced similarly faulty comparisons. In creating a picture of Armenian distinctiveness, his claims also distorted Jewish history. Jews and Armenians, he argued, 'emerge as victims for opposite reasons. The Armenians were destroyed in their natural homeland – their ancestral territories – in historic

Armenia. . . . In the Jewish case, the victims were destroyed as an immigrant population by the rulers of the host country.'[23] This claim ironically, and surely unintentionally, endorsed Hitler's rationale for destroying the Jews. The real purpose of Dadrian's comparison, of course, was to emphasize Armenian claims to 'their natural homeland – their ancestral territories'.

The reader may weary of these critiques, but their point is quite central: *ad hoc* comparisons of other cases with the Holocaust tend to reproduce a narrow exterminatory conception and get caught up in secondary features, so blurring core similarities. (Nor is this tendency confined to Armenian scholars.) In order to understand other genocides, therefore, the imperative is not to compare them with the Holocaust – which as a specific episode was necessarily unique in many respects – but to interpret them in terms of a coherent general conception. We don't need a standard that steers all discussion towards a maximal concept of industrial extermination, a standard that distorts even the Nazi genocide against the Jews. We do need a coherent, generic, sociological concept of genocide that can make sense of a range of historical experiences.

Holocausts and genocides

Even when mystifying arguments about 'uniqueness' were cast aside, the nexus of historical empiricism and special pleading that produced it continued to influence comparative research negatively. More moderate versions of exceptionalism remained pervasive. Thus Yehuda Bauer influentially claimed that the Nazi anti-Jewish campaign represented an 'extreme' form of genocide and for this reason deserved the separate designation 'Holocaust'.[24] His case seemed more reasonable because he generalized the term 'holocaust' as an ideal type that could apply to other genocides (for example, the Armenians) and allowed that holocausts could recur: 'Events happen because they are possible. If they were possible once, they are possible again. In that sense the Holocaust is not unique, but a warning for the future.'[25]

The wider remit of the term 'holocaust' gives the argument greater plausibility. As Stannard, an opponent of Holocaust 'uniqueness', polemically contended:

> as for restricting use of the word 'holocaust' to references having to do with the experiences of the Jews under the Nazis, that copyright was filed at least three centuries too late. Although 'The Holocaust', in what has

become conventional usage, clearly applies exclusively to the genocide that was perpetrated by the Nazis against their various victims, 'holocaust', in more general parlance, as a term to describe mass destruction or slaughter, belongs to anyone who cares to use it. It is a very old word, after all.[26]

However, the generalization of 'holocausts', which writers such as Stannard embrace in order to apply the term to other episodes (in his work, the destruction of native peoples became 'the American Holocaust'),[27] adds little to a social-scientific vocabulary. Its meaning is too loose to have much value as a general term for 'extreme' genocide – surely an oxymoronic idea. To distinguish 'holocausts' from 'ordinary' genocides only permits the idea of hyper-genocide, in some sense worse than 'mere' genocide, to be extended to selected other cases. It is not clear what scientific purpose such classification serves, since the difference of exterminatory from 'ordinary' genocidal killing is not always easy to determine, and it develops from and deepens genocide. Nor, of course, is it very significant to the victims: as Lopate remarked of the Holocaust, 'The fact that one's group was not targeted for extermination *in toto* is a serious distinction, but hardly much consolation to the Gypsies, homosexuals, radicals, Poles, Slavs, etc., whom the Nazis did wipe out.'[28] It seems more plausible to see extermination as a particular type of genocidal policy, which when pursued successfully leads to more comprehensive physical as well as general social destruction of a target group. The extent and forms of extermination are important questions, but hardly separate studies from that of genocide.

Thus although the sterile 'uniqueness' debate has been transcended, the debilitating effect of the Holocaust paradigm remains. Its dominant role has strongly influenced the tendency to narrow genocide to killing, which has now spread throughout the social sciences. Just as the Holocaust has been over-interpreted in terms of its final, exterminatory, phase, so genocide generally has been narrowed to extermination. Charny's reductive view that 'genocide in a generic sense is mass killing' has been widely reinvented in new definitions. Levene advanced a view of genocide as an 'actual event' of mass murder, defined by a state's 'systematic, *en masse* physical elimination' of an 'aggregate population' perceived as threatening to it.[29] In Barbara Harff and Ted Robert Gurr's textbook on ethnic conflict, '[g]enocide is mass murder carried out by or with the complicity of political authorities and directed at distinct communally defined groups.'[30] Mann used the term to refer only to the most extreme murderous politics, involving both 'total cleansing' *and* 'premeditated mass killing'. In his comprehensive analytical framework, genocide was a narrow rather than a broad term, referring only to deliberate, systematic and total extermination.[31] Thus, in the Nazi case, Mann ended up embracing – empirically – the uniqueness advocates' restriction of genocide to the Jews. Their extermination, he wrote, 'was clearly genocide, the only really large genocide attempted by the Nazis.'[32] For him, the Nazis' killing of mentally disabled Germans 'was erratic, leaving too many alive to be genocidal'. The Nazis did develop the intent to murder Gypsies, but since it 'was thwarted by an elusive quarry', with 200,000 to 260,000 deaths this was only 'attempted genocide'.[33] The mass murder of Polish elites was only 'politicide'; combined with the 'segregation' and 'wild deportations' of other Poles, the 'intended outcome was not quite genocide'. Although the numbers of Soviet prisoner-of-war and civilian victims were 'horrific', 'This was not quite genocide because there were too many Soviet Slavs to contemplate killing them all.'[34]

If only total extermination is now admitted, how should we describe the situations that would constitute genocide on Lemkin's or the Convention's definition, but which fall outside this newly narrowed remit? Officials, journalists and scholars have been quick to reinvent genocide in new terms. The most widely applied – but least coherent or useful – is 'ethnic cleansing', discussed in the next chapter. But this is only one of a wide range of new terms, and in the following chapter I argue that, in order for them to be useful, they need to be reintegrated in a genocide framework.

4

The Minimal Euphemism

The substitution of 'ethnic cleansing' for genocide

Because genocide has been narrowed down to Nazi-like extermination policies, few recent cases have been recognized. Only that of Rwanda (1994) has been overwhelmingly accepted, since the campaign against the Tutsis involved total physical destruction. Although Holocaust 'uniqueness' advocates might find it lacking – machetes seeming less clinical and modern than extermination camps – Hutu nationalists accomplished their killings with a deadly speed that outstripped the Nazis. Before this, many commentators also saw Serbian nationalist campaigns in Croatia and Bosnia-Herzegovina as genocidal. Yet the phrase most widely used to describe them was 'ethnic cleansing', which quickly achieved an extraordinarily wide currency. Barely a year into the Yugoslav wars, it was 'adopted as part of the official vocabulary of UN Security Council documents and by other UN institutions and governmental and non-governmental international organizations'.[1] Hardly used in worldwide discourse before the 1990s, it was soon employed throughout international media, policy and academic circles to describe political violence. Mann has now given it a sociological imprimatur.[2]

Origins of 'cleansing' terminology

A study of the term's emergence derives it from the Slav phrase *etnicheskoye chishcheniye* (ethnic cleansing), 'used by the Soviet authorities to describe the Azeri attempts to drive the Armenian population away from their territory in the Nagorno-Karabakh crisis of the late 1980s.'[3] However, the term entered Western discourse from Yugoslavia, where the similar word *ciscenje* (cleansing) was employed. According to Drazen Petrovic,

> The term derived its current meaning during the war in Bosnia and Herzegovina, and was also used to describe certain events in Croatia. It is impossible to determine who was the first to employ it, and in what context. As military officers of the former Yugoslav People's Army had a preponderant role in all these events, the conclusion could be drawn that the expression 'ethnic cleansing' has its origin in military vocabulary. The expression 'to clean the territory' is directed against enemies, and it is used mostly in the final phase of combat in order to take total control of the conquered territory. In general terms, the idiom 'cist' – 'clean' – means 'without any dirt' or 'contamination'. The word 'ethnic' has been added to the military term because the 'enemies' are considered to be the other ethnic communities.[4]

Moreover 'cleansing' had been used by Second World War Croatian fascists to describe their expulsions of Serbs, and by Serb critics of their expulsions by Albanian authorities in Kosovo in 1981. It could be traced back at least to the 1912 Balkan War.[5] Translated into English, the term 'surfaced in the summer of 1992 in the context of the Bosnian conflict', entering the British press vocabulary at this time, and 'began to lose its quotation marks a year or so later . . . though for the most part they were retained.'[6]

'Ethnic cleansing' was a *perpetrators' term*, embedding rather than criticizing their particular meaning of 'cleanliness' or 'purification', while failing to indicate the destructive character of the removal of groups from territories where they lived. Although international journalists, politicians, lawyers and officials did not advocate ethnic purity, their use of the term accepted this idea rather than indicating the consequences of 'cleansing' for victims. The question this raised was: why enshrine a perpetrator concept in official, legal, journalistic and social-scientific language when there were terms such as *expulsion* and *forced migration* that indicated the precise harm caused – and when *genocide* described the general social destruction involved? Thus there were always doubts about the incorporation into political, legal and sociological discourse of 'ethnic cleansing'. Petrovic noted that 'the reasoning behind this terminology and its relationship to the system of international law' were 'not very clear'.[7] Could 'ethnic cleansing' really become a neutral descriptive term – let alone a core concept of historical and political sociology?

Nevertheless 'cleansing' terminology continued to spread, and definitions piled up.[8] UN Special Rapporteur Tadeusz Mazowiecki wrote in a
1992 report: 'The term ethnic cleansing refers to the elimination by the
ethnic group exerting control over a given territory of members of other
ethnic groups.' He later modified this to 'the systematic purge of the civilian population based on ethnic criteria, with the view to forcing it to
abandon the territories where it lives.' A 1993 Commission of Experts
considered that it meant 'rendering an area ethnically homogenous by
using force and intimidation to remove persons of given groups from the
area.' A first scholarly definition was provided by Andrew Bell-Fialkoff:
'ethnic cleansing can be understood as the expulsion of an "undesirable"
population from a given territory due to religious or ethnic discrimination, political, strategic or ideological considerations, or a combination
of these.'[9] For Petrovic, synthesizing these ideas from a legal point of
view, 'ethnic cleansing is a well-defined policy of a particular group of
persons to systematically eliminate another group from a given territory
on the basis of religious, ethnic or national origin. Such a policy involves
violence and is very often connected with military operations. It is to be
achieved by all possible means, from discrimination to extermination, and
entails violations of human rights and international humanitarian law.'[10]
In his book-length study, Bell-Fialkoff expanded the concept from this
religious-national-ethnic basis, introducing the wider concept of *population cleansing*, the 'planned, deliberate removal from a certain territory
of an undesirable population distinguished by one or more characteristics such as ethnicity, religion, race, class, or sexual preference. These
characteristics must serve as the basis for removal for it to qualify as
cleansing.'[11] Mann has deployed a similarly broad concept of *murderous
cleansing*. These concepts moved 'cleansing' from a specific to a generic
meaning, parallelling the shift in genocide studies from the narrow categorical basis of the UN Convention to more generic definitions.

'Cleansing' and genocide

The new terminology's users often felt obliged to explain its relationship to genocide. Indeed the significance of this issue was recognized
when the UN General Assembly denounced 'the abhorrent policy of
"ethnic cleansing", which is a form of genocide.'[12] A review by UN
lawyers in 1993 found that 'ethnic cleansing' 'might well be considered
genocide under the convention'.[13] An International Court of Justice
judgement by Judge Elihu Lauterpacht, a Cambridge professor nom-
inated by the Bosnian government as its *ad hoc* judge, argued that

it is difficult to regard the Serbian acts [of ethnic cleansing] as other than acts of genocide in that they fall within categories (a), (b) and (c) of the definition of genocide . . ., they are clearly directed against an ethnical or religious group as such, and they are intended to destroy that group, if not in whole certainly in part, to the extent necessary to ensure that the group no longer occupied the parts of Bosnia-Herzegovina coveted by the Serbs.[14]

Lauterpacht's views were not those of the whole court but, later, judges in the International Criminal Tribunal for Former Yugoslavia recognized 'cleansing' as genocide in several cases. Thus Judge Riad equated at least its graver forms with genocide:

The policy of 'ethnic cleansing' . . . presents, in its ultimate manifestation, genocidal characteristics. Furthermore, in this case, the intent to destroy, in whole or in part, a national, ethnical, racial or religious group, which is specific to genocide, may be inferred from the gravity of the 'ethnic cleansing' practised in Srebrenica and its surrounding areas, i.e., principally the mass killings of Muslims which occurred after the fall of Srebrenica in July 1995, which were committed in circumstances manifesting an almost unparalleled cruelty.[15]

On the other hand, the ICTY's prosecutor was 'extremely cautious in laying charges of genocide' in relation to 'cleansing'.[16] Clearly this caution reflected uncertainty in the relationship of the two, and the preference of prosecutors for charges likely to stick: a conviction for crimes against humanity was preferable to an acquittal for genocide.

Scholars who adopted the term naturally emphasized the difference. For Bell-Fialkoff, genocide was identified with 'mass murder' and thus deserved 'to be treated as a separate category' from 'cleansing'.[17] Norman Naimark asserted:

A new term was needed because ethnic cleansing and genocide are two different activities, and the differences between them are important. As in the case of determining first-degree murder, intentionality is the critical distinction. Genocide is the intentional killing off of part or all of an ethnic, religious, or national group; the murder of a people or peoples (in German, Völkermord) is the objective. The intention of ethnic cleansing is to remove a people and often all traces of them from a concrete territory. The goal, in other words, is to get rid of the 'alien' nationality, ethnic or religious group and to seize control of the territory they had formerly inhabited.[18]

Here the exterminatory concept of genocide was clearly in play, and the justification of the 'new term' was to cover what was left out by this narrowed-down version of genocide. Merely (!) 'removing' or 'getting rid' of an 'alien' people 'and all traces of them' from the territory they inhabited was not genocide – without 'intentional killing off'. Looking closely at the language brings into focus the crassness of the proposed analytical distinction. The words were all synonyms for the 'destruction' of a group, understood as the essence of genocide. The scholarship of 'cleansing' was reinventing the analytical wheel, as witness this statement: 'whereas war generally matches armed men against armed men in a contest of will, machines, and numbers, ethnic cleansing usually involves an armed perpetrator and an unarmed victim – more often that not, an armed man and an unarmed woman, child, or elderly person.'[19] Substitute 'genocide' for 'ethnic cleansing' and this could have come from Lemkin. A further indicator of the confusion was Naimark's statement that the relationships between 'cleansing' and genocide were close:

> At one extreme of its spectrum, ethnic cleansing is closer to forced deportation or what has been called 'population transfer'; the idea is to get people to move, and the means are meant to be legal and semi-legal. At the other extreme, however, ethnic cleansing and genocide are distinguishable only in the ultimate intent. Here, both literally and figuratively, ethnic cleansing bleeds into genocide, as mass murder is committed in order to rid the land of a people.[20]

However, both scholars conceded the problems of their new terminology. According to Bell-Fialkoff: 'The term "cleansing" itself is ambiguous. In everyday use it has positive connotations of cleanliness and purification . . . . But when applied to human populations it refers to refugees, deportation, and detention. It spells suffering. And that is why the term is widely used: it is a euphemism that hides the ugly truth.'[21] Naimark acknowledged: 'There is nothing "clean" about ethnic cleansing. It is shot through with violence and brutality in the most extreme form.'[22] Likewise Schabas, who argued that legally 'cleansing' was not necessarily genocide, also called it a 'euphemism for genocide'.[23]

Obviously organized violence against civilians cannot be genuinely cleansing, even for perpetrators, let alone for victims or society at large. If the language of dirt and cleanliness applies, surely it is the 'cleansers' who foul social life, which needs purification *from* their violence. This emancipatory meaning of cleansing has indeed been used: for example, the purification of killers from their murderous state has been called 'war cleansing' in accounts of coping with the aftermath of African wars.[24] After the mid-1980s terror inflicted by Robert Mugabe's notorious Fifth

Brigade, Ndebele people in Zimbabwe talked of 'cleaning' the forests
in which had been the sites of so much killing and where the bones
of victims were 'left lying around'. Their idea of 'cleaning' in the aftermath of violence evoked a more traditional idea of 'cleaning' the forest,
removing animal bones, nests and dead branches, which were ceremoni-
ally burnt.[25] In social science too, *cleansing* should be defined by this
more appropriate human meaning. 'Ethnic cleansing' should remain
within inverted commas.

The question remains, however, whether – shorn of this language –
the concept refers to a distinctive reality. Yet when advocates attempted
to specify its content, there was more fuzziness. For Bell-Fialkoff, as we
saw, 'Population cleansing . . . defies easy definition. It covers a wide
range of phenomena from genocide at one end to subtle pressure to
emigrate at the other.' Moreover, 'while all types of cleansing involve
population removal, not all forms of removal constitute cleansing.'[26]
Naimark was clear that the boundary between non-genocidal 'cleansing' and genocide might be unreal:

> Further complicating the distinctions between ethnic cleansing and geno-
> cide is the fact that forced deportation seldom takes place without vio-
> lence, often murderous violence. People do not leave their homes on their
> own . . . . They resist . . . . The result is that forced deportation often
> becomes genocidal, as people are violently ripped from their native towns
> and villages and killed when they try to stay. Even when forced deporta-
> tion is not genocidal in its intent, it is often genocidal in its effects.[27]

Here Naimark let the cat out of the bag. How could 'forced deportation' ever be achieved *without* extreme coercion, indeed violence? How,
indeed, could deportation *not* be forced? How could people *not* resist?
How could it *not* involve the destruction of a community, of the way of
life that a group has enjoyed over a period of time? How could those
who deported a group *not* intend this destruction? In what significant
way is the forcible removal of a population from their homeland
different from the 'destruction' of a group? If the boundary between
'cleansing' and genocide is unreal, why police it?

Certainly the idea of peaceful, non-violent (but still forcible!) population removal had a long if dubious pedigree in twentieth-century
international relations. Schabas argued that 'the drafters of the
Convention quite deliberately resisted attempts to encompass the phenomenon of ethnic cleansing within the punishable acts.'[28] 'Mass displacement' of populations was not regarded as genocide, he concluded,
except where (as in Armenia) 'attended by such circumstances as to lead

to the death of the whole or part of the displaced population (if, for example, people were driven from their homes and forced to travel long distances in a country where they were exposed to starvation, thirst, heat, cold and epidemics).'[29] The problem was, of course, that expulsion was too common and was practised by the victorious powers that founded the UN as well as by the defeated Axis. As Schabas noted, in 1945 'as many as 15 million Germans were expelled [from Poland, Czechoslovakia, etc.] and resettled pursuant to Article XIII of the Potsdam Protocol.'[30] If forcible removal was recognized as genocidal, moral differences between victors and losers would become matters of degree. As early as 1946, Palyi, reviewing Lemkin's *Axis Rule*, suggested that '[h]is highly refined legal apparatus which is to serve against the Nazis could be turned against the Allies as well . . . . Allied practices include, in effect, even the worst of Nazi excesses – "genocide", the mass extinction of civilians, is the fate of millions of Germans driven, under inhuman conditions, from their homes in East-Central Europe.'[31]

'Non-genocidal' expulsions?

It is therefore worth examining this great Western displacement of Germans during and after the Second World War. Was Palyi's charge against the Allies justified, or was this 'non-genocidal' expulsion? There is little doubt that the USSR, which seized much of pre-war Poland as well as German territory, the Polish authorities, who grabbed much of Germany as compensation for their lost eastern lands, and the Czechoslovak government, who wished to punish the Sudeten Germans for their role in Hitler's occupation, all aimed to expel the remaining German populations from their historic homelands.[32] Indeed many expulsions had already taken place before the USA and Britain ratified the related territorial changes at Potsdam.

In a pioneering study of this neglected social disaster, Alfred de Zayas identified several phases. In the initial Soviet occupation of Germany during the final weeks of the war, Soviet forces carried out mass rapes, massacres and deportations, causing 'the disorganized flight of hundreds of thousands of civilians'; many were killed when planes bombed refugee convoys and ships.[33] This was followed by 'organized' expulsions, beginning in March 1945 and continuing until 1949.[34] The first expulsions were undertaken unilaterally by Poland and Czechoslovakia, without the consent of the Western Allies but with the encouragement of the USSR. For example, in Brünn (Brno) on 30 May 1945 the Czech National Guard marched through the streets calling on all German citizens to be standing outside their front doors at 9 o'clock with one piece of hand luggage each, ready to leave the town forever. Women had ten minutes in which to wake and dress their children, bundle a few possessions into their suit-cases, and come out on to the pavement. Here they were ordered to hand over all their jewellery, watches, fur and money to the guards, retaining only their wedding rings; then they were marched out of town at gun-point towards the Austrian border.[35]

But Austria refused to accept them and they were put in a field 'turned into a concentration camp', where they remained months later without regular rations, engulfed by a typhus epidemic. Bertrand Russell commented that 'an apparently deliberate attempt is being made to exterminate many millions of Germans, not by gas, but by depriving them of their homes and of food, leaving them to die by slow and agonizing starvation.'[36] Even Jews and anti-Nazis recently released from Gestapo camps were 'not immune';[37] indeed '[o]ne of the worst camps in post-war Czechoslovakia was the old Nazi concentration camp of Theresienstadt.'[38] Elsewhere, massacres were reported, for example at Aussig (Usti) in July 1945: 'Women and children were thrown from the bridge into the river. Germans were shot down in the streets. It is estimated that 2000 or 3000 persons were killed.'[39] Russell noted that many were deported by rail:

At a moment's notice, women and children are herded into trains, with only one suitcase each, and they are usually robbed on the way of its contents. The journey to Berlin takes many days, during which no food is provided. Many are dead when they reach Berlin; children who die on the way are thrown out of the window. A member of the Friends' Ambulance Units describes the Berlin station at which these trains arrive as 'Belsen all over again – carts taking the dead from the platform, etc.'[40]

Robert Murphy, US Political Adviser for Germany, informed the State Department:

In the Lehrter railroad station in Berlin alone our medical authorities state an average of ten have been dying daily from exhaustion, malnutrition and illness. In viewing the distress and despair of these wretches, in smelling the odor of their filthy condition, the mind reverts instantly to Dachau and Buchenwald. Here is retribution on a large scale, but practiced not on the *Parteibonzen*, but on women and children, the poor, the infirm.[41]

These expulsions were seen as 'cleansing': a Czech Communist proclamation demanded that party members 'cleanse the Fatherland of the agents of a treachery without equal in the history of our people'.[42]

Later came the post-Potsdam 'transfers', which according to the protocol should have been 'orderly' and 'humane'.[43] Nevertheless these 'exceeded by far anything either Churchill or Truman had been disposed to authorize. Thus, the contemplated westward displacement of 3 to 6 million Germans stampeded into an expulsion of 15 million.'[44] As de Zayas commented: 'The forcible removal of tens of thousands of persons would have in any event caused grave problems from the technical and humanitarian point of view. The uprooting of millions necessarily spelled chaos, misery and death.'[45] 'Of course,' he added, 'it is not easy to imagine how the involuntary uprooting of millions of persons, guilty and innocent alike, could ever be considered "humane" in any sense of the word; still, there is little doubt that much suffering and death could have been avoided if the transfers had at least been "orderly".'[46] Not all transfers were carried out brutally, but many were. Altogether, 'over 2 million Germans did not survive their displacement. Probably about 1 million perished in the course of the military evacuations and flights of the last months of the war. The rest – mostly women, children and old people – perished as a result of the ruthless method of their expulsion.'[47]

How should these atrocities be understood? Clearly this was expulsion or forced migration, 'murderous ethnic cleansing', on a gigantic scale. However, the aim was clear: 'the victorious leaders of Eastern Europe . . . were determined to annex large tracts of the old Reich and to make these areas as free of Germans as possible. They intended to waste no time in the implementation of this programme.'[48] They did not intend to kill every last German, but they did intend to destroy German communities, by means that included direct and indirect killing and many brutalities. Lemkin's two phases – 'one, destruction of the national pattern of the oppressed group; the other, the imposition of the national pattern of the oppressor'[49] – were vividly exemplified. Thus the framework fits, and one is compelled to ask for what reasons these expulsions should be regarded as more acceptable 'population transfers' or 'only ethnic cleansing'.

Clearly many have simply taken for granted that the destruction of German communities by the Soviet, Polish and Czechoslovak governments with the acquiescence of the Western Allies *must* be different from the destruction of Jewish, Slav and other populations carried out by Nazi Germany. Yet the events reminded observers of the Nazi genocide, and large-scale population transfer was indeed a prime Nazi policy. Lemkin quoted Hitler:

We are obliged to depopulate as part of our mission of preserving the German population. We shall have to develop a technique of depopulation.

> If you ask me what I mean by depopulation, I mean the removal of entire
> racial units. . . . And by 'remove', I don't necessarily mean destroy; I shall
> simply take systematic measures to dam their great natural fertility. . . .
> There are many ways, systematic and comparatively painless, or at any rate
> bloodless, of causing undesirable races to die out.[50]

Certainly it is clear that, while Hitler professed 'bloodless' means, his
aim was to cause 'undesirable races to die out'. The Soviet, Polish and
Czechoslovak regimes 'only' wanted to push millions of Germans – collectively punished for the complicity of some of them in the Nazi order –
into a rump Germany. But the intention of destroying the groups'
presence in their homelands was common and the practical consequences were very similar.

Indeed, pre-exterminatory phases of the Nazi genocide also saw vast
expulsions. Hitler's invasion of Poland, with its grandiose plan to annex
its western part to the Reich and expel those Poles not suitable to be
'Germanized' to easterly regions, where the Jews were concentrated in
ghettoes, was an immediate precedent for the Soviet and Polish campaigns against Germans. Moreover the Soviet annexation of eastern
Poland, the push factor in the expulsion of Germans from the German
regions annexed by Poland, consolidated gains originally made by the
USSR *in alliance* with Nazi Germany in 1939–40. *So instead of a categorical divide between different phases of expulsion, there were historical continuities that survived violent fluctuations in Nazi–Soviet relations.*
The main difference was that the war's outcome made larger German
populations – not only minorities within Poland and Czechoslovakia
but also people in eastern regions of historic Germany – the targets of
the new campaign. The other difference was that Great Britain and the
USA, which in 1939 protested against Poland's division, now legi-
timated it together with the accompanying expulsions, even if they
deplored excesses.

It is highly ironic, therefore, that the Holocaust and 'ethnic cleansing'
have come to be regarded as categorical opposites: one 'extreme' genocide, the other not fully genocidal. Even if 'ethnic cleansing' was not a
Nazi term, it had many antecedents in Nazism's medicalized language.
Racial purification was always part of Hitler's vocabulary: 'By the time
of *Mein Kampf*, he asserts that the stateless Jews were a "bacillus",
"disease", "plague", "parasite", "contagion" or "virus" in the host body
of other nations.'[51] The Nazis 'often used the imagery of "a virus, parasite, or a pest of some sort . . . that had to be destroyed, as vermin would
be." Heinrich Himmler thought that anti-semitism "is exactly the same
as delousing".'[52] An army handbook stated, 'The battle against the Jews

is a moral battle for the purity and health of the divinely created *Volksstum*.'[53] The Jews were a 'cancerous growth' on history.[54] Nazi policy was to render the Third Reich *Judenrein* (clean or pure of Jews).[55] Similar ideas also informed Nazi policies towards the mentally ill, infirm and chronically ill. They 'had become part of an overall triage. They were transferred and murdered whenever necessary – whenever local authorities needed sickbeds, blankets, sheets, stretchers, and basic medical equipment.'[56]

'Cleansing' language permeated German military operations in the occupied territories. Western Poland 'was to be "cleansed" of Poles and Jews, incorporated into the German Reich, and settled by ethnic Germans.'[57] In the invasion of Serbia, General Böhme ordered the 'cleansing' of the Macva region.[58] In the invasion of the Soviet Union, as soldiers surrounded villages and farms, drove Jews together and executed them next to specially dug ditches, it was recorded that 'the *Wehrmacht* did a thorough job of cleansing the countryside.'[59] Other words used more or less synonymously with cleansing were eliminating, annihilating, neutralizing and liquidating:[60] Nazi euphemisms for what the world subsequently called genocide. *The prevalence of this language only underlines the perverseness of the attempt to separate 'cleansing' categorically from genocide*. It is not just that 'cleansing' is sometimes genocidal, or that genocide is 'extreme' cleansing. Cleansing language invariably oozes genocidal intent, resonating with the idea of destroying, if not murdering, the groups to whom it is applied.

Peaceful, legal 'transfers' and 'exchanges'?

However, even if 'cleansing' is understood as genocide, the question remains, is it truly possible to enforce population movements in a non-genocidal way? Certainly the idea of peaceful 'transfer' lives on: nowhere, perhaps, with so long a history as in Zionism. From the movement's inception, its leaders envisaged displacing the Arab population of Palestine. Initially, displacement was conceived in gradual terms, as Theodore Herzl advocated in 1895: 'We must expropriate gently . . . . Both the process of expropriation and the removal of the poor must be carried out discretely and circumspectly.'[61] Moreover, as Benny Morris documented, ideas of transfer were kept largely private and in the background, as 'the Zionist public catechism . . . remained that there was room enough in Palestine for both peoples . . . . There was no need for a transfer of the Arabs.' However, Morris argued, 'the logic of a transfer solution to the "Arab problem" remained ineluctable; without some sort of massive displacement of Arabs from the area of the Jewish state-to-be, there could be no viable Jewish state.'[62] Therefore 'by the early 1930s a full-throated near-consensus in support of the idea began to emerge among the movement's leaders.'[63] This consensus

> was not tantamount to pre-planning and did not issue in the production of a policy or master-plan for expulsion; the Yishuv and its military forces did not enter the 1948 war, which was initiated by the Arab side, with a policy or plan for expulsion. But transfer was inevitable and inbuilt into Zionism – because it sought to transform a land which was 'Arab' into a 'Jewish' state and a Jewish state could not have arisen without a major displacement of Arab population.'[64]

Zionists argued that the process could be benevolent, describing Palestinian Arabs in terms reminiscent of those who denied that Eastern Europe was really a 'homeland' for its Jews. They argued, Nur Masalha noted,

> that the uprooting and transfer of the Palestinians to Arab countries would constitute a mere relocation from one district to another; that the Palestinians would have no difficulty in accepting Jordan, Syria, or Iraq as their homeland; that the Palestinian Arabs had little emotional attachment and few real ties to the particular soil in Palestine and would be just as content outside the 'Land of Israel'; that the Palestinian Arabs were marginal to the Arab nation and their problems might be facilitated by a 'benevolent' and 'humanitarian' policy of 'helping people to leave'.[65]

However '[t]he term used for "transfer" then, as now, was the Hebrew word *tihur*, which is closer in meaning to "purification" or "cleansing" of the land.'[66] While transfer thinking conditioned the Jewish population and institutions for expulsion, the 1948 war created the conditions for it to be practised. Implementation was often brutal and murderous, bitterly resented and resisted where possible, and its results perpetuated conflict between Arabs and Israelis into the twenty-first century.

Giorgio Balladore Pallieri reported that, among twenty 'population transfer' treaties between 1913 and 1945, 'il n'y a jamais eu de transfert vraiment voluntaire des populations'.[67] Nevertheless he 'concluded, with the logic of an ethnic cleanser, that there was nothing in international law to oppose the legitimacy of population transfers and they were even, in certain circumstances, desirable.'[68] Even de Zayas wrote that

> [i]t remains, of course, theoretically possible that a transfer of populations, if internationally supervised and carried out gradually, in an 'orderly' and

'humane' manner, might be compatible with international law standards.
But a transfer of population accompanied by the atrocities and inhuman-
ities that characterized the expulsion of the Germans from Poland and
Czechoslovakia would in any case constitute a serious violation of positive international law in the dimension of a 'crime against humanity'. . . .
[and] the illegality of the means ineluctably condemns the end.[69]

Even this qualified endorsement of the possibility of 'legal' transfer
reckons without human rights law. Individuals and groups enjoy
growing protection from arbitrary eviction under both international
law and the domestic law of most states. It is difficult to conceive of conditions under which mass expulsions of established populations would
be legal, and impossible to conceive that they would be just.

It is also difficult to imagine how they would not raise questions of
genocide. The most plausible *prima facie* exceptions are those that
are perpetrated by a state claiming to protect its 'own' people. Thus
prior to the destruction of German communities by the victors, some
Germans of the Baltic states and elsewhere had already opted for
German citizenship 'pursuant to the population transfer treaties nego-
tiated by Hitler's Germany with these countries between 1939 and
1941'; others had been evacuated by the retreating German army.[70] To
the extent that the people involved genuinely embraced these movements, it is difficult to see them as genocidal. However, many movements
were hardly voluntary: local Germans also had to follow the occupiers'
orders, and their lives were put at risk by 'their' state's violence against
others. Borderline situations are also created by colonial settlement,
especially when accompanied by brutal expropriation of pre-existing
populations. Clearly those who personally and knowingly benefit from
the expulsion of others can hardly benefit, immediately, from the same
protection as more established populations. However, this exception
cannot apply to successor generations. Whatever the political and economic redistributions justified by decolonization, wholesale expulsion
of long-established 'settler' communities must constitute genocide.

Another variant is when two states agree to move 'their' minorities
within each other's territories. Thus, after the First World War, the
Greek minority in Turkey was 'exchanged' for the Turkish minority in
Greece. The exchange involved the destruction of centuries-old communities and was accomplished with considerable violence and
suffering. Later, at Indian independence in 1947, millions of Muslims
from areas allocated to the new Indian state, and Hindus from the areas
allocated to Pakistan, were 'exchanged'. The process was accomplished
amidst chaos and bloodshed: hundreds of thousands died. Although the

politically 'voluntary' character of these exchanges clouds the destructive processes, it is euphemistic to describe them as neutral-sounding
'exchanges' and 'transfers'. Even if community leaders supported their
states' policies, and many individuals accepted their expulsion and sal-
vaged new lives in new homelands (as do survivors of all genocides),
these were deliberate, coercive and violent processes of community
destruction. Mutual expulsion remains expulsion; sponsorship does not
convert destruction into something else. Politically, these were atypical
episodes and, to the extent that violence was spontaneous rather than
centrally organized, maybe not fully genocidal. From the point of view
of the victims, however, they possessed many essential features.

The territorial dimension

Expulsion of populations, so readily distinguished *from* genocide, turns
out to be a central feature *of* it, and non-genocidal expulsion an illusory
category. Yet expulsion has been surprisingly neglected in genocide
studies. Lemkin's *Axis Rule* focused on the suppression of the occupied peoples as though they mostly remained *in situ*. The Genocide
Convention specified the means of genocide in terms of physical and
biological destruction, and even if this specification was not exclusive it
did not refer to expulsion. None of the principal later exponents of
genocide theory emphasized expulsion, although it had been a prelude
to and means of physical destruction in the two archetypal genocides
of the earlier twentieth century, the Holocaust and Armenia. *Therefore
the debate on 'ethnic cleansing' could still achieve an important shift in
genocide studies if it leads us to place the role of coercive territorial movement of populations high on the agenda.*
    It is actually very difficult to conceive of genocide *without* a terri-
torial dimension. People are embodied, and social groups exist in
physical space. Destroying a social group always means destroying
(partially if not totally) its presence and its economic, social and cultural power *within a given territory*. So even the most ideologically
driven genocides, generating hatred for members of a group irres-
pective of their location, actually *target* violence at the group within a
territory. The Nazis may have regarded 'international Jewry' as their
enemy, but they concretely aimed to destroy Jewish communities
within territories they had conquered. This meant removing Jews from
their homes, first from Germany itself, then from the area of Poland
annexed to Germany and eventually from the entire European empire.
Even this removal was conceived first as territorial expulsion (to

Madagascar) and only later as complete physical extermination of all Jews under Nazi control.[71]

Looked at in this light, genocide always involves territorial displacement. Mann conceived of extermination as an extreme form of displacement, but the underlying commonality is that both are ways of destroying the social group and its social power. *Genocidists generally aim both to destroy the power of their target groups within a given territory and to expel or remove them from that territory, either simultaneously or sequentially.* For the Nazis, before the Second World War, destroying Jewish power within and encouraging Jewish flight from Germany were two sides of the same coin. Later, destroying Jewish power within the Nazi empire, removing Jews from its core areas and concentrating them in ghettoes, reserved areas or camps, expelling them from Europe, and finally physically exterminating them were all different means towards the end of destroying Jewry. All of these policies had both territorial, spatial and non-territorial, non-spatial dimensions.

Theoretically it is possible to conceive of genocide that is not territorially focused but aims to destroy a group regardless of its location. In an increasingly globalized world, if armed actors regard transnational social groups as enemies, then they may aim not only to expel them from particular territories but also to destroy them wherever they are. For example, Islamist terror organizations seek to drive Americans and Westerners (sometimes represented religiously as 'Crusaders') as well as Jews from predominantly Islamic countries – in this sense they remain territorially focused. But they also try to destroy, through the symbolic power of killing, the power of these amorphous enemies worldwide. Yet such less territorial cases are, so far, relatively unimportant in the history of group destruction. They are partial exceptions that prove the rule of the centrality of territory.

5

Conceptual Proliferation

The many '-cides' of genocide

> Many authors, instead of using a generic term, use . . . terms connoting only some functional aspect of the main generic notion of genocide.
>
> Raphael Lemkin[1]

We saw that, in the 'cleansing' literature, 'genocide' has been redefined as the extreme form of a wider phenomenon. This roughly matches the legal view that genocide is a specific type of criminal political killing, to be placed alongside the broader classes of war crimes and crimes against humanity. Although these categorical distinctions are evidently insufficient for sociological purposes, they have influenced the literature by suggesting that genocide is only *one form* of violence directed at civilian groups, rather than – as Lemkin originally proposed – a *general framework* for understanding it. In response to this categorization, the rapidly expanding literature has seen an *ad hoc* proliferation of concepts to describe 'other' forms of violence. Thus 'ethnic cleansing' is only the most prominent instance of a wider trend that has confused the understanding of genocide. In this chapter, I shall explore the conceptual jungle and try to clear a path through.

New frameworks: murderous cleansing and democide

As we have seen, the general tendency has been to reject or neglect Lemkin's broad approach linking killing with social destruction. Yet the reduction of genocide to killing, and therefore a special form of violence, has led to a search for new broad master-concepts to substitute for genocide. Scholars have recognized the problem that exercised Lemkin, the need for a generic concept as a framework for understanding violence against civilians, while producing new solutions that displaced his concept. Thus Mann, we have seen, used 'murderous cleansing' as a master-concept and graded its varieties according to the degrees of 'cleansing' and violence.[2] Likewise Rudy Rummel proposed 'democide' – 'the murder of any person or people by a government, including genocide, politicide, and mass murder' – an overarching concept for all kinds of killing.[3] Because of his focus on individual deaths, Rummel used 'democide' more to measure and compare death tolls for episodes than to explain social processes. It led towards a statistical approach, abstractly piling up the bodies, rather than a sociological analysis, showing how they arose from complex political and social relations – each of the chapters of Rummel's book included an episode's body count in its title. Moreover democide was a thin concept. It took the social and group dynamics out of mass killing, so that any arbitrary governmental killing, even of a single individual, was included. It categorized killing by agent: by focusing only on governments it artificially separated governmental from paramilitary and 'societal' killings. And it separated killing from the other political coercion and violence to which it is usually intimately linked.

Both Mann's and Rummel's frameworks integrated a range of secondary concepts developed by scholars to describe the forms of political oppression and violence, including genocide as one specific form. Unlike them, I do not accept that most such concepts are straightforwardly useful. Many have only limited uses, while others are misleading and should be discarded. Even when they denote distinctive realities, they are often proposed in ways that artificially separate one from another. And conceptual proliferation is itself a problem. While there is a need for flexible language to describe the varieties of genocide, overemphasis on secondary differences confuses discussion. The invention of new terms threatens, as with 'cleansing', to delineate as separate phenomena types of action that belong to genocide. *Historically the various 'phenomena' are not discrete, but tend to be combined in one way or another. We need concepts and theories that link them rather than set them apart.*

As social scientists, we cannot legislate the wider social usages, but we can clarify our own, and thus contribute to consistent debate. In this chapter I consider the principal terms that have been used. I propose that *the many new '-cides' are, in fact, the many sides of genocide.* And although I have criticized 'ethnic cleansing', the term has one small redeeming feature: it is not yet another '-cide' word. Proliferation has proceeded unimaginatively in Lemkin's footsteps: almost all innovations have echoed his approach by adding '-cide' to an existing root.

Ethnocide and cultural genocide

Perhaps one reason that 'ethnic cleansing' was not a '-cide' term is that the most obvious word, *ethnocide*, already had other meanings. As we saw, Lemkin had mentioned this word in joining *genos* to *-cide*: he noted that '[a]nother term could be used for the same idea, namely, *ethnocide*.'[4] This usage has not caught on, although Stuart D. Stein, in an encyclopaedia entry, noted that '[t]he term *ethnocide* is generally taken to refer to the destruction of members of a group, in whole or in part, identified in terms of their ethnicity. Its use is conceptually and theoretically closely linked with the term *genocide*.' And yet, he continued, 'inasmuch as ethnocide is used to refer to the destruction of members of a group, in whole or in part, on the basis of their ethnicity, this practice would simultaneously constitute genocide.'[5] René Lemarchand's study of Burundi deployed 'ethnocide' in this sense, 'as largely synonymous with "genocide"'.[6] Yet it seems superfluous to use a special term for the destruction of ethnic groups, when these are one of the principal types understood as targets of genocide. If we followed this logic we would also need 'nationcide', 'racicide' and 'religicide' to refer to the Convention's other core types. Yet the use of terms such as 'gendercide', 'politicide' and 'classicide', which I discuss below, does imply that each type of victim group needs its own term; thus all such usages would be legitimate. This would unnecessarily fragment the discussion of anti-group violence, when 'genocide' can cover all its forms.

However, ethnocide has been more widely used in a much more limited sense, meaning *cultural genocide* (indeed it has even been replaced by the horrible word *culturecide*).[7] Ethnocide in this sense has been defined internationally: in 1981 UNESCO (the United Nations Educational, Scientific and Cultural Organization) declared:

> Ethnocide means that an ethnic group is denied the right to enjoy, develop and transmit its own culture and its own language, whether individually or collectively. . . . We declare that ethnocide, that is, cultural genocide, is a violation of international law equivalent to genocide, which was condemned by the United Nations Convention on the Prevention and Punishment of the Crime of Genocide.[8]

The references to 'cultural genocide' and the Convention make clear the term's close connections with the master-concept. We should recall that, from the earliest days when he placed 'vandalism' alongside 'barbarity', Lemkin saw cultural destruction as an element of genocide. Destroying a group necessarily involved suppressing, indeed often obliterating, its culture, both in the sense of a lived way of life, and in the sense of trad-ition embodied in signs and artefacts. Clearly it is difficult to conceive of genocide without a cultural, any less than a territorial, dimension.

However, the scope of ethnocide has also been distinguished *from* genocide, by applying it to cultural suppression *unaccompanied* by widespread violence or killing. In this sense, Charny distinguished ethnocide from genocide that – in his terms – must involve mass murder.[9] Some writers on indigenous peoples have talked instead of 'cultural genocide'; but Moses rightly questioned whether it is 'really satisfactory to equate cultural genocide and physical extermination', arguing instead for a 'dynamic' view of the relations between them, for example the potential for escalation from one to the other.[10] The logic is that *we should avoid using 'genocide' for situations where there is no attempt to destroy the group in a violent sense*: that is to say, where its members are allowed to survive physically, even in their homeland through coercive assimilation and where their culture is permitted to continue through oral transmission in families, religious communities and villages that state power does not penetrate.

To compound this confusion, ethnocide is also used for cases in which a group *is* destroyed, but *without* a developed intention to destroy it on the part of its oppressors. Thus the pre-Columbus civilizations of the 'new world' were not only suppressed by European conquerors, but their populations were decimated – and sometimes entirely wiped out – by imported diseases. Using this sense, Mann put ethnocide in the 'unpremeditated mass deaths' column of his tabulation of 'murderous ethnic cleansing'.[11]

Thus the principal meanings of ethnocide are contradictory to each other and usage badly needs clarifying. It is clear that much cultural and linguistic suppression falls short of the destruction of a group and cannot be considered genocide, although in some cases it may be its precursor. However, where deep, extensive cultural and linguistic sup-pression leads to violent attacks on a group, or to armed conflict in which violent suppression occurs, this tips over into genocide. So the idea of ethnocide as 'cultural genocide' distinct from physically violent genocide is misleading, since cultural genocide can only be the cultural dimension *of* genocide, something which is integral to every genocidal attack.

On the other hand, unpremeditated destruction, for example by unintentionally spreading disease or by poverty- and weather-induced famine, does not necessarily constitute genocide. Yet whenever a group is destroyed in these ways, questions of intention and responsibility of the powers that rule over them are acutely raised. States and armies that fail to halt the spread or alleviate the effects of disease or famine – and certainly those that deliberately take advantage of them – may come to *intend* the destruction they condone. Once again, it is a fine line. No wonder that Mike Davis used the term 'holocausts' to describe the famines of late Victorian India, when British rulers allowed starvation (originally due partly to weather conditions) to weaken the peasantry, perceiving political benefits.[12] In the more clear-cut cases of the Stalinist and Maoist 'terror famines' (Ukraine in the early 1930s and China in the late 1950s), hunger was used alongside violence in conscious policies to break the peasantry and its resistance.[13] Although sometimes seen as cases of 'unpremeditated' death or 'callous revolutionary projects', the intentional destruction of peasant social power by causing extensive hardship and death seems fairly clear, and these cases were therefore genocidal.

For all these reasons, we should question the utility of 'ethnocide'. As Stein put it, 'its close affinity with the concept genocide, and the somewhat varied and confused amplification of its meaning without adequate reference to the derivative attributions of the Genocide Convention 1948, or Lemkin's work, tends to render it superfluous for both analytic and descriptive purposes.'[14] It is better to refer to *cultural suppression* for pre-genocidal denial of culture, the *cultural dimension of genocide* for suppression that is part of a broader genocidal process, and *unintentional group destruction* for cases where groups are destroyed by disease and famine that are originally unintended.

Gendercide

Many more '-cide' words have been introduced in recent years. Their originators and proponents often see their 'new' forms as distinct from genocide. A term that illustrates the wider conceptual dilemmas is 'gendercide', first coined by Mary Anne Warren, who drew

an analogy between the concept of *genocide* and what I call *gendercide*. The *Oxford American Dictionary* defines genocide as 'the deliberate extermination of a race of people.' By analogy, gendercide would be the deliberate extermination of persons of a particular sex (or gender). Other terms, such as 'gynocide' and 'femicide,' have been used to refer to the wrongful killing of girls and women. But 'gendercide' is a sex-neutral term, in that the victims may be either male or female. There is a need for such a sex-neutral term, since sexually discriminatory killing is just as wrong when the victims happen to be male. The term also calls attention to the fact that gender roles have often had lethal consequences, and that these are in important respects analogous to the lethal consequences of racial, religious, and class prejudice.[15]

So far so good: following the analogy with genocide, gendercide would be the deliberate destruction (although not necessarily physical exter-mination) of a group of people of a particular sex or gender.

Yet there have been few such episodes in history. As Adam Jones pointed out, Warren herself focused on female infanticide, witch-hunts in medieval Europe, widow-burning in India, female genital mutilation, 'the denial of reproductive freedom' (to women), 'misogynist ideologies' and the sex selection of children.[16] While these are all widespread forms of violence and discrimination against women and girls, *none* of them amount to a definite attempt to destroy women or female children as a category of people. On the contrary, these forms of suppression were all designed to reinforce a particular, subordinate *place for* women within certain cultures. Moreover Jones's own extension of the concept of gendercide took us little further. Pointing out that 'gendercide, for all practical purposes, is limited in Warren's analysis to "anti-female gen-dercide"', he redefined the term 'gender-selective mass killing'.[17] His main purpose was to extend the analysis to the killing of men, since 'non-combatant men have been and continue to be the most frequent targets of mass killing and genocidal slaughter, as well as a host of lesser atrocities and abuses.'[18] Jones documented many cases in which men have been massacred – for example, in 1995 at Srebrenica, where Serbian forces slaughtered unarmed men of combatant age, while women, chil-dren and old men were expelled by bus to the relative safety of Bosnian government territory. Such examples are useful to correct the perception of gendered violence as mainly violence against women. Yet no more than Warren's cases concerning women do any of Jones's actually amount to the targeted destruction of *men* in general, which would be required to demonstrate the existence of gendercide. The principal genuine case is one that neither emphasize, the Nazis' attempt to destroy the homosexual population of Germany.[19] Indeed *sexual-orientation groups such as gays are far more likely to be targets of genocide than women or men as such*. Even the most misogynist of rulers is unlikely to destroy the very social category of women in the society over which they rule. Even the most violent, chauvinist feminists – the notorious but short-lived Society for Cutting Up Men (SCUM) comes to mind – are unlikely to have any serious plan to destroy men in general even in a particular place.

The proponents of the concept of gendercide have therefore been talking about forms of violence that are rather different from those that the genocide analogy logically indicates. Warren was drawing attention to widespread violence against women, but that violence was not comparable to genocide. Jones was drawing attention to the gendering of victimhood, particularly the tendency of armed forces to target civilian men, but that was one dimension of a broader genocidal process. *That genocide is gendered – women and men are targeted in particular ways relating to their gendered social roles, sexuality, age, etc. – is an important insight. However, through this violence, the perpetrators usually intend to destroy not gender groups, but ethnic, national and other groups that they have defined as enemies.* At Srebrenica, men were killed because they were male Muslims, and therefore potential fighters for the Bosnian cause and resisters to the destruction of their ethnic community. In Rwanda, Hutu nationalists raped and enslaved women not simply because they were women, but because they were Tutsis.

It seems more helpful to understand these forms of gendered violence in terms of the *gender dimension of genocide*, rather than as a separate phenomenon called 'gendercide'. The *reductio ad absurdum* of this conceptual proliferation was Jones's argument for resurrecting 'gynocide' (for women-killing) and introducing yet another variation, 'androcide' (for men-killing).[20] At this point, the general terminological madness should stop. Using separate terms for the killing of men and women takes away from the common victimization in their different gendered experiences. The point, surely, is not *who* is being killed, but the fact that people are being harmed because of how they are perceived as gendered individuals, in order to destroy their social existence as part of a community.

Politicide

Although gendercide is a newer '-cide', the problems it entails also apply to more established concepts. Arguments about the killing of political groups have long been central to genocide debate. As we have seen, Lemkin originally saw the destruction of the political institutions of a group as part of genocide, although, in the Convention drafting process, including political *groups* was the most controversial issue.[21] Soviet representatives, not surprisingly in view of Stalin's persecutions, argued strongly against. Subsequently the exclusion of political groups has led to 'unrelenting criticism of . . . the Convention's "blind spot" ',[22] and many scholars have argued for their inclusion in an expanded definition.

Certainly there appear to be significant differences between political groups and the ethnic, national, racial and religious groups that the Convention protects. Membership in most of these types is often ascribed (individual members are born into them), but that of political groups is primarily elective (people choose to belong). Political collectivities are generally associations, whereas what are sometimes called basic social groups (including social classes as well as those protected by the Convention) are – at least potentially – communities. Political 'groups' such as parties are *intensive* power organizations, mobilizing power precisely in order to enter into political conflict, whereas the cohesion of most kinds of social group depends on *extensive* power in social and cultural life.[23] Moreover political associations such as parties, pressure groups and indeed social movements often understand themselves as *representing* social groups and thus have a different character and role from groups they claim to represent. Lemkin himself argued against the inclusion of political groups, 'on the grounds that they lacked the permanency and specific characteristics of the other groups'.[24] However, these distinctions cannot be regarded as rigid. Whereas class, ethnic and especially religious communities often have associational qualities, political bodies often develop communal qualities. Parties and movements often become communities, sharing lifestyles and reinforcing political choice with all sorts of communal bonds. Partners and children of party members often become part of an extended party- or movement-community. From the standpoint of a generic theory of genocide, in any case, these differences cannot be of prime importance. *If a 'political group' is targeted for destruction in the same way as other kinds of group, then surely this is, likewise, genocide?*

Nevertheless, differences in the character of political associations do give rise to important issues. Since genocide develops out of political and military struggle – rather than simple hatred or prejudice against a particular group – political elites and activists are often the first targets of genocide. The Nazis destroyed opposing political organizations such as the Communist and Socialist parties and trade unions – eliminating them as organizations, imprisoning and even killing their activists – before they eliminated the Jewish community in Germany. In their occupation of Poland, the Nazis first targeted Polish officialdom, and especially the officer class of the army. In their invasion of the Soviet

Union, they targeted communists as well as prisoners of war and Jews. In the Rwandan genocide, the Hutu nationalists first killed opposition politicians (including Hutus) before attacking the mass of the Tutsi population. In Bosnia, Serbian nationalists eliminated political activists of the Croatian and Bosnian-Muslim nationalist parties, as the first step in the elimination of Croat and Muslim populations. *However, we don't generally describe any of these genocidal episodes primarily as killings of 'political groups'.* Party members, public officials and (disarmed) members of armed forces tend to be targeted as leaders of a larger population. Indeed, as Zygmunt Bauman pointed out, they are generally targeted as potential organizers of resistance:

> Among the resources of resistance that must be destroyed to make the violence effective (resources whose destruction, arguably, is the central point of the genocide and ultimately the measure of its effectiveness), by far the most crucial is occupied by the traditional elites of the doomed community. The most seminal effect of the genocide is the 'beheading' of the enemy. It is hoped that the marked group, once deprived of leadership and centres of authority, will lose its cohesiveness and the ability to sustain its own identity, and consequently its defensive potential. The inner structure of the group will collapse, thereby dissipating it into a collection of individuals who may be then picked one by one and incorporated within the new structure administered by the victors, or forcibly reassembled into a subjugated, segregated category, ruled and policed directly by the managers of the new order.[25]

Note, however, that Bauman rightly expressed the issue as one of a community's 'elites' in general rather than simply of political leadership.

Only occasionally has the destruction of a political group come to serve as the *defining* aspect of a whole episode of slaughter. A prime case is the mass killing of communists by the Indonesian army in 1965, in which a whole party and all those associated with it were destroyed. This could be described as *politicide*, in which a political group as such is the prime target, a term used by authors such as Harff and Gurr and adopted by Mann.[26] However, we may question whether politicide should be defined as different from genocide. Fully fledged politicides, in which a political party and the community that surrounds it becomes the prime target of a policy of destruction, are not qualitatively different from other genocides, and probably form a small proportion of cases. In this sense, it seems best to view *politicide as a variant of genocide* and *political targeting as a general dimension of genocide*, where political enemies are targeted alongside, or as the leading elements of, ethnic, class or other social enemies.

Classicide

The targeting of social classes for destruction is also unusual. If, as Marx and Engels proposed, history is the history of class struggles, nevertheless classes do not normally destroy each other. In the long history of complex civilizations, ruling groups often displaced each other violently through war and conquest and massacred their enemies – before settling down to absorb their societies into their own empires. Otherwise, new ruling groups often ascended gradually through new forms of wealth and power. In what Marxists call 'the transition from feudalism to capitalism', capitalists gradually displaced the traditional power of feudal landowners and generally assimilated them (as 'aristocracy') into a capital-based system of power. New ruling classes did not commit genocide against old ruling classes, but absorbed their forms of power, status and wealth through buy-outs, amalgamations and intermarriage as well as coercion. Even less have ruling classes generally sought to destroy subordinate social classes. Rulers needed slaves, serfs, peasants and, latterly, industrial workers: while they might defeat, sometimes bloodily, their various rebellions, they fundamentally required the reproduction of these groups' ways of life, based on labour. Marx emphasized, it is true, the violent dispossession of the English peasantry in the transition to capitalism.[27] Peasant communities and their ways of life were broken up, often brutally, with great suffering among the dispossessed. This element of violent destruction in the dissolution of peasant communities showed the potential of class relations to develop genocidally, but this does not seem common.

Likewise movements of subordinate classes have rarely assumed genocidal form. In working-class revolutionary movements of the nineteenth and early twentieth centuries, violence was deployed mainly to defeat the organized state power of the ruling class. Although movements often intended to overthrow the group power of propertied classes, violence was more often the result of outbursts of popular anger or excesses by local militants than of deliberate campaigns by revolutionary leaders. Radical socialist ideas of ending class society entailed dissolving social groups through transformative action. Marx believed that the workers' seizure of power would lead to the simultaneous dissolution of all classes: the working class would also cease to exist as a class, offering liberation to individuals of all classes. While it is abstractly possible to read back such schemes of radical social change in a quasi-genocidal sense, socialists of the pre-First World War period did not intend or generally practise them in this way.

Projects of *destroying social classes*, in a sense analogous to the destruction of ethnic, national, racial and religious groups that the Convention defined as genocide, accompanied the rise of totalitarian Stalinist parties and states. Only in their hands did the Marxist identification of a political 'class enemy' become a programme for class destruction through extensive terror and killing. The case of the peasantry is instructive. Marx had been dismissive of peasants as a class, believing their way of life to be an obstacle to the development of modern capitalist social relations.[28] Marx believed that peasants, with their individualistic attachment to the land, were incapable of collective social action or organization of production, and that their way of life needed to change. Likewise Bolshevik leaders saw the embedding of individual peasant land ownership – one of the most profound results of the Russian Revolution – as blocking the creation of modern agriculture in an industrial socialist society. And although the Bolsheviks advocated a consensual transformation of agriculture, like central rulers in all agrarian societies they were not shy of using force to subdue peasants. Already in the civil war (1919–21), they deployed terror to extract foodstuffs to feed the cities. And yet the *destruction* of the peasantry remained unimaginable until Stalin turned the party-state into a terroristic personal dictatorship. Now the regime looked to break the power of the peasants in a far more fundamental way, and to destroy existing peasant ways of life. In 1929 Stalin proclaimed the *kulaks* as the 'enemy' of the regime; pushing the party-state machine back into civil-war mode, in 1930 he launched a military-style offensive to 'liquidate' them as a class. Through deportations, mass killings and starvation, the peasantry was destroyed as a class and prepared for collectivization, its capacity for resistance broken. Further, Stalin exported food from the main agricultural areas, compounding the peasants' defeat with a terrible state-made 'terror famine' in 1932–3.[29] Altogether, 10 million peasants may have died. This kind of campaign was repeated by Mao's regime in China in the 'Great Leap Forward' of 1959–61, with a toll of probably over 30 million lives.[30] The peasantry's traditional way of life was also a target of the Khmer Rouge in Cambodia in 1975–9.[31]

Mann invents the term *classicide* for this type of murderous action; it is a logical extension of the range of '-cide' terms.[32] Clearly the idea that social classes were 'enemies', to be 'liquidated' by terror and slaughter, is a distinctive variation on the more common targeting of ethnic and national groups. But it is by no means so separate a phenomenon. The anti-peasant 'classicides' were combined with and followed by similar murderous campaigns against other social groups – both other classes and ethnic or national groups. Stalin's terror famine was not just a means of breaking the peasantry: concentrated in Ukraine, its secondary target was Ukrainian national identity. Mao's anti-peasant campaign was particularly extreme in Tibet, where it combined with suppression of national identity; he followed it with the 'Cultural Revolution', directed against the urban intelligentsia. Pol Pot's anti-peasant policies were part of a comprehensive genocide of all kinds of social groups, including ethnic and national minorities (Cham and Vietnamese) as well as other classes (such as the urban middle class) and religions.

Of course Stalinist and Maoist violence was so all-embracing that these regimes are easily assumed under other rubrics, notably 'totalitarianism'[33] and 'terror'.[34] Fein, arguing that the targets of genocide must be 'real' groups, gives Stalin's attacks on 'wreckers' as an example of a campaign against fantasy groups. Attacking such a non-group, she argues, is a phenomenon of terror rather than genocide.[35] Actually this case shows the opposite: under the pretext of attacking largely imaginary groups of 'wreckers' and pseudo-scientifically defined groups such as *kulaks*, real groups of officials, intellectuals, workers and peasants were attacked. Stalinist regimes were totalitarian, involving a general terror against society and all individuals, but, within this, particular groups (classes, nations, etc.) were targeted as special 'enemies' to be destroyed in a genocidal sense.

Because genocide is a political process, the nature of the perpetrator regime is always germane to its understanding. The genocides of Stalinist regimes were distinctive in their emphasis on 'classicide'. Totalitarian genocides are generally distinctive in their tendency to multiply enemies (for example, Nazism's wide range of genocidal targets). However, the common features of genocide are even more compelling. In the end, it is not so important which type of civilian social group is attacked. Wherever armed power organizations attempt to destroy any such group, an extreme departure from normal politics and social life is under way. Ultimately, exactly how genocidists conceptualize the groups that they attack is less important than the fact that they are able to define social groups as enemies in this way. As we have noted, fantasy is inherent in genocide. Once a regime or movement embarks on the destruction of one group, it is more likely to target others. Genocidists should not be thought of as highly rational, consistent actors: whatever the pseudo-rational core to their projects that makes them fix on particular groups as enemies, the practice of destruction has its own dynamics that often lead to shifts in targeting, identification and methods. Hence a lot of the arbitrariness that constitutes the experience of victims.

There is another reason why 'classicide', separated from genocide, has limited purchase. This is that class, like gender and politics, is a dimension of genocide in general. Even when, as in most genocides, the prime enemy to be destroyed is an ethnic or national group, genocidal practice will inevitably acquire a class aspect. Indeed in some cases, such as in Rwanda, groups that are labelled 'ethnic' from the outside are understood locally more like classes.[36] Genocidists attack particular classes differentially: the wealthy for their wealth (perpetrators are often robbers); those of high status for their symbolic roles in the victim group; and the educated generally for their capacity to articulate the group's interests and values. Class has also entered into the process of some genocides in the selection of some people to work and others to be killed. We should not forget that genocide is a dynamic, layered set of processes in which death is not the instant fate of all victims. To conclude, therefore, there is not only *classicide in the sense of class-targeted genocide*; there is also *a general class dimension of genocide* that is common to all cases.

Urbicide

Yet another '-cide' increasingly preoccupies scholars (although it doesn't find its way into Mann's table): 'urbicide'. Urban centres, originally fortified centres of power, have always been pivotal to warfare, and modern war has targeted industrial and capital cities with bombs and nuclear missiles.[37] Yet in certain conflicts, other sides of the city have become central: plurality, multi-ethnicity and cosmopolitanism have become targets of anti-urban violence. Since, Martin Coward contended, '[h]eterogeneity . . . can be said to be the defining characteristic of urbanity, the destruction of urban life is the destruction of heterogeneity.'[38] He emphasized 'the destruction of buildings and urban fabric as elements of urbanity' – the cultural dimension – but this should be seen alongside the destruction of plural urban populations themselves. Anti-urbanism can be traced through Nazi attacks on intellectual and artistic 'decadence', Stalinist attacks on 'bourgeois' culture, and Maoist anti-urbanism (forcing the intellectuals to return to manual labour in the country), finding its most extreme expression in the Khmer Rouge's emptying of Pnom Penh in 1975. It was evident in Serbian nationalists' campaigns against Sarajevo and other cosmopolitan urban centres in Bosnia-Herzegovina. Nationalists generally locate their nation's heart in its traditional rural hinterlands, mobilize greater strength in the countryside and small towns, and face cosmopolitan resistance in the cities.

It can therefore be argued that 'urbicide' is a distinctive anti-urban violence. However, anti-urbanism is intertwined with other dimensions of genocide: it has strong cultural and class elements; it often combines with the attack on political elites, who of course are urban; and it is generally combined with more conventional ethnic-national targeting. It represents the tendency towards the multiplication of group 'enemies', since anti-cosmopolitanism is the other side of exclusive nationalism that targets 'enemy' ethnic groups. Even less than 'politicide' or 'classicide', however, does 'urbicide' represent a set of political processes that can be clearly distinguished from genocide's common ethnic-nationally targeted forms. Urban communities are rarely if ever targeted separately from other kinds of targeting. Therefore 'urbicide' is best understood as the *anti-urban dimension of genocide*.

Auto-genocide

We could pursue the full range of '-cide' concepts, although it is likely that, by the time this book is published, more new terms will have been added. But the discussion is in danger of becoming repetitive and I will mention only one more term. The curious idea of 'auto-genocide' is applied principally to the Cambodian case. The term's strangeness is that, taken literally, it suggests self-destruction: and while individuals often take their own lives, collective suicide is much rarer – and no one has suggested that this has happened in any genocide, including in Cambodia. The term has been defined instead as 'mass killing of members of the group to which the perpetrators themselves belong'.[39] The idea is still sociologically unenlightening, because a campaign of killing necessarily arises from – or at least generates – a deep cleavage between killers and killed, which may be assumed to override any prior common identity. The idea derived, however, from the UN Convention's presumption of ethnical–national–racial–religious targets in genocide. Given this definition, it could be concluded (on a narrow reading) that killing by members of the 'same' ethnic group could not be genocide. Thus Schabas argued: 'Confusing mass killing of the members of the perpetrators' own group with genocide is inconsistent with the purposes of the Convention, which was to protect national minorities from crimes based on ethnic hatred.'[40] Alternatively, if it was concluded nonetheless that there was genocide, this had to be seen as 'auto-genocide'. The term was probably coined by a UN rapporteur,[41] trying to squeeze the Cambodian case past a definition that appeared not to allow it.

Of course, all this demonstrated the widely acknowledged inadequacy of the Convention's restriction of the 'groups' covered. Indeed a reflection on the nature of the Cambodian terror, commonly seen as genocide, brings us up squarely against this failing. For Ben Kiernan has shown that part of the Khmer Rouge campaign – the destruction of the Cham minority – was in any case 'genocide' in the Convention's terms.[42] It seems reasonable to see the campaign against the Vietnamese minority in the same light. Thus we are left with the argument that some Khmer Rouge anti-group violence was 'genocide', some not. Whether or not legally this distinction is unavoidable (as Schabas argued),[43] sociologically it is nonsense. The Pol Pot regime organized a comprehensive campaign of destruction against virtually all recognizable social groups – ethnic-national, class and religious – in Cambodian society. It is bizarre to describe this campaign as 'genocide' when it affects ethnic-national or religious minorities, as 'auto-genocide' when it affects ethnic Khmer, and as 'crimes against humanity' concerning the targeting of educated and urban populations and traditional peasant ways of life. This approach leads to an artificial conceptual fragmentation of anti-group violence that had common authors, a single ideological frame and a combined trajectory. What we need are concepts, theory and analysis that enable us to understand the integral processes of such episodes.

Genocide as a framework

Thus the proliferation of '-cide' concepts has done as much to confuse as to clarify the understanding of violence against civilian social groups. Sixty years ago, at the beginning of the discussion, Lemkin complained: 'Many authors, instead of using a generic term, use currently terms connoting only some functional aspect of the main generic notion of genocide. Thus the terms "Germanization", "Magyarization", "Italianization", for example, are used to connote the imposition by one stronger nation (Germany, Hungary, Italy) of its national pattern upon national group controlled by it.' Although now scholars classify events as 'ethnic cleansing', 'ethnocide', 'gendercide', 'politicide' or 'urbicide', rather than genocide, it is clear that what is referred to by all these concepts are closely related forms of political violence, which tend to occur in combination with each other. Lemkin's conclusion is still appropriate: 'these terms are also inadequate because they do not convey the common elements of one generic notion.' He complained that the terms he was criticizing 'treat mainly the cultural, economic, and social aspects of genocide, leaving out the biological aspect, such as causing the physical decline and even destruction of the population involved.'[44] Today's conceptual proliferators reverse this error, identifying genocide only with physical destruction, separating off social and cultural destruction, or treating the destruction of one kind of group as different from the destruction of another. More than ever, we need a common theoretical framework to understand violence against civilians. I have explained why some of the more prominent alternative proposals are unacceptable. *It is better to use genocide as the master-concept, accepting that its meaning has expanded from the narrower meaning of genos as nation or ethnic group, to cover the destruction of any type of people or any group.*

So far this book has involved a critique of the current theoretical tendencies in the study of genocide. We are now ready to turn to the more difficult question: how can the idea of genocide, as a generic framework for understanding violence against civilian groups, be understood sociologically? This is the subject of the second part of this book.

Part II: Sociology of Genocide

6

From Intentionality to a Structural Concept

Social action, social relations and conflict

the attempt at a *rational reconstruction* of a *procedure in use*
Thomas Burger on Weber's theory of concept formation[1]

Underlying all the problems examined in the first part of this book is incoherence in how the concept of genocide is grasped. This arises partly from the paradox that, although the literature's concerns are fundamentally sociological, lawyers and historians have drafted its key propositions. There has been little systematic reflection informed by sociological understanding. As we have seen, most writing has stayed close to the Genocide Convention. Yet its central contention, that 'genocide means [certain kinds of] acts committed with intent to destroy, in whole or in part, a national, ethnical, racial or religious group, as such', begs a series of key sociological questions. In this part of the book, I explore these and propose a new framework for understanding genocide.

I begin with the foundational assumption that genocide is *intentional action* aimed at the destruction of social groups, together with its implication that genocide is defined by the *subjective meaning* attached to it by the actors conventionally described as 'perpetrators'. I argue, with the aid of Weber's understanding of social action, that while establishing this subjective meaning is an unavoidable starting point, it is only a preliminary stage of conceptualization. Intentionality does not therefore provide an overall framework for understanding genocide. We need to move, I propose, to the main stage of sociological conceptualization,

structural concept formation. This means moving away from the subjective meaning of genocidal action (for the perpetrators) to understanding
the typical *social relations* of genocide (not only among perpetrators, but
crucially between them and the victims, and indeed among victims), and
therefore the structure of *social conflict* that these set up.

Intention in the light of a sociology of action

Before opening up the sociological discussion, it is important to see
how these issues have been approached legally. Here it is clear that 'the
mental element', genocidal intention, defines genocide. According to
the Rome Statute of the International Criminal Court, which codified
genocide and other serious international crimes, this element has two
components: knowledge and intent. Knowledge 'means awareness that
a circumstance exists or a consequence will occur in the ordinary course
of events.'[2] In genocide, it involves awareness that the acts committed
will lead to the destruction of the target group. It is entwined with the
second element, intent, because a crucial element of knowledge is
awareness of the existence of a 'plan' to destroy a group. Genocide has
been seen legally as an organized, not a spontaneous, crime;[3] it could
not be committed by an individual acting alone.[4] As the International
Criminal Tribunal for Rwanda declared, 'although a specific plan to
destroy does not constitute an element of genocide, it would appear
that it is not easy to carry out a genocide without a plan or organization.'[5] As Schabas argued, even if the terms 'with intent' had not been
included in the definition of genocide, it was inconceivable that such an
enormous crime could be committed unintentionally.[6]

However, the legal understanding of 'intent' is narrow: the reference
to 'intent' in the text indicated that the prosecution needed to go beyond
establishing that the offender meant to engage in the conduct, or to
cause the consequence. The offender must also be shown to possess a
'specific intent' (*dolus specialis*).[7] Schabas cited the explanation by a
trial chamber of the Rwanda Tribunal that '[s]pecial intent of a crime
is the specific intention, required as a constitutive element of the crime,
which demands that the perpetrator clearly seeks to produce the act
charged', so that (it continued) the 'offence is characterized by a psychological relationship between the physical result and the mental state
of the perpetrator.'[8] This could be seen as demanding a standard of evidence about the perpetrators' mental states that would be difficult to
achieve. 'In practice', however, Schabas pointed out, 'proof of intention
is rarely a formal part of the prosecution's case. The prosecution does

not generally call psychiatrists as expert witnesses to establish what the accused really intended. Rather, the intent is a logical deduction that flows from evidence of the material acts. Criminal law presumes that an individual intends the consequences of his or her acts, in effect deducing the existence of the *mens rea* from proof of the physical act itself.'[9] Moreover the Rwanda chamber maintained that, in the absence of a confession, the accused's intent could be inferred from presumptions of fact. The chamber reasoned that 'it is possible to deduce the genocidal intent inherent in a particular act charged from the general context of the perpetration of other culpable acts systematically directed against that same group, whether these acts were committed by the same offender or by others.'[10] So although the legal requirement to show 'specific' intent is formally a strict understanding of intention, it need not be as tight as it first seems.

Nevertheless the legal idea moves 'intent' beyond its ordinary meaning, in ways that unnecessarily restrict understanding. This tight concept of intention is sometimes reinforced by sociologically unrealistic concepts of *collective* intention. The Yugoslav Tribunal's reasonable argument, that individual perpetrators did not have to share genocidal intentions to be considered participants in genocide, provoked legal insistence that only those who specifically shared the intention could be guilty of the crime.[11] And although Schabas was clear that intent could not be *equated* with motive,[12] his view emphasized a central link between the two, which in turn contributed to an excessively tight concept of intention. For him, organizers and planners must necessarily have 'a racist or discriminatory motive, that is, a genocidal motive'.[13] In one sense this demand seems obvious, even tautological: how could any organization plan genocide without discriminating against the victims or having dehumanized concepts of them? And yet it pushes back towards a more absolute concept of organizing intentions as necessarily informed by *consistent values or beliefs* that drove specific decisions – implicitly, the kind of racist values typified by Nazism. Although in both legal and social thought the idea of intention normally refers to the conscious rationale of an action, insisting on the linkage with underlying motives converts intention into something larger, more rigid and absolute.

Thus specific intentions, decisions and actions must be linked together in grand plans behind which a single *grand intention* can be seen. The Convention's emphasis on intention, which on the surface is no more than an insistence that genocide should be regarded as deliberate, policy-driven action, is converted into an assumption that policy and its drivers are coherent and consistent over a large range of actions and often a long period of time. Genocide then entails *the absolutist idea of a singular, heavily value-laden original intention that informs all the actions of a perpetrator organization over a whole historical period.* Yet assuming singular intentionality blocks any serious sociological investigation of genocide as the complex, intentional action of multiple actors, and many scholars have indicated its difficulties. Collective actors who commit genocide are engaged in political and military struggles; their aims and policies are necessarily complex and evolve according to the exigencies of conflicts in which they are involved. Thus we cannot *assume* consistent motives for action or the racist coherence of actors' values and ideologies; nor can we draw straight lines from the latter to particular 'plans' and 'intentions'. On the contrary, the degrees of coherence and consistency in actors' underlying motives, values or ideologies, and the framing of specific actions, are *empirical* questions. Not surprisingly, historians and sociologists have often emphasized the *incremental* nature of decision-making in genocide: policies develop over time and adapt to changing circumstances.[14] It is not necessarily, or even usually, the case that an entire historical episode of genocide, carried out over many months or even years, can be explained by a singular 'decision', 'intention' or even 'motive'. As Mann argued, '[m]ost accounts of murderous cleansing, especially genocide, are overorganized and overpremediated. Early events, early decisions are too often read back from the ghastly known end result.'[15] From his careful case studies, he concluded: '*Murderous cleansing is rarely the original intent of perpetrators.* . . . Murderous cleansing typically emerges as a kind of Plan C, developed only after the first two responses to a perceived ethnic threat fail . . . . To understand the outcome, we must analyze the unintended consequences of a series of interactions yielding escalation.'[16] This argument does not, however, 'downplay intentionality' (as Mann unnecessarily conceded),[17] but only the unrealistic, absolutist version of intentionality prevalent in genocide studies. Genocide was intentional, aiming to 'wipe out' an entire group, culturally as well as physically,[18] but since it was never the ethnonationalists' initial solution, 'we must be able to reconstruct the successive flow of their goals.'[19] Because the singular concept is not plausible, *a complex, situational account is the only way to continue making sense of the 'intentional' element.*

The emphasis on intention inherited from international law derived originally from the fact that genocide was seen in the same way as war crimes, which were recodified at Geneva around the same time as the Genocide Convention was drafted. The idea of intentionality in genocide follows that of 'wilful intent' in war. As Kenneth Rizer emphasized, 'the use of the word "wilful" in regard to killing or causing suffering' is a central feature of the Geneva Conventions. In order to violate them, 'one must *deliberately intend* to kill or cause suffering to civilians. In other words, if one *really* intends to destroy a military target that resides in an urban area, and civilians happen to die or be hurt as a result of poor aiming, mistaken target coordinates, inaccurate bombs, etc., this isn't technically a violation as it isn't a *wilful* attack upon the civilians.'[20] The idea that a power organization must intend a population's destruction for killing to constitute genocide reflects the same thinking. If it brings about destruction without intending to – for example when colonial armies bring disease or misguided policies cause famine – then on the Convention criteria this does not constitute genocide. However, the qualification to this kind of defence in the laws of war is also enlightening: 'If the destruction [of civilian populations] is *avoidable* however, presumably through better weapon selection, tactics, etc., then the commander could still be held liable under Article 2 of the 1907 Hague Conventions.'[21] Likewise, if leaders know that their policies may lead (or are leading) to the social and physical destruction of a group, and fail to take steps to avoid (or halt) it – as Mao Zedong, for example, knew of the effects of the Great Leap Forward but continued his policies – then they come to 'intend' the suffering they cause and may similarly be guilty. The matter is complicated, moreover, by the relationship between genocide and war. Types of act that constitute genocide – killing and other harm against civilians – also occur in war, where they may not always be criminal, or, if they are, they may be easily be seen as war crimes or crimes against humanity. This is another reason why the law of genocide has been encumbered with the idea of 'special intent'.

Some sociologists have reacted to these difficulties by abandoning the idea of genocide as intentional action. As Fein noted, to 'avoid the whole question of inference of intent, [some authors] propose that we simply eliminate intent as a criterion.'[22] But can we really, as Tony Barta suggested, 'remove from the word the emphasis on policy and intention which brought it into being'? However sympathetic we are to his alternative proposal, for 'a conception of genocide which embraces *relations* of destruction'[23] (I explore its significance below) the meaning of genocide is firmly lodged in the idea of destruction as the intentional, organized policy of particular actors. Rather than abandon the whole idea of intent, we need to contextualize it properly. As Fein argued, sociologists may have 'needlessly confused the meaning of intent', and she is right to insist on a more usual understanding, distinguished once more from motive:

> Intent or purposeful action – or inaction – is not the same in law or everyday language as either motive or function. An actor performs an act, we

say, with intent if there are foreseeable ends or consequences: for what purpose is different from why or for what motive is the act designed.[24]

We need, therefore, 'the sociological concept of purposeful action' as a 'bridge' between the legal concept of intent and a broader understanding.[25] This concept derives, of course, from Max Weber's action-centred sociology, and it is his theoretical framework that provides the essential template for understanding 'intention' – and enables us finally to transcend intention as genocide's defining element. Weber insisted that, for both sociology and history, the object of cognition was the 'subjective meaning-complex' of action.[26] For him, subjectively meaningful action is the essential subject matter of social enquiry. If we wish to grasp social relationships and structures we must first identify the meanings at work in the actions that make them up. In this sense the emphasis on perpetrator intention in genocide follows Weber's proposal that we start from the subjective meaning-complex. *Yet genocide studies generally fail properly to explore the significance and limitations of this starting point. Because they remain in thrall to legal discourse, they get stuck at this beginning and fail to follow through and develop coherent general concepts.*

Although it is generally agreed that genocide is meaningful action, it is not even established that it constitutes *social action*. Some interpretations, as we have seen, present genocide as totally 'one-sided' – the perpetrators simply 'act on' the victims, who are by definition passive. On this reading, genocide appears not to fit Weber's definition: 'Action is [only] social in so far as, by virtue of the subjective meaning attached to it by the acting individual (or individuals), it takes account of the behaviour of others and is thereby oriented in its course.'[27] Yet genocide *is* socially oriented, in a double sense. First, perpetrators' actions are typically part of complex social organizations, and individuals' actions are oriented to those of fellow perpetrators. Secondly, their actions are oriented to the behaviour of the target group, focused on *its* social organization, culture and power that they wish to destroy, and 'taking account' of the behaviour of that group's 'members' in response to the destructive policy. It is what the target group represents *socially* that constitutes the rationale for destroying it.

Thus the social character of genocidal action already indicates that understanding only perpetrators' intentions may be insufficient to explain it. Their orientation to victims implies social *relationships* in which the other actors' actions and beliefs may also be important. Moreover, in understanding the 'meaning-complexes' of genocidal action we need to take account of Weber's explanation that meaning may be of two kinds. Historians of particular genocides have been concerned with what he calls 'the actual existing meaning in the given concrete case of a particular actor', or 'the average or approximate meaning attributable to a given plurality of actors'. However, in formulating the law of genocide and in the definitional debates, authorities have also proposed what Weber called 'theoretically conceived *pure types* of subjective meaning attributed to the hypothetical actor or actors in a given type of action'.[28] *The prevailing idea of genocide – action informed by an intention to destroy social groups as such – is precisely a pure, ideal-typical representation of the subjective meaning involved in a general class of actions.*

Thus the genocide literature has unwittingly followed Weber, and his 'rational reconstruction of a procedure in use' is valuable guidance. His conception of ideal types can be invoked to understand the conceptualization of genocide. Sociological analysis, he argued, both abstracts from reality and at the same time helps us to understand it, showing with what degree of approximation a specific historical phenomenon can be subsumed under general type concepts. As an example, he argued that a single historical phenomenon might be at the same time 'feudal', 'bureaucratic' and 'charismatic'. In order to give a precise meaning to these terms, it was necessary for the sociologist to formulate pure ideal types of the corresponding forms of action, involving the 'highest degree of logical integration by virtue of their complete adequacy on the level of meaning.'[29]

However, four crucial consequences for the status of the concept of genocide follow from understanding it in this way. First, 'precisely because' of their ideal-typical character, real phenomena rarely correspond exactly to the ideally constructed pure type.[30] Hence it is unsurprising that particular genocidists vary from type in their understanding of their actions, and that therefore individual campaigns appear 'unique'. Second, logical ideal types are always constructed with a view to adequacy on the level of meaning.[31] The concept of genocidal action abstracts a particular set of meanings from the historical muddle, complexity and variation in the meanings of many perpetrators. Weber stressed that, although ideal types 'may be rational or irrational as the case may be, [f]or the purposes of a typological scientific analysis it is convenient to treat all irrational, affectually determined elements of behaviour as factors of deviation from a conceptually pure type of rational action. . . . Only in this respect and for these reasons of methodological convenience is the method of sociology "rationalistic".'[32] As we saw, *ideal types have formulated genocide's meaning in a rational way, as a singular goal of group destruction, single-mindedly pursued in a linear, systematic fashion.* This concept has purchase because genocide tends to reduce power relations to violence, and because perpetrators tend to be bureaucratically organized 'rational' actors subordinating means to ends. However, as Weber went on to explain, it is 'important to avoid . . . [the error] which confuses the unavoidable tendency of sociological concepts to assume a rationalistic character with a belief in the predominance of rational motives.'[33] *Genocidists invariably have multiple goals and deviate from their rationalistic pursuit. The ideal-typical concept of 'rational', 'intentional' genocide can be no more than a heuristic tool enabling us to grasp the complexity of real cases.* Not understanding this is one reason for the prevalence of the 'overorganized and overpremediated' – one might better say *overrationalized* – paradigm of genocide.

Third, there is the question of the *sense* in which genocidal action is 'rational'. As is well known, Weber distinguished two types of rationality. The first type (*zweckrational*) was action that is rational in terms of its orientation to a system of discrete individual ends. This type of action makes use of expectations about external situations and the behaviour of others as 'conditions' or 'means' for the successful attainment of the actor's own rationally chosen ends. The second type (*wertrational*) was action that is rational in terms of its orientation to an absolute value. Thus it involves a conscious belief in the absolute value of some ethical, aesthetic, religious or other behaviour, purely for its own sake.[34] Weber's English editor, Talcott Parsons, commented that the keynote of the distinction lay in the absoluteness with which the values involved in *Wertrationalität* are held: the sole important consideration to the actor is the realization of the value. In so far as it involves ends, rational considerations of efficiency are involved in how means are chosen. But 'there is no question either of rational weighing of this end against others, nor is there a question of "counting the cost" in the sense of taking account of possible results other than the attainment of the absolute end.'[35] In the case of *Zweckrationalität*, on the other hand, Weber saw action as motivated by a plurality of relatively independent ends, none of which is absolute. Hence, rationality involves on the one hand the weighing of the relative importance of realizing the different ends and, on the other hand, considering whether undesirable consequences would outweigh the benefits to be derived from the projected course of action.

As we have seen, genocide has often been understood in *wertrational* terms, as though the murder of the target group was an absolute and singular value. Thus Bauman contended: 'Modern genocide is genocide with a purpose. . . . The end itself is a grand vision of a better, and radically different, society.'[36] Even Mann argued that when people were willing to risk or inflict death in pursuit of their values, 'instrumental reason may be relegated to the back burner.'[37] However, considering Weber's idea of *Zweckrationalität,* one can only be struck by how very clearly it applies to many genocidal organizers, including the Nazis. Although racist ideologies appear to involve absolute values – an appearance strengthened because they are 'substantively irrational' from a human, social point of view – these may often be pursued alongside other more instrumentally rational goals (military, political, economic). Grossly inhuman ends and outcomes seem absolute, but it is not so strange to think of them being pursued in terms of instrumental rationality.[38] As Bauman acknowledged, '[r]acism is a policy first, ideology second. Like all politics, it needs organization, managers and experts.'[39] He might have added that it needs to be calibrated with other policies, involving the same kinds of pragmatic calculation. Genocidists are organized political actors often weighing their actions in the way that Weber suggests. The variety of their collective and individual ends, as well as other factors, means that their actions often deviate from type. Mann, for whom Weber's distinctions seemed very relevant, included *both* his types of rationality in a long list of perpetrator motives.[40]

Limits of intentionality

The principal consequence of understanding intentionality in the light of Weber's methodology is to recognize its necessary limits. As Fritz Ringer put it, '*the rational action of the individual,* while methodologically significant as a point of departure, was never more than a *limiting case* in his overall scheme.'[41] Thus we may look at perpetrators' 'intentions' and the subjective meaning of their acts as the *beginning* of our attempts to explain genocide. But such investigations can never be more than a starting point. The reasons are bound up with the difference between historical explanation and sociological conceptualization.[42] For Weber sociology was 'a generalizing, regularity-seeking discipline, rather than an "idiographic" one, and its method was essentially typological', although it was also 'interdefined' with history, and 'facilitated the causal analysis of singular historical phenomena'.[43] However, as Burger put it: 'The difference between sociology and history is not just one of degree. . . . For the task of sociology is *the construction of a special kind of general concept* whereas the goal of history is the formation of individual concepts.'[44] Indeed,

If historical accounts are not possible without the use of ideal types, a generalizing social science – sociology – is an indispensable cognitive

requirement. Without the latter there is no need for it because its generalizations have no value in themselves. At the same time, history cannot be
written without them. History and sociology thus are complementary;
the latter supplies an element without which the former cannot do, but
without the former the latter is pointless.[45]

Moreover without clear definitions, words would be 'vague thought-
images created to meet the unconsciously felt need for adequate expression whose meaning is only concretely felt but not clearly thought
out.'[46] Clearly defined terms enabled 'the conceptually clear description
of *individual* historical developments, whenever this is necessary and the
merely felt mental picture is too unprecise [*sic*] for a particular purpose
in question.'[47] As Carlo Antoni put it: 'In relation to history, this sociology might be viewed as a kind of terminology.'[48]

Thus while a rational ideal type of genocidal action constructed
around perpetrators' intentions is a necessary first step in explanation,
we also need causal interpretations. For Weber, a correct causal interpretation of typical action meant that the process which is claimed to be
typical is shown to be both adequately grasped at the level of meaning
and, simultaneously, causally adequate.[49] An intention-interpretation
might suggest causes, since ' "purpose" is the conception of an *effect*
which becomes the *cause* of an action. . . . Its *specific* significance con-
sists only in the fact that we not only *observe* human conduct but can
and desire to *understand* it.'[50] Yet intention-propositions can never be
conclusive; at the most, they provide us with hypotheses. Although
without 'the conviction that certain values are embodied in certain phenomena, these phenomena would never become the object of historical
investigation',[51] these values have *no overriding role* in explanation. On
the contrary, the thrust of Weber's argument *denies* them any special
methodological status. The fact that he 'called his sociology "interpretative" (*verstehend*) must not be misinterpreted. It was primarily
intended to indicate that its concepts always make reference to actors'
subjective meanings which are connected with the phenomena designated by the concepts. It does *not imply* that *Verstehen* is a method.'[52]
Thus in genocide studies, while we must refer to perpetrator intentions,
this is *never sufficient* as a method.

This discussion points us to a crucial tension between genocide's definition by intentional acts and the larger historical enterprise of comparative genocide studies, aimed at understanding whole historical
episodes and their variety. For the latter, a more developed *sociological*
conceptualization is needed. As Burger pointed out, 'behind Weber's
methodological elaborations stands the conviction that historiography

must not limit its concerns to individual occurrences and actions but must pay attention to the impact of "structural" features and "collective" phenomena in the course of historical development. Weber's sociology, accordingly, appears above all as an attempt to conceptualize, on the basis of a methodological individualism, *the structural and collective aspects of historical reality* that were neglected by the guardians of the institutionalized historiographical tradition.'[53] Moreover, the difficulties in matching individual genocides to the general concept reflect intrinsic difficulties in forming *general concepts* of historical, compared to natural, phenomena.[54] In order to be able to form general concepts,

> Weber relies on the device of constructing a course of action as it would take place if only one or a few clearly specified considerations of the many which are in operation in any concrete instance governed an actor's (actors') conduct . . . . Such a picture he calls an ideal picture, for its content does not represent what numerous empirical phenomena have in common, but what they *would* have in common without the causal influence of what – *for the purposes of concept formation* – are disturbing influences.[55]

Thus he called concepts such as 'feudal', 'charismatic', 'capitalistic', 'bureaucratic', 'Christian', ideal types because 'they are neither truly general concepts [as in the natural sciences] nor individual ones [as in history].'[56] The same applies to 'genocide'. Like other sociological ideal types, it does not 'describe the elements which the instances of a class of phenomena have in common in the empirical world, but the elements which they have in common in an imaginary world, a utopia.'[57] Whenever sociologists want to describe how social forms *in general* are structured, they are required to build models, 'mental constructs, consisting of a number of elements standing in particular relationships to each other, which are designed to represent, for descriptive purposes, a specific segment of empirical reality and the interdependencies existing in it.' Thus the sociological model 'does not correctly *describe* this segment; it *stands* for it.'[58] *The concept of genocide is a model that stands for the structure of social action and social relationships that empirical genocide involves.*[59]

A sociologically adequate concept of genocide needs to build understandings of types of action and relationships into a general account. This will take us still further from the subjective meaning for perpetrators. In Weber's transition from talking about action and *Verstehen* to talking about social relationships, he 'no longer concentrated on the *content* of human action as it appears in the actor's subjective understanding.' Instead he talked 'about the social forms separated from their [subjective] content'.[60] In order to pursue the comparative study of the major historical social systems, Weber 'was forced into the business of elaborating a systematic formal sociological language in terms of which comparisons could be made.'[61] Viewed in this light, Weber can be understood to have proposed a series of *stages* in comparative and historical investigations. In the first 'he sought to describe the social systems he was dealing with in language as close as possible to that used by the actors themselves.' *Genocide studies, in its overriding concern with establishing 'intentionality', is mostly stuck at this preliminary stage, but what is more important is 'what happens at the second stage'.*[62] Here conceptual construction *selects* from the available meanings and *exaggerates* what it selects: 'of the complex meaningful considerations within the minds of the empirical actors to whose actions an ideal type refers, only one or a few elements are assumed to operate, and that the actions which are thought of as resulting from them, therefore, embody certain meanings more purely than the empirically existing actions.'[63] So the question is the *criteria* by which these 'meaningful considerations' are selected in the construction of types. Weber was clear that '[t]he generalizations required by historians are of a special kind; they do not really state what attributes a plurality of phenomena have in common but what value-relevant (culturally significant) features they share.'[64] This criterion of *cultural or value significance* means that '[t]he goal of ideal-typical concept construction is always to make clearly explicit *not* the class or average character, but rather the unique particularity of cultural phenomena.'[65] As Jeffrey Alexander suggested, even prototypical evil can be understood only inside of symbolic codes and narratives, whose frames change substantially depending on social circumstances.[66]

So the question is, what constitutes the 'unique particularity' of genocide? In my critiques of Holocaust exclusivity, 'ethnic cleansing' and '-cide' proliferation, I have advocated a generic concept of genocide as violent conflict, in which the armed, organized side engages in intentional social destruction of the unarmed, group side – which the latter necessarily resists. I implied, therefore, that *these features have more general value significance than other criteria by which scholars have classified political violence* – such as the extent of killing, the role of expulsion, the various ways that targeted groups are defined, the type of perpetrator ideology, and so on.

In emphasizing these values, I am advancing to Weber's 'second stage', structural concept formation. Yet I am also acknowledging *with genocide there is a particular difficulty in accomplishing this movement.* Generally in this stage, historians and sociologists who have access to more than one account, in a way that participant actors do not, find that it is possible to translate the language of the particular accounts into a common language and to agree among themselves on the description in this new language of any particular social system. . . . What we find is that it is possible to develop an agreed sociological language and a limited number of agreed categories which explain, not just this or that particular situation or social system, but all the major historical social systems.[67]

However, with genocide, translating the competing accounts of 'participants' into an agreed sociological language is obviously difficult. Although the labelling and interpretation of cases (e.g. the idea of Holocaust 'uniqueness') often owe much to victim groups' perceptions, emphases on intentionality and one-sided action lead scholars to deal in perpetrators' language (ironically, victim-driven claims of 'uniqueness' are substantiated not through victim experience but in terms of perpetrator intentions, as in Katz's work). Mann has even given the field a one-sided *verstehend* definition, embracing 'ethnic cleansing' as a comprehensive analytical concept.

However, generally we cannot be satisfied with such 'phenomenological empiricism', which 'looks only at the actor's own definition of his situation',[68] and in no case is this truer than that of genocide. In Lemkin's original formulation, *perpetrator language was very radically 'translated' into a framework that claimed universal value and cultural significance. His part-criminological etymology of 'genocide' – the analogy with homicide – criminalized perpetrators and delegitimated their accounts. It took account of victim experience (if not action) and implied the bystander action of international political and legal authorities.* The concept that I have advocated assumes a similar framework of universal human values. However, because my goal is sociological understanding, and because we now have a history of genocide studies and debate which has clarified issues further, my structural concept represents a further development of Lemkin's original idea.

Social relations and a structure of conflict

How then do we constitute an appropriate structural concept? We should begin by emphasizing, of course, that genocide studies have not defined the phenomenon exclusively through perpetrator intentions. Rather there has been an oscillation between representing genocide as a type of *action* characterized by its intentions and as a type of *outcome* – so that the label 'a genocide' has often been reserved for a few big, largely 'successful' episodes. Indeed this has even led some to *define* genocide in general by outcome, as in Vahakn Dadrian's statement that it is 'the *successful* attempt by a dominant group . . . to reduce by coercion or lethal violence the number of a minority group whose extermination is held desirable . . . .'[69] This reduction of genocide to an outcome has often been reinforced by the elementary failure to recognize that, as a noun, genocide has both a generic meaning and particular cases. In general it refers to the entire phenomenon: the idea of genocide and the whole class of actions and forms related to it, from the first inkling of genocidal thought and the smallest genocidal attack right up to gigantic murderous enterprises like the Holocaust. It follows that a particular episode, whether 'successful' or not, may be designated 'a genocide' and we can talk plurally about 'genocides'.

However, this concept of genocide as outcome has not been presented as an alternative to the absolutist, intentionalist concept. Rather it usually assumes that we can use a simple concept of intention to explain genocidal results, while historical cases in which the attempt is unsuccessful are defined out of the picture. Yet *it is precisely this assumption of an uncomplicated nexus between perpetrator intentions and outcomes that makes much of the literature sociologically unconvincing*. It omits two crucial elements. The first is the relational processes of genocide, including the actions of others, conventionally called 'victims' and 'bystanders', whose actions intervene between perpetrator intentions and outcomes. The second is the structural contexts, including the political and military conflicts in which perpetrators and victims are involved, which are typically about more than the perpetrator–victim relationships themselves.

Thus genocide studies need to make the crucial 'transition that occurs . . . from the discussion of action to the discussion of social relationships.'[70] Weber wrote:

> The term 'social relationship' will be used to denote the behaviour of a plurality of actors in so far as, in its meaningful content, the action of each takes account of that of the others and is oriented in these terms. The social relationship thus *consists* entirely and exclusively in the existence of a *probability* that there will be, in some meaningfully understandable sense, a course of social action.

For a relationship to exist, it was essential that there should be at least a minimum of mutual orientation of the action of each to that of the others, although the content of this mutual orientation could be most varied.[71] Of course some may resist seeing genocide as involving 'relationships', but the subjective meaning need not necessarily be the same for all the parties who are mutually oriented in a given social relationship. There is no requirement for reciprocity: on the contrary, a social relationship may be 'objectively "asymmetrical" from the points of view of the two parties'.[72] In this sense, *we must talk about genocide in relational terms.* Although it is commonly believed, as the very language suggests, that the action of the 'perpetrators' is independent of the responses of 'victims', in reality the actions undertaken by each affect those of the other. As Raul Hilberg put it, 'It is the *interaction* of perpetrators and victims that is "fate".'[73] Or, as Levene argued, 'a perpetrator–victim dynamic' may account for why genocides escalate in their murderousness.[74] *Victims have no choice but to orient their actions to the overwhelming power of the enemy that attacks them. Yet victims' actions, too, affect those of perpetrators.* Bauman illustrated this, showing how Jewish elites' 'rational' response – recognizing their weakness by collaborating in policing the ghettoes – enabled the Nazis to co-opt them and so affected the nature of the latter's genocidal policies. Instead of 'beheading' the Jews by destroying their elites, as most genocidists have done, for a period the Nazis found that '[d]eploying the rationality of the victims was a much more rational solution' than wholesale murder.[75] But in the longer term, submission could not give the Jews salvation: '[u]nder sharply asymmetrical power conditions, the rationality of the ruled is, to say the least, a mixed blessing. It may work to their gain. But it may as well destroy them.'[76] Morover this is not the only type of victim group response to affect perpetrator behaviour. The polar opposite type, armed resistance by the suppressed groups, may also have profound consequences for civilian populations. Thus Alan Kuperman has argued that armed struggle has 'provoked' genocide in such cases as Rwanda.[77]

Recognizing the relational character of genocide moves us towards an account of the kind of *structure* that it involves. Structure in common speech often means 'organization' or 'institution', and of course 'genocide' does not describe a durable social institution in the same way as feudalism, state or bureaucracy. Sociologically, however, structure has a broader meaning, the general 'structuring of social relations across time and space' in which recurring patterns of social action are reproduced.[78] In the case of genocide this is a *structure of conflict*, primarily the qualitatively asymmetric conflict of armed power and unarmed civilian society, but also entailing the possibility of armed resistance and alliance with other armed powers that 'evens up' genocidal conflict into something more symmetrical. As such, genocide is best compared with, and understood in relation to, other structures of conflict – especially of large-scale, violent political conflict. The distinctiveness of genocide is established by its differences from these other types, especially war, the more fundamental type of conflict and power with which it shares so many features. Genocide is therefore a structural phenomenon in the sense that it is *a recurring pattern of social conflict, characterized by particular kinds of relationships between actors, and with typical connections to other conflict structures in society.*

Obviously, proponents of intentionalism introduce some elements of a structural concept into their explanations; if they did not, they would have little plausibility. Much of the genocide literature operates with the shorthand account of 'perpetrators', 'victims' and 'bystanders', understood as referring simultaneously to both individuals and collectives, which we have used so far. Yet it is not clear what theoretical work these terms are doing. They tell us little about the content of the relationships and less about the social forces at work, although there are common assumptions about how these should be specified. 'Perpetrators' are generally understood as comprising states and armed movements – but Mann and others have shown that they also include parties and paramilitaries, together with their social constituencies and the populations that they mobilize. 'Victims' are understood essentially as 'groups' targeted for 'destruction' – yet it is clear that victim populations are often socially heterogeneous and affected individually by group targeting in complex ways. In order, therefore, to arrive at a more adequate account of the structure of genocide, we need to examine further how its typical actors are identified and their relationships are understood. This will be the subject of the next chapter, which examines in more detail the conceptualization of 'groups' and 'destruction' and genocide's character as 'conflict' and 'war'.

7

Elements of Genocidal Conflict

Social groups, social destruction and war

Because of the 'one-sidedness' of genocide, there may be resistance to utilizing the general sociological term 'conflict'. However, genocide's gross power asymmetry does not eliminate conflict relationships; it produces them in particular forms. In the next chapter I suggest how to fill the conceptual gap – in the sociology of stratification, conflict and war as well as genocide studies – that is opened by thinking about this qualitatively asymmetrical form of conflict. But here I continue with my task of exploring the sociological implications of the terms of genocide studies, and providing accounts adequate to support a structural concept. It is time to approach the issue that appears to define genocide's sociological character: the nature of 'social groups'.

Social groups in genocide

The 'group' character of genocide's targets is almost universally agreed. Although the Convention's range of protected groups is widely seen as too narrow, critics generally retain the idea of genocide as an attack on groups. Instead they define this either more broadly (adding other types) or generically (referring to social groups in general). Yet Schabas pointed out that in the Convention's drafting history there was no 'meaningful discussion about use of the term "group"',[1] and hardly anyone has attended to the concept, for example exploring whether it has an agreed sociological meaning. While the question of whether attacked groups are 'real' social entities or collectivities conceived by perpetrators has attracted attention, this issue has not been resolved in a developed theoretical manner.

Legal discussion has tended towards conservative readings, but even here 'group' is seen as problematic. Schabas argued that what Lemkin really sought to protect were 'national minorities': 'Use of terms such as "ethnic", "racial" or "religious" merely fleshed out the idea . . . .' He 'referred to "groups" as the entity that deserved protection . . . . But sometimes Lemkin mentioned "minority groups", suggesting that he viewed the two concepts as somewhat synonymous.'[2] While some have regarded 'groups' as an improvement on 'archaic' minority terminology, Schabas asked: 'Given that minorities constitute the principal beneficiaries of genocide law, it might be asked why the drafters of the Convention did not opt for this designation, already well-recognized in international jurisprudence.'[3] For him, such a narrow, straightforward idea of protected social entities was preferable to the open-ended concept that the Convention bequeathed. There was a note of regret in his comment that '[c]ertainly the label "group" is flexible, enabling the Convention to apply it without question to the destruction of entities that may not qualify as "minorities" . . . .'[4] His view was that

> Concerns about the scope of groups protected by the Convention may represent a passing phase in the law of genocide. For several decades, the Convention was the only international legal instrument enjoying widespread ratification that imposed meaningful obligations upon States in cases of atrocities committed within their own borders and, as a general rule, by their officials. The temptation was great to subsume a variety of State-sanctioned criminal behaviour within its ambit due to the absence of other comparable legal tools. This problem has diminished in recent years with the progressive development of international criminal law in the field of human rights abuses.[5]

We may question whether these developments have proceeded so far that we no longer need to extend the law of genocide. While it is possible to charge those who destroy 'ethnic' groups with 'genocide' and those who destroy other groups with 'crimes against humanity', the incoherence to which this leads will not benefit international law. From a sociological point of view it is nonsensical and law cannot afford to turn its back on sociological understanding.

One advantage of 'group' over 'minorities' is that it designates vulnerable populations in general, not according to their numerical proportion in the population of a territory. This allows us to deal with 'majorities' as well as 'minorities' being attacked – including most of the cases Lemkin considered in *Axis Rule*. More broadly, it allows us to recognize that social categorization is not simple: if Lemkin 'fleshed out' national terminology with 'ethnic', 'racial' and 'religious', these were not, as Schabas implausibly observed, 'really all efforts to describe a singular reality'.[6] The need for multiple definition was that populations might be defined – by themselves, by their attackers or by observers – in terms of any or a mixture of these terms. Thus a range was necessary to capture the breadth of the phenomenon. In any case, the multiple 'group' concept is now part not only of international law, but also of political and social-scientific discourse. Despite its difficulties, it has facilitated legal, political and scientific understanding of a broad swathe of violence. Although we are not obliged to retain all recent conceptual and linguistic innovations, abandoning the 'group' concept, like abandoning 'genocide' itself, is neither plausible nor desirable. To adopt a generic definition, including all social groups, is the only coherent solution, since any attempt to draw new lines will face the same problems as Schabas's narrow view that 'ethnic' would suffice to describe the protected groups. Other terms will always enter the discussion because social targets are variably perceived and have permeable boundaries.

In any case, proponents of restriction have developed a rationale that goes beyond particular categories: the 'reality' of the target groups. As Fein put it,

> the victims of genocide are generally members of *real groups*, whether conceived of as collectivities, races or classes, who [themselves] acknowledge their existence, although there may be administrative designation of their membership as German authorities designated Jews for 'the Final Solution' including some people of Jewish lineage who no longer considered themselves Jews . . . . Had there not been an actual Jewish community with its own institutions, German authorities could not have defined and enumerated Jews, for there was no objective indicator of their alleged criteria of Jewishness – race – which divided 'Jews' and 'Aryans' categorically.[7]

This view has a long pedigree. As we have seen, Lemkin himself argued against including political groups because they 'lacked the permanency . . . of the other groups'.[8] For Schabas, '[f]undamentally, the problem with including political groups is the difficulty in providing a rational basis for such a measure. If political groups are to be included, why not the disabled, or other groups based on arbitrary criteria?'[9] So he assumed that political groups could not be defined 'rationally' and the criteria for defining the disabled must be 'arbitrary', while simultaneously acknowledging the difficulty of the 'reality' criterion: even '[t]he four groups listed in the Convention resist efforts at precise definition.'[10] 'On closer scrutiny', he recognized, 'three of the four categories in the Convention enumeration, national groups, ethnic and religious groups, seem neither stable nor permanent.'[11] Indeed he nodded towards the subjective basis of group definition, quoting Weber to the effect that an ethnic group is one whose members 'entertain a subjective belief in their common descent.'[12] And Schabas reduced the reality criterion to absurdity by arguing that '[o]nly racial groups, when they are defined genetically, can lay claim to some relatively prolonged stability and permanence.'[13] From a sociological point of view, the solidity of 'race' is especially illusory; even if it has regained some currency in genetic research, virtually no serious sociologist credits race as a social category. Weber had already dismissed it half a century before the Convention:

> It is by no means true that the existence of common qualities, a common situation, or common modes of behaviour imply the existence of a common social relationship. Thus, for instance, the possession of a common biological inheritance by virtue of which persons are classified as belonging to the same 'race', naturally implies no sort of communal social relationship between them. . . . In the case of the Jews, for instance, except for Zionist circles and the action of certain associations promoting specifically Jewish interests, there thus exist communal relationships only to a relatively small extent; indeed Jews often repudiate the existence of a Jewish 'community'.[14]

Historians of European Jewry might qualify Weber's account, but his case that many who might be seen as Jewish by 'biological inheritance' (itself more problematic than Weber acknowledged) did not necessarily belong to a Jewish 'community' is difficult to contradict.

Despite such manifest problems in automatically ascribing communal life to the Convention's group types, let alone all 'social groups', the idea that this is an imperative for genocide theory has survived. Fein sought to give 'real' groups a more adequate foundation:

> From the root of *genus* we may infer that the protected groups were conceived (by Lemkin and the UN framers) as basic kinds, classes, or subfamilies of humanity, persisting units of society. What is distinctive sociologically is that such groups are usually ascriptive – based on birth rather than choice – and often inspire enduring particularistic loyalties. They are sources of identity and value; they are the seed-bed of social movements, voluntary associations, congregations and families; in brief, they are *collectivities*. . . . Further, these collectivities endure as their members tend to reproduce their own kind.[15]

Immediately, however, Fein backtracked, recognizing that 'collectivities need not be self-reproducing to be cohesive over a given span of time' and that '[t]here is no categorical line, in fact, between the enduring character of ascribed (heritable) identities and elected or achieved identities: both may be constructed or passed on generationally.'[16] Yet despite all these difficulties, the assumption persisted that genocide requires that the target be a 'real' group. It has recently been redefined by the Rwanda Tribunal, dealing with difficulties of defining Tutsi as an 'ethnic group', in the claim that 'the intention of the drafters of the Genocide Convention . . . was patently to ensure the protection of *any* stable and permanent group.'[17] Thus the idea that the particular target group had to fit into some preconceived category of 'real' group has been replaced by the idea that it must possess its *own* form of stability and permanence.

Even the advocates of a 'real groups' criterion recognize, therefore, its problems. Fein acknowledged that 'the specification of groups covered should be consistent with our sociological knowledge of both the persistence *and construction* of group identities in society, the variations in class, ethnic/racial, gender, class/political consciousness and the multiplicity and interaction of people's identities and statuses in daily life.'[18] While recognizing groups' constructed and complex characters is useful, it only opens up the sociological dilemma. It is necessary to return to two fundamental questions: What is a social group? And in what sense does genocide presuppose their existence?

The first thing to note is that contemporary sociology makes little use of 'group'. It does little serious work except in a sense far removed from genocide – small-group interaction in social psychology.[19] The only major authority for a relevant understanding of 'groups' is, again, Weber, who developed this concept out of his concepts of action and relationships. He proposed that social relationships could be 'communal' or 'associative',[20] 'open' or 'closed',[21] and proposed that 'groups' involved a particular kind of closed or restricted relationship:

> A social relationship which is either closed or limits the admission of outsiders by rules, will be called a 'corporate group' (*Verband*) so far as its order is enforced by the action of specific individuals whose regular function this is, of a chief or head (*Leiter*) and usually also an administrative staff. . . . Whether a corporate group exists is entirely a matter of the presence of a person in authority, with or without an administrative staff.[22]

What is significant is that this concept presupposes rules, organization and authority. It is not far from the concept of the group, with its way of life and institutions, seen by Lemkin as 'comprehensively attacked' by Nazi occupation policies. However, in its demand for closure or rule-bound membership and its insistence on (generally bureaucratic) organization,[23] Weber's concept was considerably tighter than Lemkin's. While nation-*states* with their citizenship rules and bureaucracies might be seen in this light, nations and ethnicities as such do *not* constitute 'corporate' groups in this tighter sense (although religions might). Although these types of 'group' might be real in the sense of being subjectively validated – people may think of themselves as belonging to them and orient their actions towards them – this is a weaker and looser sense of 'group' than Weber proposed. So although Weber had an idea of 'groups', it does not fit with the way groups are understood by the advocates of 'real groups' in genocide theory.[24]

In genocide studies, 'groups' cover what in sociological discussion are seen as very disparate sorts of entity: populations defined by 'whole' national societies (as in *Axis Rule*), 'minorities' ('whole' ethnic or national communities within nation-states) and also 'groups' such as religious communities and classes within nation-states. 'Group' is therefore a catch-all, an abstract label used in such a broad and loose sense that it lacks real content. Unsurprisingly a recent definition by Levene abandoned 'group' altogether, replacing it with 'aggregate population'.[25] This is unsatisfactory, since it is through presumed 'group' identities, rather than randomly, that populations are attacked. Yet we must recognize that the lowest common denominator of 'group' is no more than a *category* of a population, seen as having some common social characteristic. Such abstract categories of this kind are of course common in sociology, as in Weber's ideas of a class as 'any group of persons occupying the same class status'[26] and a status group as 'a plurality of individuals who, within a larger group, enjoy a particular kind and level of prestige by virtue of their position and possibly also claim certain special monopolies.'[27] Marx's concept of social classes as groups defined by their relationship to the ownership of the means of production is similar. *Such categories are all defined by objective criteria; they are not necessarily 'collectivities', foci of identity and communal life.* The actors to whom they refer *may*, under certain circumstances, subjectively grasp the criteria by which observers identify them as groups – or they may not. Commonly some 'members' will subjectively identify with these 'groups', others will not. Marx distinguished between a class-in-itself, objectively defined by its role in the relations of production, and a class-for-itself, subjectively conscious of this role and acting in its terms. In reality, members of the working class have varied greatly in their 'class consciousness'. As Marx recognized, at any given time many proletarians were not class conscious to any significant extent.

The same is true of other categories invoked in the genocide debate, such as 'nation' and 'ethnic group'. Indeed the difficulties of 'objective' definition have long given rise to subjective criteria, as in Benedict Anderson's view of nations as 'imagined communities'.[28] Although lodging nations in the imagination does not make them any less real, it does make it difficult to say *who precisely* constitute them at any given moment in time. Nor does it overcome the problem that some people imagined as belonging to the nation may not see themselves as such, and that people see the nation and their own memberships in different ways. Even if the reality of the nation is *intersubjectively* established among some members, this does not overcome the problem of ascribing membership to people who do not share the identification.

These kinds of difficulty have long been recognized in genocide studies. However, they are fundamentally compounded by the fact that it is the perpetrators' concept of the group that *initially* defines the genocide – as Chalk and Jonassohn's definition emphasized – although the attacked's and observers' conceptions may also matter to the outcome. Mann resolved the issue pragmatically by having it both ways: 'An ethnicity is a group that defines itself or is defined by others as sharing common descent and culture.'[29] But he argued that 'the relevant collective actors are many, and some emerge in the process of escalation itself. Identities based on the relationship to the state, class, occupation, region, generation, gender and so on weave in and out of ethnic identities, rechanneling ethnicity as they do.'[30] Even Schabas acknowledged: '[d]etermining the meaning of the groups protected by the Convention seems to dictate a degree of subjectivity. It is the offender who defines the individual victim's status as a member of a group protected by the Convention.'[31] Despite this, he dismissed the 'purely subjective' approach that, '[i]f the offender views the group as being national, racial, ethnic or religious, then that should suffice.' Its flaw, he argued, 'is allowing, at least in theory, genocide to be committed against a group *that does not have any real objective existence. ...* the subjective approach flounders because law cannot permit the crime to be defined by the offender alone. It is necessary, therefore, to determine some objective existence of the four groups.'[32] However, Guénaël Mettraux demonstrated the uneasiness of the legal demand for objective existence by arguing that groups need only possess 'a semblance' of it.[33]

In reality the fact that perpetrators define their own target groups does *not* entail that they define the crime. The degree of 'reality' of the perpetrator-defined group is simply not relevant to the definition of genocide as a social phenomenon. *Genocide is an attempt to destroy a group of people, regardless of how far groups defined by perpetrators correspond to 'real' groups, intersubjectively recognized by their members or objectively identifiable by observers.* Criminologically and sociologically, genocide is established by acts of violence against certain people accompanied by political goals that express enmity towards a group. Perpetrator, victim and bystander definitions are relevant, of course, to the *dynamics* of genocide: the ways in or extent to which target groups are 'real' may affect how perpetrators proceed, how individuals and societies are affected, how much resistance is organized, and whether perpetrators are brought to justice.

Genocide theorists who cling to the 'reality' criterion share genocidists' own theoretical error. 'The search for categorical certainty proceeds', Nigel Eltringham suggested, 'from man's ever-present disposition, a taken-for granted assumption (or "habit of the mind") that social distinctions are *a priori*, natural, self-evident, necessary and *always* present. If, however, we are to escape what René Lemarchand calls the "confinement of the apparently obvious", we must recognise that such classifications are made/invented by us.'[34] The practice of these theorists belies this assumption: 'Problems arise . . . when we "misplace concreteness" and set out to "prove" that our abstract concepts (our "ideal types") really do *correspond* to reality, rather than being contingent approximations.'[35] When genocidists attempt to enforce the classifications to which they hold, they actually *create*, or reshape, what they already imagined as existing. As Fein pointed out, the 'German authorities . . . defined and enumerated Jews, for there was no objective indicator of their alleged criteria of Jewishness – race – which divided "Jews" and "Aryans" categorically.' Likewise, Eltringham suggested, the 'self-ascriptive construction of an "imagined community" was forestalled in Rwanda where a "sanctioned identity" – inscribed on ID cards/birth certificates – determined one's "ethnic" affiliation.'[36] In the attempt to fit these cases into the categories of the Convention, or some other definition of the victim groups of genocide, theorists are (despite their different intentions) making the same mistake: 'To get diverse groups to fit the "ethnicity" box involves a sleight of hand on the part of the analyst-classifier.'[37]

Fein's case was that Nazi authorities could not have defined Jewishness 'had there not been an actual Jewish community with its own institutions'. Certainly, Nazism did not conjure its ideas of Jewishness out of thin air, but drew on a long history of anti-Semitic thought; and both historic anti-Semitism and Nazi policies interacted with Jewish ideas of tradition and community. Like all ideology, genocidal thought constructs its fantasies from real elements. However, the degree to which genocidists' ideological constructions fit the attacked's own ideas of community varies. Indeed, genocidists often evoke a collective identity in their target 'group' that had hardly existed: Jewish communal identity became much stronger after the Holocaust than it was beforehand. But what is more striking than the element of 'reality' is the deeply *fantastical* character of all genocidal thought. In order to target a social group for social and physical destruction, perpetrators must fundamentally depart from reality. They must see masses of individuals and families living in disparate communities through the distorting lens of pseudo-classification, in order to convert them into a collective 'enemy' of a kind whose ways of life and physical existence must be brutally crushed. To achieve this transformation, discordance between the perceptions of perpetrators and victims is inevitable. *This means that genocidists invariably misrepresent both individuals and 'real' groups: their perceptions are very different from those of the people targeted. The disjunction generally has a dual character: different definitions of collective identity (and non-identity) and different ideas of individual affiliation (and non-affiliation).* And even when there is little disagreement about group membership – for example, Armenians and Ottoman Turks may not have disagreed much about who were Armenians – perpetrators act out a false perception of a whole population as a dangerous enemy of their nation. Such beliefs take many different forms, but they reflect *a fundamental irrationality: the perception of a social group as an enemy to be destroyed, in the manner that normally only another armed enemy would warrant.* Because essentially unarmed civilian populations can never really equate to armed enemies (even if they have some degree of sympathy for them), genocide is only possible where the genocidists fundamentally misrepresent the target group in their own minds, to their supporters and ultimately, through violence, to the target group. Of course, the irony is that oppressive, violent and murderous action will inevitably produce real enemies among its victims.

The destruction of groups

If 'intention' and 'group' raise fundamental sociological issues, so does group 'destruction', which lies at the heart of the idea of genocide. From the beginning, Lemkin's use of the common suffix '-cide' suggested that the destruction of groups was similar to the killing of individuals denoted by established terms such as infanticide and patricide. Genocide involved the 'killing' of a social group, as the UN General Assembly made clear when it asserted: 'Genocide is a denial of the right of existence of entire human groups, *as homicide is the denial of the right to live of individual human beings.'*[38] Yet this powerful analogy, like all analogies, had a potential to mislead. At that time, there was a greater propensity than today to consider societies as organisms, in which the functioning of the whole determined the activities of the parts and the well-being of the individual was subordinated to the whole. This view was formulated most starkly in fascist, Stalinist and indeed genocidal ideologies, but there was a more general belief in the holistic nature of national societies and individuals' subordination to them. This holistic tendency was represented in sociology, too, but in reality human groups or societies were not so like biological organisms. Human societies were constituted through social relations between individual human beings: 'societies' and 'groups' are ways of thinking about how these relations bind individuals together. As Weber had written,

> For other cognitive purposes . . . it may . . . be convenient or even indispensable to treat social collectivities . . . as if they were individual persons. . . . But for the subjective interpretation of action in sociological work these collectivities must be treated as *solely* the resultants and modes of organization of the particular acts of individual persons, since these alone can be treated as agents in a course of subjectively understandable action.[39]

Social groups are *not* like individuals. It follows that 'killing' or 'destroying' them is not like killing embodied human beings, either. We have seen that there is a powerful trend in genocide theory to reduce 'destruction' to its 'physical' and 'biological' dimensions. The logical conclusion is that genocide is seen simply as mass killing, as in Charny's definition. However, this position is sociologically incoherent even in its own terms. *Because groups are social constructions, they can be neither constituted nor destroyed simply through the bodies of their individual members.* Destroying groups must involve a lot more than simply killing, although killing and other physical harm are rightly considered important to it. The discussion of group 'destruction' is obliged, then, to take seriously Lemkin's 'large view of this concept',[40] discarded in genocide's reduction to body counts, which centred on social destruction. A more appropriate way of interpreting group destruction is therefore to see it as involving *a nexus between the destruction of collective ways of life and institutions and bodily and other harm to individuals.*

Just as we should reject a view of genocide as only killing and physical harm, we should resist defining the suppression of a group's culture as genocide when it is done without physically harming the members of the group. Certainly, this much more common repression has affinities with genocide and may be its precursor. Modern nation-states have *generally* come into being by undermining traditional ways of life. Nations were not 'attempts to fill the void left by the dismantling of earlier community and social structures', as E. J. Hobsbawm once suggested.[41] As Eugen Weber commented, 'this actually reverses the order of events.' In regard to France, he pointed out, 'the political nation of the Ancien Régime functioned side by side with traditional community and social structures. The ideological nation of the Revolution had to compete with these. It was not invented on their dismantling; its invention implied their dismantling.'[42] Moreover in this process, 'Finally there was force. Finally, but also originally and throughout.'[43] But in most cases this 'force' was administrative, economic, political and ideological. Certainly, the suppression of the Vendée counter-revolution in 1793 involved widespread killing, making this for Levene 'an archetype of modern genocide'.[44] But generally in the nineteenth century there was coercion to wear down old ways and assimilate people and communities into the nation. It was 'dismantling' aimed at integration, not Lemkin's 'synchronized attack' aimed at social destruction. It was 'cultural imperialism' but it was not a war against the peasants. Thus if, as Levene suggests, 'the origins and continued momentum towards the potentiality for genocide in the modern world has been intrinsically bound up with the strivings . . . of societies towards some form of grounded, territorially grounded coherence',[45] there remains *a fundamental difference between the general modern homogenization of national societies and the extreme form that these processes take in genocide.*

Thus Fein was right to criticize writers who 'extend the connotations of genocide to cover all kinds of acts undermining collectivities as a result of social policy – "sociocide", "linguicide", "cultural genocide" – so that genocide becomes not only unbounded but banal, an everyday occurrence.'[46] *The idea of group 'destruction' implies the kind of deep social catastrophe that is usually marked by extensive violence and killing.* Nevertheless, defining the nexus of social destruction and violence is more difficult than it might seem. Lemkin wrote that '[g]enocide is directed against the national group as an entity, and the actions are directed against individuals, not in their individual capacity, but as members of the national group.'[47] Another way of looking at this, I have suggested, is that violence against individuals is a *means* to the end of group destruction. However, if 'groups' are not necessarily clearly demarcated, coherent communities or associations, and perpetrators' perceptions of their 'enemy' groups are partly fantastical misrepresentations of 'real' groups, then *the match between anti-group campaigns and action against individuals will not necessarily be tight.* There is a strong danger – inherent in the over-rationalized concept of intentional action – of presenting genocide as more instrumentally rational than it really is. Since perpetrator organizations, together with the individuals and small groups directly perpetrating physical violence, generally have plural goals, aims and motives, a victim's experience of violence will not always be capable of simple interpretation in terms of the action against a singular target group. *Understanding needs to take account of individual victims' own experience and perceptions, especially their understandings of violence as arbitrary, senseless and irrational.* This reflects the inhuman, bureaucratically organized character of genocidal campaigns, but also their often chaotic, apparently random practice on the ground. These contradictions play out in how individuals are attacked and experience their victimization. The contradictions between self-ascribed and genocidist-ascribed identities also affect experience. People targeted by Stalin's campaigns may not have recognized themselves as *kulaks*, but they may have felt a common situation as peasants, the 'real' group target of the attack. The meaning of Nazi anti-Semitism to a secular 'Jew' or so-called *Mischling* (part-'Jew') caught in Hitler's race laws could be different from its meaning for a self-identifying Jewish person.

The paradox is that *both* an anti-group drive *and* harm to individuals are essential to genocidal action, but a tension between them is inevitable. To 'kill' a group means to destroy its supposed power, common ways of life and institutions: *the extent of physical killing that this entails will vary according to the perpetrators' aims and ideology, the type of control they have over the target population, and their practical success.* Few genocidists even aim to kill all the members of their target groups. As Bauman put it, ' "Ordinary" genocide is rarely, if at all, aimed at the total annihilation of the group; the purpose of the violence . . . is to destroy the marked category . . . as a viable community capable of self-perpetuation and defence of its own self-identity.'[48] Even if they do, the killing of all members of any large-scale group is inconceivable: some will always survive, either by losing their group identity or by moving beyond the reach of genocidal power. *A successful genocide is generally one that destroys a group's territorial basis, its presence in its homeland.* The Armenian genocide of 1915 is a striking example, but despite the campaign's murderousness many individuals survived and so did Armenian identity in the diaspora, where it was reinforced by the awareness of the community's disaster. So while the destruction of a group cannot occur without the destruction of individuals, it cannot generally involve the physical destruction of all of them, either. *Thus variation in the relationships between group destruction and individual killing is intrinsic to genocide, rather than defining the difference between genocide and other forms of repression.*[49]

Finally, granting a role to individual victims' experiences and perceptions is not the same as giving *priority* to victims' points of view, still less to collective appropriations of victim experience by those who claim to speak for particular victim groups. As Dirk Moses argued, different victim groups make incommensurable, indeed competing, claims, and group traumas contribute to blocking conceptual development (as well as mutual recognition), leading to unproductive conflicts such as that over Holocaust uniqueness *versus* the status of indigenous genocides. A critical perspective is necessary that ultimately transcends that of victims, as well as of perpetrators and their descendants.[50]

Genocide as war

I have argued that genocide involves a conflictual structure of social relationships. Weber argued that a relationship can 'be referred to as "conflict" in so far as action within it is oriented intentionally to carrying out the actor's own will against the resistance of the other party or parties.'[51] He went on to distinguish 'peaceful' conflict, 'in which actual physical violence is not employed', from 'the bloody type of conflict which, setting aside all rules, aims at the destruction of the adversary.'[52] Although genocide may have 'peaceful' phases during which perpetrators mostly achieve their immediate goals without physical violence, obviously it constitutes 'bloody' conflict. We should note moreover that Weber, writing before the invention of 'genocide', defines bloody conflict through the same term, *destruction*, which was later adopted by Lemkin and the Convention in that process. But in what sense can genocide be regarded as a form of social conflict, and what are the implications of its destructive, bloody character?

A common view is to regard genocide as an extreme form of conflict *between social groups*, particularly ethnic groups. Thus Vahakn Dadrian argued that, '[f]irst and foremost, genocide presupposes intergroup conflict with a history of growth and escalation . . . [and] serves as a radical device to resolve that conflict: in this sense, genocide is functional.'[53] In the genocides of the Jews and Armenians, 'the religious identities of both peoples were pregnant with the rudiments of conflict, with a potential to erupt in major conflagrations.'[54] And yet attempts to explain violence by ethnicity as such, or even by histories of ethnic conflict, are now largely discredited. What Villia Jefremovas wrote of Rwanda has been echoed in other cases: genocide 'did not arise out of ancient hatreds but through overt political manipulation, ruthlessly orchestrated by a morally bankrupt elite.'[55] Yet in their textbook on 'ethnic conflict', Harff and Gurr argued that 'politically active ethnic groups coexist within modern states',[56] and that three-quarters of the groups surveyed in the 1990s were politically active.[57] They treated 'ethnic groups' as such as political actors, although the term 'ethnic conflict' in their title often became 'ethnopolitical conflict' in the text – the slippage indicating uncertainty as to whether ethnic groups are themselves political actors or form the social basis for organized political actors. They certainly saw the social characteristics of groups – identity, cohesion and economic status – as explaining conflict in general, and its extreme, genocidal forms in particular, alongside the character of the state, the kind of force it uses, etc. Similarly Mann framed genocidal conflict (and other gradations of 'murderous cleansing') within 'inter-group relations',[58] arguing that competition for territory between movements based on rival ethnicities was the prime explanation. However he didn't claim that the mere co-presence of two or more ethnicities produces genocide; rather he acknowledged that 'murderous ethnic conflict concerns primarily *political power relations*.'[59] Thus Mann's account, although presented as a question of 'inter-group' relations, was concerned with organized conflict and war between armed movements, the inter-group aspect relating to their modes of mobilization and legitimation. He proposed that genocide is not conflict between ethnic groups as such, but *political and military conflict* in which genocidists generally mobilize ethnicity.

There is indeed an emerging anthropological and sociological consensus that 'the notion of ethnic conflict is . . . misleading', since it 'implies that ethnicity can be seen as the cause of such conflicts, and that ethnic conflicts are apolitical, somehow distinctive from other wars fought over resources or political power.'[60] On the contrary, much work has shown that 'ethnicity is the ideological form, not the substance of the conflict',[61] and 'popular ideas of ethnic antagonism have emerged *during* conflicts rather than themselves *causing* conflict.'[62] Even if ethnic ideas exist beforehand, they are strengthened and gain practical significance during violent episodes. What we often need to examine is, as Jocelyn Alexander, Jo Ann McGregor and Terence Ranger put it, 'why notions of identity which were once fluid, inclusive, mutually compatible and weakly ethnicized have at times been replaced by understandings of coherent, mutually exclusive peoples with a history of rivalry, persecution and revenge.'[63] Mann agreed that, 'if ethnic groups do become more homogenous as conflict escalates, this is precisely what we must explain.'[64] Thus genocide is not ethnic conflict but conflict between armed power organizations and civilian groups that *mobilizes* social differences as ethnicity.

This conclusion leads us to another stage in the argument. First, as Mann noted, war is the major context of genocide and other murderous politics: the vast majority of genocidal episodes in fact occur in the context of more conventional warfare.[65] Second, as 'bloody conflict' aiming at 'the destruction of the adversary', genocide is conceptually linked to the ideal type of warfare proposed by Clausewitz, for whom 'War is nothing but mutual destruction.'[66] We can therefore give a more precise sociological definition: *genocide is not only a form of social conflict, but also a form of war*. An adequate conceptual framework will relate genocide to the forms of war and militarized power with which it is intimately related. Ideal-typically, war is the contest between armed power organizations, in which each armed actor projects violence against the other in order to destroy its power. Of course, war never involves only armed forces: they always have some degree of support from social groups, so that groups and their members, though not combatants, are participants in war. Moreover in most war, the projection of violence extends to some degree, whether by accident or design, to the social groups supporting armed forces, so that civilians as well as combatants are victims. The difference between war and genocide is not the destructive character of the action, the violent modality, or the typical actor (since armed power organizations exist primarily for war). *The difference lies in the construction of civilian groups as enemies, not only in a social or political but also in a military sense, to be destroyed.* Genocide remains as Lemkin first categorized it, an extreme form of war that departs from the ideal-typical form of war in this fundamental sense.

Thus although genocide is not an exclusively modern phenomenon, its development has been closely linked to modern forms of war. As the mobilization and participation of social groups in total war became more extensive, so the tendency to target social groups was more systematic. Economically, enemy civilian populations were seen as central to the supply of military machines. Politically, civilian groups were seen as key supporters, attacking whom would weaken the armed enemy. Technologically, modern weapons gave states and other armed actors a vastly greater range of means – from aerial bombardment to biological diffusion – to destroy civilian populations. I have therefore argued that modern war, in both its interstate and guerrilla-counterinsurgency forms, should be seen as *degenerate war*. This was still war, because its primary focus remained the conflict between armed power organizations, but civilian targeting had become integral to its prosecution.[67] The fine but still important difference from genocide centred on *who was the enemy*. In degenerate war, the core enemy remained the opposing organized armed force: the 'enemy' civilian population was targeted as a means towards the defeat of a state and army. Thus although mass slaughter of civilians – for example at Dresden or Hiroshima – was evil and illegitimate, it could still be understood at least partially under the rubric of war. Civilians were part of the enemy: but no civilian group was an enemy distinct from the enemy state.

Genocide in contrast *constructs unarmed civilian populations as the objects, in their own right, of the types of armed violence normally applied only to armed enemies.* James Reid suggested that, in the destruction of the Armenians, the Young Turk regime was applying the modern German military concept of the 'annihilation' of the enemy to a civilian group.[68] Indeed Isabel Hull portrayed this approach as a general tendency in German military thinking of the late nineteenth and early twentieth centuries.[69] The essential barbarism of such ideas, evident also in the Stalinist notion of the 'liquidation' of the *kulaks*, lies in this extension of the generally legitimate armed violence of war to a group who are not – and cannot be – an enemy in a military sense.

The shock of genocide is therefore not just the civilian bodies piled high, which we find in most episodes of modern war. It is turning the logic and methods of war directly against civilian groups as such, as enemies in themselves, in their own right. Genocide is war against civilian groups. Hard power is used to destroy soft power. Killing, violence and coercion are used to destroy the power of dense social networks, traditions and ways of life. *These are not careless, incidental or indirect consequences of war between states and armies, but deliberate campaigns by armed power against civilian groups, with the aim of destroying their kind of power.* Thus the distinctiveness of genocide is striking despite the larger history of slaughter in war. This can only be because, for all the degeneracy of war, we can still grasp its core rationality of state against state, army against army. An armed campaign directed at civilians, more or less because of their characteristics as a group, is a fundamental step even beyond what we understand to be wrong with war. Once groups are targeted, the campaign may seem like war – it exhibits the *instrumentally* 'rational' discrimination of members from non-members, of steps that aim towards the end of destroying power, which is reminiscent of war. But we know that behind it lies the *substantively* irrational delineation of civilian groups as enemies to be violently 'destroyed'.[70] Irrational beliefs are a general feature of social action, and war provides particularly rich material for their study. Yet genocide removes the last vestiges of rationality and legitimacy that cling to more conventional war.

8

The Missing Concept

The civilian category and its social meaning

The last chapter leaves genocide theory with a dilemma. If we reject the definition of genocide's targets by particular types of identity, or by the criterion of real groups, we seem to be left with no common denominator other than that these groups are defined by their attackers. Yet while genocidists do indeed define the particular characters of target groups, they obviously do not define genocide in general. For a crucial commonality of both group and individual victims has been omitted from the discussion. Although people are targeted for their particular identities rather than because they are 'civilians', *all groups or populations targeted in genocide are overwhelmingly civilian in character, and it is their civilian identity that makes their targeting genocidal*. It is the fact that the perpetrators of genocide are generally armed and militarily organized, while victims are generally unarmed and militarily unorganized, that marks off this form of political violence from others. *The missing link of genocide studies is the core social distinction between combatants and civilians (or non-combatants).*[1]

Surprisingly, although this conceptual distinction has been developed in the law of war and extensively deployed in analysis and debate, it has not had a central place in the discourse on genocide. Moreover it has never been properly investigated, even in the context of war, in *sociological* theory. Here I seek to remedy these omissions. I first discuss the necessity for, and implications of, the civilian concept in genocide theory. I then underpin the idea as a general sociological category: I examine how the concept of 'civilian' has been developed; I argue that this is not just a legal category, but one generally produced in the social relations of armed conflict; and I discuss its place in a general account of social distinctions. This in turn leads to further conclusions about genocide as social conflict.

The civilian enemy

I have argued that to appreciate the irrationality of genocide we need to grasp the idea of *the civilian enemy*. Of course, the construction of enemies is a general feature of social conflict in civil society. It is normal for social actors to see others' interests and values as opposed to their own, and to aim to increase their power vis-à-vis that of others. It is common for rulers, governments, elites and parties to see particular social groups as obstacles to their interests and policies: they therefore tax, pass laws and take administrative action to reduce groups' social power. Social groups in turn often perceive governments as enemies, so hostility between governments and sections of society is commonplace. And yet enmities in such conflicts are normally framed – and therefore contained – by the assumption of mutual coexistence. Even where enmities are deep and historic, informed or reinforced by cultural differences, there is usually no questioning of 'hostile' groups' rights to exist. All sorts of misinterpretations and irrational beliefs may inform perceptions of difference and clashes of interest. But these are limited by some semblance of sharing a single social space and common humanity.

Yet genocide takes the construction of social groups as enemies beyond normal limits. Groups are enemies for armed power in a sense that fundamentally transcends usual social conflict: they are to be destroyed in an essentially military manner. Enemy groups' economic, social, political and cultural power is shattered by the application of concentrated power, by violence towards members of the group, and especially by killing. *For all the barbarism and irrationality of war, genocide is something more: a form of anti-war, war against particular civilian groups as such, because of the social identities ascribed to given civilian populations.*

There is, of course, a good reason why genocide's anti-civilian character has not been foregrounded. On first inspection, taking perpetrator ideas as our guide, genocide seems to obliterate the combatant–civilian distinction. Genocidists deny the civilian idea by imposing on the target population a singular, absolute, death-justifying identity. They regard unarmed civilians as part of an aggressive, combatant enemy. They often deny the difference between fighters and civilians, treating the latter as though they are also armed enemies. Yet, as we have seen, genocide cannot be defined solely by the actions or beliefs of the perpetrators. Genocide involves relationships between these actors and others – conventionally described as victims and bystanders – and their perceptions also count. Certainly genocide often reinforces victims' identifications with particular attacked communities. At the same time, however, they are necessarily aware of the disparity between their own unarmed condition and their attackers' armed character: to this extent their civilian identities are also reinforced. *Victims typically define themselves simultaneously both through their particular identities and as civilians.* Likewise, bystanders such as international organizations and social scientists recognize particularistic identities, but *when we criminalize destructive actions we forefront the civilian identity of the attacked populations.*

This raises a perplexing issue. If we define genocide as conflict between armed power organizations and particular civilian groups, are we simply choosing a victim and bystander perception of civilian status over a primarily perpetrator focus on particularistic identities? In developing our structural concept, are we 'translating' only from the victim and bystander viewpoints, and simply reversing perpetrator perceptions? This might be legitimate – clearly genocide demands deconstruction as much as *Verstehen* – but it flies in the face of the idea of giving initial priority to actors' subjective framing of their actions. So an important question for my 'civilian' definition is whether the idea actually figures in perpetrators' own minds. Of course, the idea that genocidists make no distinctions among the enemies they destroy is clearly too simple. The genocidal mentality generally, even obsessively, classifies. Many perpetrators define numerous social enemies – for the Nazis, not only Jews but also Gypsies, Slavs, communists, homosexuals and more; for the Khmer Rouge, city-dwellers, Vietnamese, Cham, Buddhists, indeed virtually every recognizable 'group' in Cambodian society. Even apparently singular genocidal targets, such as the Armenians for the Ottoman Turks, entwine with conventional international enemies and overlapping social categories such as Christians. Even when there is one main group target, people who do not belong to it are targeted for adjacent reasons, as in Rwanda where Hutu opposition politicians were killed before the mass attack on the Tutsi population, or in Bosnia where cosmopolitan urban centres were attacked at the same time as Muslims. Moreover there is copious evidence that genocidists distinguish *among* their group enemies: they treat men differently from women, the young and old differently from those of working age, the wealthy and educated differently from the poor and uneducated, and so on. Remember that ethnicity is the ideological form, not the entire substance, of genocidal violence.

Once we examine their practice, it is clear that *genocidists are well aware of the difference between a civilian enemy and a conventional armed enemy*. The paradox involved in defining civilian groups as 'enemies' in an essentially military sense and waging 'war' upon them is evident not only to victims and bystanders, but also to perpetrators. They know the difference generally because it is recognized by all major traditions of belief and thought, all discourses of war, all cultures and societies. They are aware of the distinction because of how armed power is institutionalized in all modern societies, and how the distinction also works between them and their 'own' society. However, *the most striking evidence for civilian recognition is the way that genocidists actually organize genocide*. They understand the big difference between 'destroying' an armed enemy and 'destroying' a civilian group. Much more limited violence, with much more basic weapons, will intimidate and kill unarmed civilians. There is no technological or tactical rivalry, no arms-racing or strategic contest, and no need constantly to establish superiority in these senses. The challenges, for genocidists, are political, logistical and administrative, and if gruesome new technologies of extermination are devised to answer these, these are of a different order from the technologies of destruction in even the most degenerate modern war. In organizing genocide, leaders and policy-makers comprehensively recognize the civilian character of the population that they attack, choosing different methods from those they deploy against armed enemies. Of course civilian recognition is nearly always implicit. For public consumption, at least, perpetrators simultaneously represent their victims as linked in nefarious ways to armed enemies, and conceal or deny their own violence. *Universal denial is, however, key confirmation that genocidists are generally aware at some level that their targets can be considered civilians* – often through the related idea of 'women and children'. Whatever novel ideology they have concocted to justify their barbarism, they are not so far removed from the historic norms of their societies – or from widely diffused understandings of the legitimate scope of war – as to be able to block out all understanding of the distinction between combatants and civilians.

For all these reasons, scholars of genocide should insist on the centrality of the civilian status of its targets. Certainly, genocidists never proclaim their determination to destroy 'civilians' as such. Evidently, they identify particular nationalities, ethnicities, classes, political groups, religions and other social categories as their enemies. However, the process of genocide is never simply defined by these particular categories. In an extreme case of multiple targeting, SS *Einsatzgruppen* reports in the wake of the invasion of the Soviet Union identified no fewer than forty-four overlapping 'target groups': these included, Mann aptly commented, 'some ethnic, some political, some vague'.[2] When an *Einsatzgruppen* killer pulled his trigger, could victims always tell – or care – whether they were killed as Slavs, as communists or as Jews, even if the perpetrators later produced grisly reports claiming to itemize the numbers of victims in different categories? Can we, historians and sociologists many decades later, make these distinctions with certainty? Instead *we should focus on what all genocidal campaigns have in common: not the destruction of a particular group type (the groups attacked vary greatly between cases) but the civilian character of the attacked population.* It is important to understand this character in a double sense. Not only are attacked 'groups' generally civilian, but so too are the vast majority of individual victims, who may not actually regard themselves as belonging to any particular group that is being targeted, or whose killing may not always be linked to the membership of a particular group. As Mann noted of the SS killings with their overlapping targets, 'almost all victims were harmless civilians, neither armed nor even Communist.'[3] Although victims are targeted for their supposed particular identities, the civilian character – not a particular identity type – is the *common* feature of both group targets and individual victims across *all* genocidal episodes. The focus on civilian enemies demarcates genocide from war and defines its comprehensive immorality and illegality. Thus the concept of 'civilian' is central to the understanding of genocide.

Civilians in international law

Nevertheless, the suspicion may linger that civilians and combatants are legal rather than sociological categories: formal ideas of significance to lawyers and human rights campaigners rather than articulations of real cleavages in social relations. Certainly it is in international law that we find most guidance as to their meaning: again we need to evaluate legal ideas before we can sociologically reformulate the civilian concept. 'Civilians' and 'belligerents' are, Karma Nabulsi has argued, 'the two most commonly used categories in the normative order of international humanitarian law.'[4] A broad consensus now exists around these terms, yet, Hugo Slim contended, 'what these terms meant in the past, when the laws were originally created, is still poorly understood.'[5] Although the origins of civilian immunity go back to the tenth century (in the thirteenth, Pope Gregory IX had given it a 'clear statement' with eight classes of protected non-combatants), the modern legal development of the distinction between combatants and non-combatants was only weakly influenced by concerns about civilian protection. If this body of law is seen today 'as a set of rules to mitigate the excesses of war and as the correct means of introducing humanitarian protection for civilians caught up in its devastation',[6] these categories originally meant something rather different.

Historical and ideological context 'is therefore crucial for understanding these concepts'.[7] As Geoffrey Best commented,

> The concept of 'the civilian' as someone essentially other than the combatant, invented by the European founders of the international law of war in the course of the seventeenth and eighteenth centuries, has ever since then held a fixed lodging in all thought and writing about war, especially in what is thought and written about the ethics and the international law of war. But times change, and the meanings of words change with them. We go on using the same words, but they may not mean what they once did.[8]

As recently as the early twentieth century, the main focus of international law was not humanitarian. When the modern laws of war were defined at The Hague in 1907, '[t]he central problem engaging the lawmakers . . . was most emphatically *not* the protection of civilians but defining what types of combatants the laws were to cover.'[9] The drafters were conservatives, even reactionaries: 'Central to their position was a desire to limit the rights of belligerency to a particular class of participant – the soldier – and to exclude all others from the right to become actively involved in war.'[10] Civilians were originally a residual category, those with no place in fighting: 'A key principle underpinning the entire system of the laws of war was the distinction between lawful and unlawful combatant. This norm criminalized civilian participation (political or military) in resistance to military occupation.'[11]

The 'humanitarian' interpretation only really came into its own with the Fourth Geneva Convention, the 'Civilians Convention', of 1949. Mid-twentieth-century jurists 'had a far different view' from their predecessors: 'Civilians were now seen as a distinct category under international law.'[12] '[T]he most significant development at Geneva', Nabulsi pointed out, 'was the outright banning of most of the traditional tools used by occupying armies to punish civilian resistance.'[13] The inspiration was the desire to prevent repeats of the unprecedented attacks on civilians by the Axis occupiers – the same motive that propelled Lemkin to define genocide. It was no coincidence that the Geneva Conventions followed within months of the adoption of the Genocide Convention and the Universal Declaration of Human Rights: all reflected the same imperative to protect unarmed populations from excesses of organized, armed power. These transformations 'confirmed this postwar era as the beginning of "international humanitarian law" rather than that of "the laws and customs of war" as at The Hague.'[14] The Geneva Conventions

> explicitly endorse the principle of distinction 'between the civilian popu-lation and combatants and between civilian objects and military object-ives.' They also require the protection of civilian livelihoods, and respect for essential human rights and humane treatment. In defining civilians, they also seek to remove as much ambiguity as possible by requiring that 'in case of doubt whether a person is a civilian, that person be considered a civilian', and that 'the presence within the civilian population of indi-viduals who do not come within the definition of civilians does not deprive the population of its civilian character.'[15]

Central to the civilian conception is the idea of 'innocence', deriving, Slim pointed out, from the Latin *nocens*, to harm, and meaning that 'the innocent are the non-harming.'[16] Thus 'ideas of distinction, restraint, non-combatance and innocence are . . . the key ingredients in the con-struction of the civilian idea.'[17] This idea of the civilian became a uni-versal, or 'superordinate', social identity – 'a belief that all of us, no matter what side we are on, have a greater common identity as human beings than the particular identities that war bestows on us as "enemies" or "allies".'[18] Yet the civilian category has been highly con-tested in both law and military practice. Although mostly the difference between a person who fought and one who didn't was clear, several developments compromised the distinction and 'blurred' civilian iden-tity. Total war was based on mass armies composed of men conscripted from the general population, while in civil and revolutionary war many civilians became irregular combatants. Moreover there was extensive, non-military *civilian participation* in war. Politicians and soldiers often believed that 'the 'civilian' person's moral, political or material rela-tionship with the enemy war effort, whether as munitions worker, food grower, voter, ideological sympathiser or loyal parent of a fighter . . . compromises the civilian ethic. . . . In this view, although such enemy individuals may be unarmed, they may still be harmful in other ways.'[19] Michael Walzer was prepared to countenance the extension of com-batant status to civilian munitions workers in their workplaces, while they were actually making weapons. He was also prepared to say that this 'plausible line . . . may be too finely drawn'.[20] Such views led to the erosion or qualification of civilian protection, with the invention of 'a new legal person, the quasicombatant, away from whom some propor-tion of legal protection was thought fit to be taken. Defining that proportion, however, proved difficult, and the blurring of the clear old distinction seemed to most jurists and war moralists self-destructive.'[21] Indeed, Best commented, '[t]hat such an awkward hybrid should have been proposed at all was the significant thing.'[22]

These difficulties have not prevented thinkers from proposing elaborate variations on the quasi-combatant idea. Even Best argued:

> Separability of civilian from combatant can prove physically almost impossible. It approaches being so wherever total national defence preparations fail to provide for the protection of such civilians as must be quite beyond combatant participation: those nursing mothers and young children, cripples and greybeards who regularly form *the irreducible residue of, so to speak, arch-civilians* whenever the civilian category comes under critical scrutiny.[23]

Since 'the law knows [the civilian] by only the simplest test', Best asked if, in this kind of situation, ethics should 'complement it by inviting distinction between civilians who may with some truth be said to have brought war upon themselves and civilians upon whom war comes more like a hurricane from afar?'[24] Ted Honderich took up this invitation, trying to 'improve on' the categories of combatant and non-combatant by replacing them with more complex concepts:[25]

- *non-combatants* – 'not armed or otherwise personally life-threatening at the time of their deaths, and are not in the army or police or any other life-threatening organization, say a terrorist one. We could decide to add that they are not officers of state or certain organizations either.'
- *unengaged combatants* – 'not armed or personally life-threatening at the time, but are in the army or other life-threatening organization. Maybe they make bombs or maintain helicopters. We could add that they may be officers of state, overwhelmingly more responsible for wrongs than are engaged combatants.'
- *half-innocents* – 'not armed or otherwise personally life-threatening at the time of their deaths, and not in the army or the like. These non-combatants and unengaged combatants, however, are by choice or consent benefiting or profiting from wrongful killings by their state or their people. They are as well-named as being half-guilty. They may be settlers on the land of those people they are not personally threatening.'
- *clear innocents* – 'not life-threatening at the time, not in the army or the like, and are not by choice or consent benefiting or profiting from wrongful killings by their state or their people. They include almost all children.'

Honderich contended that *civilians*, 'for what this fifth category is worth, may be non-combatants, half-innocents, or clear innocents. They may be none of these, but rather combatants and not half-innocents or clear innocents.' Actually, this confused the core concept. Although civilians are not always politically innocent, they are *always fundamentally innocent in a military sense, since they are unarmed and non-combatant.* And although people who are not members of formal armed organizations may take up arms, thus becoming combatants, to call them 'civilian combatants' makes the secondary question of organizational membership more important than the primary issue of combat role. *'Civilians' who take up arms cease to be civilians. Likewise members of military organizations who are disarmed cease to be full combatants.* Once captured, for example, legally they can no longer be subjected to violence and are entitled, like civilians, to be treated humanely.

Sociologists look at people's social action and relations above their formal affiliations to determine whether they belong to the civilian category. Although Honderich's refined categories enable us to explore issues of the degree of 'choice and consent' exercised by civilians, he was disarmingly correct to acknowledge that they 'may still not be of great use, since we are likely to be unable to say who was or is in what category at the time of a conflict.' And *for the central purpose of the civilian idea in international law, namely determining against whom it is justified to use violence, the more complex categories are simply confusing.* They open the way to legitimating the more extensive targeting of civilians: in Honderich's hands, in a case for 'terrorism for humanity' directed against the civilian beneficiaries of repression; in the hands of others, such as Barry Buzan, in a case for bombing the civilian supporters of terrorists.[26] Indeed the notion of a 'blurred' rather than a singular identity has often facilitated a direct rejection of the civilian idea. Many do not accept this as an overriding identity: rather they 'choose to trump the notion of civilian identity with a single, death-justifying identity that people cannot negotiate away. This singular perception of the enemy is paramount in racist, genocidal or totalitarian ideology.'[27] Even in democratic states, the effectiveness of terror as a strategy has meant that '[m]any politicians have pursued a policy of civilian atrocity and massacre simply because it works.'[28] Arguments have often centred 'on the more practical concerns of technical impossibility and military necessity'.[29] It is often thought too difficult (or inconvenient?) to put civilians first. Despite these difficulties, however, Best rightly concluded that '[t]he principles of discrimination between the real civilian and the real combatant remain crucial to a morally acceptable law of war.'[30] I shall give this legal argument sociological support. While social discrimination during conflicts is certainly complex, *the simple civilian–combatant distinction is the core social division that is regularly produced in armed conflict.* Understanding this distinction is the necessary foundation for an effective sociology, not only of war, but also of genocide.

Social production of civilians

How can we establish that the civilian idea actually has a strong meaning for societies involved in war and genocide? Before I return to the civilian–combatant distinction in genocide, I make a further detour. This question of civilians is *generally* neglected in modern sociology. Although the discipline readily accepts the distinctiveness of military institutions and values – hence the sociological importance of 'militarism', indicating the extensive influence of military culture on society[31] – it has given little attention to how these are produced. The tendency to substitute organizational affiliation for combatant role in defining civilians is reinforced by military sociology's formal institutional bias. 'Civilian' becomes a residual category: someone who is not a member of a military organization. Social relations between combatants and non-combatants in armed conflict are neglected. However, sociological studies of genocide, such as Mann's, and recent theories of war, such as Mary Kaldor's, have shown the importance of paramilitarism.[32] *It is therefore necessary for sociology to develop generic conceptions of combatants, as people participating directly in armed conflict, and of civilians, those who do not participate directly in armed conflict and whose non-participation primarily defines their conflict role.*

In order to show how these concepts express, ideal-typically, empirical social relations, I examined evidence of combatant–civilians relations not – first of all – in genocide, but in the most difficult possible case: the type of war situation in which discriminating combatants from civilians might be *least* viable. My initial focus therefore was on popular guerrilla war, and the relationships between armed movements and *supportive* civilian populations – the opposite of the relation between genocidal movements and their targets. This question has much exercised the law of war, for whom the irregular combatant has been a problematic figure. Earlier denied the protection of his regular counterpart, the irregular combatant has latterly been accorded a distinctive status: a fighter who may merge with the civilian population except when actually fighting. But for sociology, too, popular guerrillas are a limiting case; my discussion focuses on cases where armed movements might be thought to have been particularly *embedded* in national and local communities and levels of popular support might be assumed to have been high: anti-Nazi resistance in occupied Europe during the Second World War. This is a context in which one would expect boundaries between civilian and combatant to be *subjectively* blurred. If studies of even these movements provide evidence of the meaning of the combatant–civilian distinction, we may reasonably argue that it is generally significant in modern armed conflict.[33]

My interest is therefore the extent to which 'combatants' and 'civilians' are *informally* produced in the social relations of irregular conflict. On first reading, accounts of anti-Nazi resistance suggested blurred boundaries. 'Recent historians have shown', Jacques Semelin summarized, 'that what is called *resistance* is a highly complex phenomenon in which armed and unarmed forms of opposition intertwine.'[34] It 'does not tolerate rigid categories. . . . *the* resistance is a misnomer . . . instead there were *resistances*',[35] and 'the similarities between civilian and guerrilla resistances are stronger than the differences.'[36] Much resistance activity by civilians supported armed actions, so there was a 'great overlapping of armed and unarmed ways of fighting'.[37] Although civilians adopted 'what is commonly called nonviolent resistance', this 'term is not adequate, however, because this form of resistance has often been chosen for lack of a better alternative . . . the situation of being weaponless created conditions encouraging unarmed methods of action.'[38] Yet despite Semelin's pointers to the interdependence of the two forms of struggle, he concluded that 'civilian resistance is not always a simple complement to armed struggle.' It also included 'autonomous civilian resistance', that is, 'social mobilization and noncooperation to defend civilian goals.' Thus we could distinguish *civilian resistance*, 'defined as the spontaneous process of resistance by civilian society using unarmed means, and mobilizing either its principal institutions or its people – or both at the same time.'[39] There could be an objection, he recognized, 'that it seems insufficient to define civilian resistance only by its means.' However 'the autonomous actions of civilian resistance . . . were oriented toward goals that were explicitly "civilian" ':[40]

> Civilian resistance was rarely directed against the occupation forces openly: it did not have the means to drive them from the territory. The goal of this spontaneous struggle was instead to preserve the collective identity of the attacked societies: that it is to say, their fundamental values.[41]

Thus civilian resistance denoted *civil society*'s spontaneous process of struggle by unarmed means. It could be collective, invoking a 'radical attitude of noncooperation and confrontation', or individual 'dissidence' or 'disobedience'.[42] It 'generally derives from both institutions and the masses': '[i]nstitutional and popular resistance provide indispensable support for each other. . . . the complete picture of civilian resistance amounts to a dialectical mobilization of society from the top and the bottom in a strategy of noncooperation.'[43] What made unarmed combat possible was, 'above all, the feeling of solidarity within the group. A population's degree of social cohesion becomes the prime condition of its civilian resistance.'[44] The greater the cohesiveness of a civil society, 'the more it can resist an armed attack on its own.'[45] Deep internal conflicts in societies played into the occupier's hands, but there was also 'a cohesion of occupied people based on the specific traits of the aggression and the occupation conditions accompanying it. . . . aggression itself is a factor that contributes to cohesion.'[46] Civilian resistance 'denotes all kinds of opposition . . . that are practiced without weapons; these include economic, legal, academic, religious, medical and other forms.'[47] Adam Roberts saw this as 'civilian defence', involving non-cooperation with an enemy or occupier, civil disobedience, industrial action, and ideological opposition.[48]

Yet if we distinguish civilian from armed resistance, the question remains of civilians' relationships *with* armed action. Much civilian resistance 'does not reject violence as a strategic principle' but only 'by necessity'.[49] Guerrilla movements may still be seen partly as 'the recourse to weapons by civilian populations'.[50] As H. R. Kedward argued: 'All wars of liberation against occupying forces are, to varying degrees, wars of civilians. . . . Alongside the irregular soldiers, known variously as franc-tireurs, guerrilla fighters, maquisards and partisans, there are what might be called the irregular civilians. . . . It is this wider notion of irregularity, indeed the whole concept of transgression, which opens up the possibility of a deeper and more exploratory search.'[51] Thus the boundary between civilian and combatant was crossed, and even civilians who did not take up arms *supported* armed struggle. This support has often been amplified in post-war accounts, as '[r]esistance against Nazism has become one of the modern archetypes of liberating violence. . . . The leaders of such movements are depicted as adventurous heroes and defiant warriors living in the shadows of an unacceptable tyranny.'[52] Mythologies around resistance heroes depict armed combat 'in a simplistic way, verging on caricature',[53] but they contribute to 'founding myths' of post-war societies, 'associated with images of redemptive violence, that is, violence perceived to be necessary'.[54] In France, the *maquis* depended on their '[h]uman undergrowth or infrastructure . . . the action of people who protected, supported, fed, clothed, and cared for the maquis, intensified and enlarged the popular revolt . . . . The search for the maquis lay, and still lies, through and within these structures, within the fundamental interconnections between the maquisards and the local population.'[55]

Armed resisters' mode of operation, based on *coups de main* for food and other essentials,

produced a model of relationships between the maquis and the population which . . . sustained the image of tough and resolute groups of fighters 'out there', descending on their chosen objectives in surprise attacks before disappearing back into the woods as mysteriously as they had come. This image gave substance to the adventurous mystique of the outlaw as it was positively rendered in the maquis discourse, and it also provided the mix of fact and fantasy with which Vichy fashioned its negative portrait of the outlaw, as a terrorist victimizing the law-abiding rural society.[56]

Yet Kedward emphasized that that model 'was inadequate as a representation of reality. Alongside it, or, in more structural terms, underneath it, was the model of the maquis as the armed embodiment of the ever-widening popular and rural resistance.'[57] In their cooperation, the fighters and the general civilian population were bound together by the 'shared risks' of guerrilla action, as 'many maquisards in the woods experienced the same kind of anxiety for their womenfolk exposed to German reprisals as women traditionally felt for the fighting men at the front.'[58]

Yet even Kedward's highly sympathetic study also underlined the *ambivalence* in civilians' attitudes towards guerrilla violence, often perceived as simultaneously necessary *and* threatening. If few supported collaborationist or occupier repression, there was nevertheless 'acute anxiety'[59] within the population:

a much greater proportion of the rural population . . ., constituting in many areas a majority, felt fear and anxiety at the maquis presence, but without fundamental hostility. Acts of industrial sabotage and armed clashes . . . were not seen by the population in terms of banditry, but any proximity of such events to their homes not unnaturally produced fears of reprisals. Such was the severity of German and Vichy repression . . . that public sympathy for the maquis frequently went hand in hand with very considerable, and justified, fear.[60]

Thus *the felt community of risk always contained tensions between combatant and civilian roles.* What started as a division of labour led to differences of experience and also of ideology: 'Central to the discourse

of the maquis', Kedward described, 'was the sense of purity and
freedom from compromise that accompanied the move to the hills,
experienced as a decisive break with hesitations.'[61] Although unlike a
conventional army, in this *movement away* from normal social life
maquisards still 'had direct access to the life and politics of the home
front'. Nevertheless,

> Uniforms, armbands, a weapon in the hand, and a sudden confrontation
> with what they variously described as the terror and exhilaration of being
> under fire, brought maquisards closer to the traditional soldier's mental-
> ity, with its highly ambivalent attitude to the home front, at once dismis-
> sive of the politics of civilian life and yet also insistent that combat and
> sacrifice gave soldiers a moral right to a say in the running of their
> country.[62]

For a few weeks at the end of the war, as the maquis became increasingly
powerful, there was a 'period of public apprehension' and 'expressions
of fear and anxiety' in many towns: 'most major towns presented some
examples of arbitrary intimidation and abuse of military power. . . .
Inevitably the tendency of civilians at the time was to generalize from
such actions, just as the tendency of maquisards looking back is to min-
imize them.'[63]

Thus although Kedward's careful and nuanced account largely
endorsed the armed resisters' own accounts of their intimate relationship with their society, it also explored this relationship's contradictions. It showed how, despite underlying social cohesion and common
aims and values, *differences of role and experience between combatants
and civilians produced serious social differences*. Of course it could be
argued that these reflected older tensions between the rural society in
which the maquis emerged, and the more conventional armed forces of
the French state. In the late nineteenth century, with 'little sense of
national identity to mitigate the hostility and fear most country people
felt for troops', conventional soldiers had already been 'treated like an
army of occupation, with little or no sense that they represented any
kind of common weal.'[64] Even before that, 'civilian armies' during the
French Revolution – bands of urban, highly politicized *sans-culottes* –
had been resented in rural society, as they 'represented the Terror on the
move, the village Terror. They aroused fear and such was the intention
of their creators.'[65] Thus anti-militarism was an old tradition: but it is
still striking that it was reproduced, even if in muted and ambivalent
forms, vis-à-vis an armed force created directly *out of* rural society and
reflecting *its* common hostility to the occupation.

This significance is heightened by the relatively favourable circumstances of the French struggle: Allied invasions put the Germans on to the defensive, enabling resistance forces to play a part in victory without paying the full price of all-out war against a formidable occupier. And yet still the ambivalence was there, *particularly in* that moment of victory. Studies of more difficult situations for the occupied populations and resistance, as in Poland, show deeper tensions between civilians and combatants. It is instructive that Joanna Hanson, in her study of the Warsaw Uprising of 1944, *defined* 'the civilian population' as 'the very large group of Varsovians who were caught up in the events of the Uprising, having had no influence on its creation.'[66] Social difference between civilians, who had little or no control, and combatants, who were actors in the military struggle and so could influence its outcome, were deepened through the struggle and resulted from its core characteristics. Semelin argued that the difference did not arise simply from arms: '[i]n themselves, arms are inert objects. The power relationship between two adversaries is not, therefore, simply the result of one being armed and the other not.' And yet, as he went on to say: 'The determination to resort to the arms at one's disposal will most likely put the person without weapons at a concrete disadvantage.'[67] The creation of an armed organization utilizes weaponry to forge power vis-à-vis other armed forces, but it simultaneously creates new power relationships between its members and civilians. The tensions that produce this difference are also reported in many contemporary accounts of armed struggles where there is an underlying sympathy of the population for the fighters.[68]

Civilians, combatants and social stratification

This has been an extensive detour. But my argument is that, *if even resistance movements reproduce social difference between armed and civilian forms of action, and hence between combatants and civilians, then these should be considered generally significant ideal types for sociology.* They offer a broader foundation for understanding the civilian question, not only in war but in genocide. Yet social theory has not regarded these distinctions as fundamental. Instead, it has tended to confine the relevance of armed conflicts to the reproduction of pre-existing social distinctions – of nationality, ethnicity, religion, class, gender, etc. We have seen how stubbornly some theorists have insisted on the objective 'reality' of certain group types as a prerequisite of genocide. And yet we have also seen how critics have emphasized the social construction of ethnicity and its transformation *through* armed conflict. The most general conclusion we can draw, taking these conclusions together with my argument about the social production of civilians, is that armed conflict does not merely reproduce existing social differentiation, but strongly affects its forms. *Violent conflict simultaneously transforms pre-existing social distinctions and produces its own new distinctions between combatants and civilians.* In turn these differences become of general significance for society, institutionalized in distinctions between members of armed forces and non-members, the unmobilized citizenry.

Yet these findings lead us to a new question: what are the relationships between strengthened particularist identities, reinforced by armed conflict, and the civilian identity that it also produces? Clearly all armed actors seek to mobilize social constituencies and heighten identities (ethnic, national, etc.) that maximize their support. In the resistance cases, successful strengthening of national identity was accompanied by social production of a civilian identity: the two coexisted, with real tensions but without fundamental conflict. In other cases, however, national identity may be undermined by an unpopular war, and so civilian identity may be brought directly into conflict with it. It is evident that these relationships will vary. The question echoes the general debate in sociological theory over how 'old' social distinctions are overlain with 'new', brought to a head by Ulrich Beck's claim that risk exposure was replacing class as the principal inequality of modern society.[69] Beck radically contended that '[i]n risk society relations of definition are to be conceived analogous to Marx's relations of production',[70] placing new emphasis on how risk was reflexively defined by actors. *In armed conflict the risk relations between combatants, who partly define their own risks, and civilians, who are largely exposed to risks that others define, are central to social relations.*[71] Hence social reproduction of the civilian–combatant difference may be seen as an example of how differences of risk are socially instantiated. The general question is how these new relations mesh with pre-existing social differences – about how far, as Mary Douglas put it, '[p]erceptions of high risk reinforce already existing social divisions.'[72] Clearly, people who increasingly think of themselves as 'civilians' do not thereby cease to recognize other social distinctions; but the interaction between conflict-produced (civilian) and pre-conflict identities is an empirical question. For example, Hanson concluded that there was no 'real proof of a great divergence in attitude and behaviour between the various classes'; [73] rather the actual experiences of the Warsaw Uprising and its defeat conditioned changing and contradictory attitudes among civilians as a whole. In other cases, class and other social divisions might make more substantial differences to civilian experience and consciousness.

Civilian resistance and genocidal war

The qualitative asymmetry of genocide's armed power projection against civilians has profound consequences for its character as *conflict*. On the one hand, *pure* genocidal relations – where the asymmetry is unmodified by other power relations – leave open principally civilian resistance, as it is often difficult for a civilian population alone to improvise effective armed resistance, and many 'arch-civilians' (young children, the infirm, the disabled) are in any case excluded from it. Civilian resistance may be a viable method of thwarting particular genocidal policies, enabling escape and survival, and sustaining moral and social cohesion among the victims. In all these senses, civilian resistance is simply unavoidable; it is inconceivable that any population will not attempt to protect itself against violent attack. However, civilian resistance alone is almost certain to be inadequate to defeat or overthrow overwhelming armed might. Civilians will inevitably look for armed responses, not only through their own resistance but also through alliance with organized armed actors. Once a genocidal campaign is well under way, only armed action is likely to halt it. This understanding gives us another reason to emphasize the intimate connections of genocide to war. *If genocide is 'war' against civilians, it tends to even up – through armed resistance or intervention – into a more normal war.* This consequence places a premium on the ability of a civilian population not only to improvise military resistance but also to find military allies, to connect resistance to 'normal' war. Populations attacked outside a situation of prior armed conflict are more likely to rely exclusively on their own resistance, and are therefore less likely to defeat genocide. The Soviet peasantry was attacked by Stalin, for example, almost a decade after the end of Russia's civil war; the regime was able to mobilize the militarized party-state inherited from that struggle, but there was no extant armed force within or outside Soviet territory to aid peasant resistance. Despite determined, often violent, opposition, the peasants lost.

Very commonly genocide is an extension of more conventional – albeit degenerate – war. Genocidists' perceptions of social groups as enemies are conditioned by their association of those groups with more 'normal' armed enemies, whether 'international' or 'domestic'. Sometimes it is difficult to distinguish when degenerate war, in which populations are attacked as a means of defeating an armed enemy, passes into genocide, where the group is an enemy in itself and its destruction becomes a distinctive policy goal. Certainly, much armed conflict combines war and genocide, and it seems useful to use the term *genocidal war* for conflict in which genocidal campaigns, at least on one side, are intertwined with more conventional warfare.

Interactions of war and genocide complicate the situations of threatened populations as well as of would-be military interveners. Armed resistance to pre-genocidal repression may help push oppressive regimes towards genocide, as with the Kosovo Liberation Army's campaign against Serbian rule. Even before this, Albanian critics of the KLA pointed out that the armed struggle's cost was 'paid for by ordinary people: human rights organizations say that 95 per cent of Albanians killed were civilians and only 5 per cent from the KLA.'[74] Once this repression provoked NATO intervention and in response Serbian policies escalated to all-out destruction of the Albanians, of course the KLA and NATO campaigns were vindicated in the eyes of civilians, who would not have returned home without them. Yet the KLA's campaign had helped bring Kosovo to its genocidal state, supplanting a blocked policy of civilian resistance[75] and exposing civilians to state violence. This example shows that, while only an armed response may halt genocide, armed action at lower levels of conflict may actually part-cause it. Conversely, while civilian resistance may be relatively weak in the face of an overt genocidal onslaught, at earlier stages of a conflict it may be more likely to slow down or avoid the movement towards genocide.

9

Explanations

From modernity to warfare

I have argued that we need to move from a concept of genocide as intentional action to one that describes the conflict this action sets up. In exploring this conflict, I emphasized the civilian character of the genocidal 'enemy' and its implications for resistance. This led me back to the fact that – despite its differences from 'normal' and even 'degenerate' war – the typical *meaning* of genocidal action is close to that of action in war, the *structure* of genocide as conflict is close to that of war, and the *context* of genocide often is, or becomes, war. So my approach understands genocide as considerably dependent on more fundamental types of conflict (war) and power (military power). In Weber's terms, the concept of genocide is an 'individual' ideal type (similar to capitalism or bureaucracy), referring to what happens in a number of instances in a broad historical epoch, rather than a 'generic' ideal type (similar to 'war' and 'military power') specifying a component element of many forms of power.[1] From the point of view of historical understanding, my ideal type of genocide is a heuristic device 'intended to refer to a class of complex empirical phenomena'.[2] Hence the ideal type becomes a hypothesis, or should be 'used as a heuristic device in order to *find* the correct hypothesis.'[3] It suggests a type of explanation centred on war and military power relations.

Of course, genocide is still a *general* concept of a range of complex historical phenomena, even if it seems slightly confusing to follow Lemkin in arguing for a 'generic' version of this 'individual' type. Yet we should recognize that genocides – like 'the majority of cases of action important to history or sociology'[4] – are 'qualitatively heterogeneous'[5] in secondary senses, even if variations should be seen as 'differences of degree in respect to action which remains qualitatively the same'.[6] Indeed as I turn to the question of explanation, addressed in hundreds of case and comparative studies, the heterogeneity seems to become more significant. *Identifying commonalities does not mean that we find near-identical individual explanations for all genocidal events.* Historians naturally elucidate specific causal contexts for each episode: the same type of action occurs in a variety of contexts (even if many are war-related) and so explanations vary considerably. So, before we examine the possibilities of general explanation, we need first of all to consider some of the variation identified, since 'variants' are often sub-types delineated by specific causal contexts. Without finding causal common-alities that transcend the variation, it is difficult to justify *any* general explanatory framework.

Types of genocide

Some variations (the '-cides') were discussed in chapter 5. However, variation has also been specified more broadly, in many typologies which have multiplied the sub-categories of genocide. Thus Chalk and Jonassohn noted that genocides varied by the types of society in which they occurred, by perpetrator, by victims, by groups, by accusations against them, and by results for the perpetrator society. They also pro-posed a classification of genocides by *motive*:

1 to eliminate a real or potential threat;
2 to spread terror among real or potential enemies;
3 to acquire economic wealth;
4 to implement a belief, a theory, or an ideology.[7]

Of course, since motives as well as intentions are complex, any histori-cal episode will probably show up all these motives in distinctive com-binations. In contrast Charny proposed a matrix combining scope (the scale and breadth of targeting) and context (colonialism, war, etc.), specifying the following major types:

1 genocidal massacre ('mass murder on a smaller scale');
2 intentional genocide ('an explicit intention to destroy a specific targeted victim group': either against a single group or 'multiple' or 'omnicide');

3 genocide in the course of colonization or consolidation of power;
4 genocide in the course of aggressive or unjust war;
5 war crimes against humanity;
6 genocide as a result of ecological destruction and abuse.[8]

All these distinctions can be multiplied in turn by further cross-tabulation. Conversely, studies of specific episodes can be used to challenge 'types': for example, Alison Palmer, finding genocide against Aboriginal peoples in Queensland to be quite different from the extermination of the Herero in German South-West Africa, questioned whether 'colonial genocide' is really a distinctive type.[9] The only solution then is to develop a more elaborate typology, as Samuel Totten and his colleagues did when they argued that genocides against indigenous peoples can themselves be divided into 'retributive', 'developmental', 'conservation-related violations', 'environmental destruction' or 'in the context of a struggle between a state and an indigenous group or collectivity of several collaborating groups that are resisting the actions of the state.'[10]

I do not intend to enter systematically into these debates, although they are important concerns for comparative research. Rather I want to emphasize how the typologies reflect beliefs that motives and causes are complex and heterogeneous. They underline the potential difficulties of general explanation. In what sense, then, can social scientists really propose this? In order to answer this question, and justify my argument for the primary role of military relations, I shall examine some explanations already proposed. We need to note, first, that very different questions are being asked, such as: Are there general reasons why the *phenomenon* of genocide has developed? Can certain features provide the principal elements of explanation for all *particular* episodes? Why do perpetrator organizing *centres* initiate genocides? Why do *individual* perpetrators commit genocidal crimes?[11] In what follows I evaluate explanatory frameworks bearing in mind these questions, although I do not summarize arguments systematically in relation to each.

Modernity

Although some authorities have found much genocide in earlier history,[12] others question whether systematically murderous policies towards ethnic and other groups were so common.[13] However, it is widely argued that, although mass killing is hardly novel, it is only in modernity that we get *systematic* policies to destroy social groups 'as such', distinct from policies to defeat armed enemies in war. Although few social theorists have directly addressed this question, Michel Foucault represented a common view when he suggested that genocide resulted from distinctively modern power relations. Indeed Foucault linked genocide to modern war – 'wars were never so bloody as they have been since the nineteenth century, and all things being equal, never before did regimes visit such holocausts on their own populations'[14] – and both to profound transformations of the mechanisms of power in modern times. Sovereign power was now

> power bent on generating forces, making them grow, and ordering them, rather than one dedicated to impeding them, making them submit, or destroying them. There has been a parallel shift in the right of death, or at least a tendency to align itself with the exigencies of a life-administering power and to define itself accordingly. This death that was based on the right of the sovereign is now manifested as simply the reverse of the right of the social body to ensure, maintain or develop its life.[15]

For Foucault therefore genocide represented a manifestation of modern *bio-power*, reflecting the fact that 'life and its mechanisms' had been brought 'into the realm of explicit calculations and made knowledge-power an agent of transformation of human life.'[16] The corollary of the state's management of life forces was a new management of death: 'One might say that the ancient right to *take* life or *let* live was replaced by a power to *foster* life or *disallow* it to the point of death.'[17] Foucault had clearly absorbed the experiences of total war and totalitarian genocide:

> Wars are no longer waged in the name of a sovereign who must be defended; they are waged on behalf of the existence of everyone; entire populations are mobilized for the purpose of wholesale slaughter in the name of life necessity: massacres have become vital. . . . the existence in question is no longer the juridical existence of sovereignty; at stake is the biological existence of a population.[18]

In this context he made his sole direct mention of genocide: 'If genocide is indeed the dream of modern powers, this is not because of a recent return of the ancient right to kill; it is because power is situated and exercised at the level of life, the species, the race, and the large-scale phenomena of population.'[19]

However, if genocide is a manifestation of the general 'power over life', by which the state takes upon itself the task of regulating and maintaining its subjects' minds and bodies, we still need to ask why this is exercised in a genocidal manner. Foucault's explanation that genocide is the *other side* of the modern state's 'function of administering life', replacing capital and corporal punishment with correction, seems insufficient. Why should state forms that increasingly eschew capital punishment resort to the 'orgies' of destruction and murder that characterize genocide?[20] Foucault's relatively unexamined idea of genocide appears over-influenced by particular pseudo-scientific, eugenic strands of genocidal thought and the exceptionally rationalized murder of the extermination camps. Although totalitarian rulers such as Hitler, Stalin, Mao and Pol Pot did sometimes appear to be mobilizing power to raise and cull entire populations like livestock, scholars have shown that even their genocidal decisions were pragmatic, launched in contexts of political conflict and war. Elsewhere genocide has been influenced less by ambitious ideological concepts and even more by specific political aims. Genocide is practised by regimes and armed groups that hardly have totalitarian ambitions or capabilities; conversely, today's Western states certainly 'manage life' but they do not practise genocide. Foucault's linkages were suggestive but they didn't explain the rise of genocide or why genocides are initiated.

If Foucault's formulations were too general, they encapsulated a widespread belief in the *enabling* implication of modernity. This view of modern society as a necessary if not sufficient cause was seminally explored by Zygmunt Bauman, for whom 'the Holocaust was an outcome of a unique encounter between factors by themselves quite ordinary and common'[21] and 'a rare, yet significant and reliable, test of the hidden possibilities of modern society'.[22] He contended 'that every "ingredient" of the Holocaust – all those many things that rendered it possible – was normal . . . in the sense of being fully in keeping with everything that we know about our civilization, its guiding spirit, its priorities, its immanent vision of the world.'[23] Bauman specified this 'modern' focus in terms of mentality, technology and organization, building on Raul Hilberg's conclusion that the machinery of destruction 'was structurally no different from organized German society as a whole. [It] was the organized community in one of its special roles.'[24] The Holocaust was a textbook case of 'scientific management', 'a paradigm of modern bureaucratic rationality',[25] exemplified by the department in the SS headquarters in charge of the destruction of European Jews, 'officially designated as the Section of Administration and Economy. . . . Except for the moral repulsiveness of its goal . . ., the activity did not differ in any formal sense (the only sense that can be expressed in the language of bureaucracy) from all other organized activities designed, monitored and supervised by "ordinary" administrative and economic sections.'[26] Thus the case entirely fitted Weber's description of modern administration:

> in the last resort – *the choice of physical extermination as the right means to the task of* Entfernung [removal, elimination] *was a product of routine bureaucratic procedures*: means–end calculus, budget balancing, universal rule application. To make the point sharper still – the choice was an effect of the earnest effort to find rational solutions to successive 'problems', as they arose in the changing circumstances. . . . *it arose out of a genuinely rational concern, and it was generated by bureaucracy true to its form and purpose.*[27]

Moreover bureaucracy provided the 'moral sleeping pills' that made possible the Holocaust's 'technical-administrative success'.[28]

Yet, like Foucault's idea, Bauman's concept of the Holocaust was over-rationalized. Although he recognized that only '[t]he *possibility* of the Holocaust was rooted in certain universal features of modern civilization; its *implementation* on the other hand, was connected with a specific and not at all universal relationship between state and society',[29] his account narrowed down its meaning and made it difficult to compare with other equally modern genocides. When he wrote that 'the Holocaust left behind and put to shame all its alleged pre-modern equivalents, exposing them as primitive, wasteful and ineffective by comparison. . . . It towers high over the past genocidal episodes in the same way as the modern industrial plant towers above the craftsman's cottage workshop'[30], he focused entirely on the industrialized extermination of the Final Solution. We got little sense of the activities of the *Einsatzgruppen*, shooting huge numbers alongside improvised ditches and burning them alive in their villages. Yet this direct slaughter was the first phase of extensive mass murder, the decisive shift of gear that paved the way for Auschwitz.

The activities of the *Einsatzgruppen* were not only closer to pre-modern paradigms. They proved a more enduring model than the extermination camps for later *génocidaires*. In Rwanda, notoriously, machine-guns and machetes proved quite as murderous as the gas chambers were, without the need for bureaucracy on the German scale (although the organizers did employ modern political organization and mass media). In Bosnia, Serbian nationalists destroyed non-Serbs while slaughtering only a minority, through intimidation, expulsion, torture, rape and killing in improvised concentration camps. In contemporary destructions of indigenous peoples, the methods and organization have been much more basic than those of the Final Solution. Not surprisingly, a student of these genocides has argued that Bauman's 'thesis linking genocide to a specific level of state formation, technological efficiency, rationality, and subjectivity is belied' by other examples.[31]

Yet, as Moses argued, the argument between these positions is unproductive, since genocide cannot be generally defined by particular victim experiences.[32] Rather, Donald Bloxham commented, Bauman's conception of genocide's 'gardening' culture, in which ill-fitting human beings are 'weeded' out, is more generally enlightening than his emphasis on bureaucracy: 'The modernity or otherwise of genocide is a function of mindset not machinery.'[33]

Such critiques have led to an alternative version of the modernity thesis. According to Nancy Scheper-Hughes, genocide is not an exceptional, high-bureaucratic realization but an *endemic* feature of modernity. She suggested 'a genocide continuum' composed of 'small wars and invisible genocides' conducted 'in the normative social spaces of public schools, clinics, emergency rooms, hospital wards, nursing homes, court rooms, prisons, detention centers, and public morgues. The continuum refers to the human capacity to reduce others to nonpersons, to monsters, or to things, that gives structure, meaning and rationale to everyday practices of violence.' The human species has developed 'a genocidal capacity' seen in 'all expressions of social exclusion, dehumanization, depersonalization, pseudo-speciation that normalize atrocious behavior and violence toward others.'[34] According to Scheper-Hughes,

> the preparations for mass killing can be found in social sentiments and institutions from the family, to schools, churches, hospitals, and the military. . . . the 'genocide continuum' . . . refers to an evolving social consensus toward devaluing certain forms of human life and lifeways . . . ; the refusal of social support and humane care to vulnerable and stigmatized social groups . . . ; the militarization of everyday life . . . ; social polarization and fear.[35]

The kernel of truth in this argument is that, once we recognize the possibility of genocidal outcomes, it is alarmingly easy to imagine how everyday social relations could facilitate them. But once again these can only be enabling conditions. The key question is, *in what circumstances can devaluing and dehumanization mutate into systematic, organized violence?* Since the former are common and the latter relatively exceptional, this kind of argument from modernity to genocide shares the over-abstraction of Bauman's version that it criticizes.

Culture and psychology

More prevalent overall explanations concern not modern social relations in general but their particular forms. Very common outside the academic literature but widely criticized within it is the assumption that ethnicity and ethnic conflict are root causes. Yet, as we saw in chapter 7, general cultures and identities – even when entwined with histories of conflict – are always *insufficient* to generate violence. The consensus has been stated by Mann: 'murderous cleansing does not occur among rival ethnic groups who are separate but equal. Mere difference is not enough to generate much conflict. . . . For serious ethnic conflict to occur, one ethnic group must be seen as exploiting the other.'[36] The most that can be claimed for *general* cultural and identity factors is that, when suffused with historic enmities, they may facilitate genocidal policies. Other resources in the same cultures may, of course, work in the opposite direction.

Nevertheless there is another sense in which culture may be more instrumental. Christopher Taylor has argued that the Rwanda genocide

> cannot be reduced solely and simply to the competition for power, dominance and hegemony among antagonistic factions. Much of the violence . . . followed a cultural patterning, a structured and structuring logic . . . many of the representations concerning bodily integrity that I encountered in popular medicine during fieldwork in Rwanda [before the genocide] emerged in the techniques of physical cruelty employed by Hutu extremists during the genocide. I do not advance the argument that the political events of 1994 were in any way caused by these symbols, or by Rwandan 'culture' conceived of in a cognitively determinist way in the manner of Goldhagen's controversial analysis of the Nazi genocide. These representations operated as much during times of peace as during times of war.[37]

Rwanda had a 'culture of terror' during many years leading to 1994; many 'narratives in circulation' justified violence. As Liisa Malkki showed, techniques of violence used *against Hutus* in Burundi in 1972 – modes of impalement, cutting foetuses from mothers' wombs, forcing parents to eat children's flesh, forcing parent and child to commit incest – became part of a learned pattern of violence.[38] 'Many of the same forms of violence, the same techniques of cruelty', Taylor pointed out, *used by Hutu nationalists*, 'were encountered in Rwanda during the 1994 genocide.'[39] Taylor's account offers a good general way of conceptualizing the causal significance of culture: although never the principal explanation why genocide is initiated, it can provide supporting evidence as to why genocidal constituencies are receptive, and explain much about how it is practised.

Likewise social psychology can provide evidence on why individual leaders are prone to genocidal tendencies and why 'ordinary men' participate in them.[40] Yet if 'ordinary psychological processes and normal, common human motivations and certain basic but not inevitable tendencies in human thought and feeling (such as the devaluation of others)' contribute to genocide, they cannot be, as Ervin Staub argued, 'the primary sources' of genocide.[41] If the tendencies themselves are 'not inevitable', genocidal consequences are much less so. For these, the central element of explanation must be the exceptional social *contexts* in which common psychological tendencies become implicated in extensive violence and killing.

Economy

Another more specific version of the 'modernity' thesis is economic explanation, a mode deeply embedded in social-scientific thought. Few doubt that genocide has recurring economic aspects: the systematic theft of Jewish personal possessions during the Holocaust is emblematic, and recent genocides have provided many further examples of how perpetrators seek to enrich themselves at victims' expense. And yet the difficulty Marxists found in explaining the Holocaust in terms of capitalism has also generally deterred scholars from explaining the occurrence of genocide – as opposed to individual perpetrators' actions – in predominantly economic terms. Mann represented a mainstream view when he argued that '[e]conomic power relations were *uniquely* the prime mover' of colonial genocide.[42] However, contemporary genocides against indigenous peoples – which often involve new forms of settler colonization within quasi-imperial states – have been seen within a similar frame. Thus for Mark Levene contemporary genocide, far from being 'a series of unrelated aberrations', needed to be viewed 'as one critical byproduct . . . of what is actually a very dysfunctional international system.'[43] The economically competitive global system produced pressure, he argued, for 'fourth world' nation-states to destroy marginal peoples in the name of state-building, developmental agendas. Thus there were 'general wellsprings and processes' of genocide in the 'Western dominated and regulated international system'.[44] Jefremovas's 'resource crunch' thesis about Rwanda was an individual explanation of a similar kind. Population growth within the context of severely limited resources accounted for the willingness of people to take up arms against their neighbours: 'Factors such as the growing landlessness, disparities between rich and poor, the ambitions of an increasingly ruthless elite losing their grip on power, regional politics, and regional dynamics played a central role in the genocide and political slaughter.'[45] She was right to argue that 'the socioeconomic aspects of the killings also should not be ignored. . . . As the killings gained momentum, the violence became more complex and less linked to purely political ends.'[46] Yet the prime motivations of the genocide's organizing centre remained political and military. The key general question is how far, as Levene argued, economic pressures account for why elites turn genocidal. The problem was, once again, excessive abstraction. Since most economically pressured poor states *don't* commit genocide, we always need to elucidate the political-military context within which genocidal policies are formulated. If economic pressures enter into the decision-making of states, parties, armies, militias and others, nevertheless genocide still requires them to formulate political and military policies against indigenous peoples.

Another way of representing cultural and economic factors has been to consider them as preconditions. Alexander Hinton suggested 'we might use the term *genocidal priming* to reference the set of interwoven processes that generate such mass violence. To "prime" something is to make it ready or prepared . . . . By genocidal priming, then, I refer to a set of processes that establish the preconditions for genocide to take place within a given sociopolitical context.'[47] Nevertheless, when Hinton came to specify 'primers' he referred not only to 'socio-economic upheaval' but also to 'segregation and differential opportunities for groups', 'legislation that polarizes social divisions' and 'dissemination of messages of hate'. Thus *'priming' involved not so much general background pressures and relations, such as those of ethnicity and development, as active pre-genocidal policies that 'stoked' the fires of conflict.* As in all close narratives of major episodes, the movement was away from generally enabling conditions towards political contexts in which genocidal policies developed. Genocide is always a deliberate policy and organized action and so needs to be explained primarily within political conflict, however economic and cultural relations feed into these. It is hard to better Mahmood Mamdani's words:

> My critique of those who tend to accent the economic and the cultural in the understanding of the genocide is that their explanation obscures the moment of decision, of choice, as if human action, even – or, shall I say, particularly – at its most dastardly or heroic, can be explained by necessity alone.[48]

Politics

If much points towards politics as the prime locus of explanation, this should not mean a simple invocation of state power. As Dadrian pointed out, the vast majority of scholars involved in genocide depict the state as the supreme author. . . . The flaw in this approach is that it issues from a perspective in which the relationship of formal authority to informal authority is not properly assessed. . . . [however,] in origin, structure and function, the state is not geared to conceiving, organizing and implementing a monstrous crime such as genocide represents. As a rule, formal authority precludes such a recourse to criminality. In order for a state to get involved in the business of genocidal enactments, it has to undergo structural changes and transform itself into an engine of destruction. In other words, it has to be criminalized. The only instrument capable of generating such a transformation is a type of informal authority that is in ascendance and in rivalry with the authority of the state. . . . monolithic political parties that were animated with revolutionary and radical designs.[49]

Thus genocide is less a matter of state institutions than of *regime*: restructuring into radical party-states transforms states into genocidal instruments. This points towards a focus on politics in a broader sense, as in Mann's sociology of 'cleansing'. For him, of course, the world's genocides remain 'thankfully few', but were surrounded by more numerous cases of 'less severe but nonetheless murderous cleansing'.[50] Although I disagree with this categorization, when Mann referred to 'murderous cleansing' he meant more or less what I call genocide, and it is possible to examine his account as the most developed general framework to address its political causation.

Mann argued that, while all four main sources of social power – economic, political, ideological and military – were involved, the primary locus was political. His account of this was very specific: 'Murderous cleansing is modern, because it is the dark side of democracy.'[51] His case rested primarily on a reading of the connections of ethnicity with democracy. Murderous ethnic cleansing was a hazard of the age of democracy because in conditions of multiethnicity the ideal of rule by the people 'began to intertwine the *demos* with the dominant *ethnos*', generating organic conceptions of the nation and state that encouraged the removal of minorities.[52] However, 'stabilized institutionalized democracies' were the type of modern polity least likely to commit 'cleansing'. Instead, 'cleansing' mostly resulted from the perversion of democracy. Indeed Mann went so far as to assert that regimes that are actually perpetrating murderous cleansing 'are never democratic, since that would be a contradiction in terms.' Indeed, as escalation towards murder proceeds, all perpetrating regimes become less and less democratic. Mann's theses connecting democracy and murderousness 'therefore apply beforehand, to the earlier phases of escalation of ethnic conflict.'[53] Indeed, for Mann, 'cleansing' was implicated more in the creation of modern democracy than in its institutionalized state. Democracies that are now stable often have ethnic 'cleansing', if not murder, in their pasts. Most of them committed sufficient violence in the past to produce an essentially mono-ethnic citizen body in the present: 'Liberal democracies were built on top of ethnic cleansing, although this took the form of institutionalized coercion, not mass murder.' The colonial expansion that established the 'new world' was especially murderous where 'settler democracy' took hold: 'The more settlers controlled colonial institutions, the more murderous the cleansing. . . . It is the most direct relationship I have found between democratic regimes and mass murder.' And the argument has a twenty-first-century twist: regimes newly embarked upon democratization are more likely than stable authoritarian regimes to commit 'murderous ethnic cleansing'.[54]

One of Mann's main contributions was a less state-centric political account, showing how social forces coalesced into genocidal blocs. He emphasized three main levels of perpetrator: (1) radical elites running party-states; (2) bands of militants forming violent paramilitaries; and (3) core constituencies proving mass though not majority popular support, while ordinary people were 'brought by normal social structures into committing murderous ethnic cleansing.'[55] He argued that ethnonationalism is strongest where it can capture other senses of exploitation, and that the most serious defect of the literature on ethnonationalism has been its neglect of class relations. Yet although ethnic differences always entwine with other social differences (especially of class, region and gender), ethnic hostility 'arises where ethnicity *trumps* class as the main form of social stratification, in the process capturing and channelling classlike sentiments towards ethnonationalism.'[56] This happens through political struggle: a danger zone of murderous cleansing is reached when movements claiming to represent two established ethnic groups both lay claim to their own state over all or part of the same territory, and at the same time this claim appears to have substantial legitimacy and some plausible chance of being implemented. Almost all dangerous cases, Mann argued, are bi-ethnic, deepened by persistent rival claims to sovereignty. Thus murderous ethnic conflict concerns primarily political power relations, though as it develops it also involves ideological, economic and eventually military power relations as well.[57]

Hence Mann's 'essentially political' explanation.[58] Ethnic 'cleansings' were 'in their murderous phases usually directed by states, and this requires some state coherence and capacity.'[59] Large-scale murderous policies involved the *centralization* and *homogenization* of diverse social and state forces, welding them into more cohesive blocs. This is why 'radical elites running party-states' were crucial: it was they who unified normally fragmented state structures and mass constituencies to pursue exceptional goals. His proposal that murderousness should be considered the product of 'unexpected escalations and frustrations', during which individuals 'are forced into' choices, offered situational accounts of how exterminatory intentions crystallized in the most extreme cases.

Through his broader sociological account, Mann proposed a complex theory of *political escalation* towards murderousness through several stages. The movement from 'the danger zone' to 'the brink' happened 'when one of two alternative scenarios plays out. Either the less powerful side is bolstered to fight rather than to submit by believing in the possibility of external aid, or the stronger side believes it has such overwhelming power and legitimacy that it can force through its own 'cleansed' state at little risk to itself.[60] Going 'over the brink' into actual 'perpetration' occurs where the state has been factionalized and radicalized in an unstable environment usually leading to war.[61] *In Mann's theory of escalation, violent outcomes did not result from deep-rooted structures. Instead he emphasized their contingency.* Out of political and geopolitical crises, radicals emerge calling for harsher treatment of perceived ethnic enemies. Where ethnic conflict between rival groups is well established 'it is usually somewhat ritualized, cyclical and manageable. Truly murderous cleansing in contrast, is unexpected, originally unintended, emerging out of unrelated crises like war.'[62] We appear to have come full circle from modernity's macro-implication. And yet *explaining genocide as the contingent outcome of political-military crises brings concreteness to the idea of it as a general possibility of modernity.* Through crises, 'ordinary' people with 'mundane' motives are brought by 'normal' social structures into committing 'cleansing':[63]

> Perpetrators of ethnic cleansing do not descend among us as a separate species of evildoers. They are created by conflicts central to modernity that involve unexpected escalations and frustrations during which individuals are forced into a series of more particular moral choices. . . . murderous ethnic cleansing comes from our civilization and from people, most of whom have been not unlike ourselves.[64]

Although Mann's rich socio-political account offered a more plausible sociological framework, major problems remained. His detailed explanations frequently appeared partially at odds with his general theses. In the darkest episodes, the 'dark side' had only tenuous connections to democracy. The homogenizing processes of murderous politics involved totalitarianism: the most murderous regimes were 'a few highly authoritarian regimes' that deviate from the norm of stable authoritarianism and mobilize majoritarian groups into a mass party-state mobilizing the people against 'enemy' minorities.[65] As Mann recognized (in a careful assessment of how far his theses fitted different cases), it was difficult to squeeze the archetypal genocide, the Nazi Holocaust, fully into his schema. Although Hitler had indeed perverted democracy, his anti-Jewish campaigns flowed more from Nazi ideology than from a history of 'ethnic conflict' between Germans and Jews. Even if these were 'two fairly old ethnic groups', it was hardly the case that they 'both laid claim to their own state over all or part of the same territory.' Indeed, as Bauman had emphasized, by 'the very fact of their territorial dispersion and ubiquity, the Jews were an inter-national nation, a non-national nation.'[66] The nature of the Jewish *exception* to the ethnic rule was what made them targets: 'The world tightly packed with nations and nation-states abhorred the non-national void. Jews were in such a void: they were such a void.'[67] In this sense, although a framework of politicized ethnic conflict might apply, ethnic *competition* was inappropriate.

Likewise Mann's principal theses did not explain the mass murders of Stalinist totalitarian states. He described most not as 'ethnic cleansing' but as 'classicide', because their targets were social classes, and explained them as 'mistaken revolutionary projects'. Thus the perversion of socialism was a class variant of the more common perversion of democracy. Socialist ideals of democracy also became perverted 'as the *demos* became entwined with the term *proletariat*, the working class, creating pressures to cleanse other classes.' This was then a second 'general way in which democratic ideals were transmuted into murderous cleansing.'[68] However, while the idea of the proletariat was instrumental in the Stalinist perversion of democracy, it was hardly its motive. 'The proletariat' stood for the rule of the party and leader, who substituted themselves for the working class. The idea of proletarian power as such did not create 'pressures to cleanse other classes'. When both the proletarian idea and democracy had most meaning, immediately after the Revolution, the communists sought an alliance of the working class with the peasantry. Although the Bolsheviks quickly turned on the peasantry, seriously destructive policies ('classicide') only emerged from the party-state later, as Stalin consolidated his rule. Mann gave too much credence to the 'proletarian' element of Stalinist ideology, and this weakness raises questions, too, about whether the substitution of 'ethnos' for 'demos' can bear the explanatory weight that he gave it.

Mann disarmed criticism by acknowledging that, given the 'messiness and uniqueness' of societies, his theses could not be scientific laws; they did not even fit perfectly all his case studies.[69] Yet we can raise some overall objections. Not only did he over-emphasize the significance of the ideological substitutions of nation and proletariat for the people. His 'ethnic competition' framework did not really fit the major cases of mid-twentieth-century political mass murder, which occupied much of his book, although it worked well for Rwanda and Yugoslavia. Yet if genocide and classicide were maximal and near-maximal forms of 'cleansing', and his general theses could not really explain them, their general relevance was brought into question.

Warfare

Another fundamental question is whether Mann correctly identified the primary locus of genocide among his four types of power. I have noted his emphasis on the contingency of violent outcomes, and especially his claim that 'truly murderous cleansing' emerges 'out of *unrelated crises like war*'.[70] The last phrase was a giveaway: as so often in the sociological tradition (although unusually in Mann's work), war was seen as an exogenous variable, an almost accidental destabilizer of ongoing political processes, giving the push to elites to radicalize and pursue mass murder.[71] But wars were hardly 'unrelated' in reality: genocidal powers were often fighting conventional wars against states or armed movements to which target populations were believed to be linked. Perpetrator regimes, even when not fighting conventional wars, were generally highly militarized – this was a key to how they homogenized and centralized power to pursue concerted anti-civilian violence. Even 'democratic' settlers were ubiquitously armed. There was nothing accidental about the role of war in genocide.

Many of Mann's own arguments pointed in this direction. He recognized that, because military power was 'socially organized, concentrated lethal violence', it 'proves decisive in the later stages of the worst cases of ethnic cleansing. Armies, police forces, and irregular extrastate paramilitaries are the main agencies.' He foregrounded 'escalation' (originally a concept of war) in accounting for the development of murderous crises, and although some was narrowly political, much was military. Indeed

Most 20th-century cases of ethnic cleansing occurred during wars or during the chaotic transfer from war to peace. . . . Ideologically tinged wars reduce shared rules and convert civilians into enemies. . . . Civil wars and wars of secession with a strong ethnic component are dangerous for ethnic groups trapped behind enemy lines. The lure towards murderous ethnic cleansing increases when it can be accomplished at low military cost, with little fear of retaliation. . . . Military campaigns may generate tactical lure towards atrocities against civilians that were not originally intended. . . . Guerrilla warfare lures guerrillas to kill civilians. . . . These . . . are all features of military power that may produce murderous cleansing.[72]

Yet at the most general level of analysis, in his formulation of his 'theses' and in locating the primary type of power as 'political', this role of war was absent. This was curious because, although other sociologists have also emphasized the distinctiveness of warfare as a source of power, Mann's exploration of this issue was the most thorough. In his major work, he dissented from Marxian and Weberian theories that (identifying economic, ideological and political as the main types of power) amalgamed military power into the political category:

My first deviation from orthodoxy is to suggest *four*, not three, fundamental types of power. The 'political/party' type actually contains two separate forms of power, *political* and *military* power: on the one hand, the central policy, including the state apparatus and (where they exist) political parties; on the other hand, physical or military force. Marx, Weber and their followers do not distinguish the two, because they generally view the state as the repository of physical force in society. To equate physical force with the state often seems to make sense in the case of modern states that monopolize military force. However conceptually they should be regarded as distinct.[73]

Mann saw this distinction as necessary to cover cases where political and military power did not fully coincide. He has used it to emphasize the importance of paramilitarism as the distinctive feature of fascist politics[74] and an autonomous form of violence in 'cleansing'.[75] What Mann did not explore was the difference in the modes of power that politics and warfare represented. It was left to theorists of war – following Clausewitz, whose sociologically seminal work has hardly been acknowledged – to explore the special significance of physically violent power-projection.[76] It is evident that genocide, as a type of power, belongs to Weber's 'bloody' category of social conflicts and to Mann's physical, violent 'military' category. This does not mean of course that genocide involves only physical violence – an idea I have argued against throughout this book. Nor does it mean that physical violence is pre-eminent in its practice at any given moment – quite clearly, genocide involves administrative, political, economic and ideological phases, especially of preparation prior to the use of violence and of consolidation after its deployment. What it means is that the use (and threat) of physical violence and killing defines the 'destruction' of social groups: it is not generally possible to conceive of genocide without them. In this sense genocide is like war: although both involve many phases and moments in which violence is not prominent, they are ultimately defined by aims of destruction which only make sense in violent terms.

The fact that genocide should be *categorized* as a bloody, violent type of conflict does not mean, of course, that it is to be *explained* solely by military power relations. Clearly cultural-ideological, economic and political types of power are all involved in genocide. *However, the main explanatory locus of genocide should not be simply political, as Mann contended, but the interactions of political and military power.* Although political and cultural-ideological processes are central to defining populations as 'enemies' and to setting up genocidal conflict, once the aim of destruction begins to be implemented, there is an essentially military process of violent power-projection. Political institutions delegate much direct policy implementation to military organizations – whether conventional armed forces, paramilitaries, or police, party and governmental officials deployed in a quasi-military role. Genocide, like war, involves constant feedback from the 'military' direct perpetrators to the 'political' central organizers. The question of where we should look for the larger causal context follows, although not simply, from this understanding. *The most common direct causal context is not simply political conflict, but conflict that has already become violent*:

1 Where a power organization is involved in war with another armed organization, it is more likely to define a population that it identifies with the latter as an 'enemy' to be destroyed.
2 Where a power organization is already involved in war, especially when it is deploying military forces extensively against civilian populations linked to armed enemies, it is more likely to extend violent campaigns to 'civilian enemies'.
3 Where a political organization has become highly militarized, even if it is not directly involved in war, it is more likely to see civilian social groups as 'enemies' in a quasi-military sense, and thus to project power violently against them.

Of course, in each case one will need to examine concretely the linkages between war and genocide, as well as the wider range of political, economic and cultural processes involved. But *in answer to the general question, what is it in modernity that enables genocide, an important part of the answer is: modern war, especially 'degenerate' total war*, in which civilians have come to be routinely and comprehensively targeted, and states and political institutions have been militarized.[77]

My proposal to study genocide in the context of war and militarization bears on a wider question. Too often the study of genocide abstracts the conflicts between armed power organizations and social groups from larger contexts of conflict. 'The Holocaust' is a prime case: Nazi policies towards the Jews have been taken as a discrete process, barely connected even to genocidal policies against other groups, let alone to the context of total war – although without the war the Nazis would not even have controlled most European Jews, let alone escalated their anti-Jewish policies to extermination. But studying other genocides involves the same problem – Rwanda is grasped through a simple relationship between the regime and the murdered Tutsis, ignoring the war with the Rwandan Patriotic Front that framed it from beginning to end; the anti-Muslim policies of Serbian forces in Bosnia are seen as involving genocide, but at one remove from the wars between Serbian, Bosnian and Croatian armies; and so on. In so many contexts, wars and genocides are intertwined. It is important to *distinguish* them, because a destructive policy against a social group is fundamentally different from a campaign against an armed enemy. Yet it is also important to understand the usually intimate *relationships* between these different types of campaign. *War and genocide are often woven together in the same campaign, so that, to describe it as a whole, it is inadequate to talk only of 'war' or of 'genocide'. Instead, we need to use the concept of genocidal war that I introduced above: two distinct types of policy integrated in a single campaign.* Genocidal war is the form in which genocide is widespread today: most genocides and many wars are best understood in these terms. In some situations opposing forces practise 'mutual' genocide, i.e. each armed force, claiming to represent one ethnic group, commits genocide against the ethnic group that its enemy claims to represent. Here one genocide calls forth another – as between armed groups claiming to represent Tutsis and Hutus in Rwanda and Burundi, or between Serbian forces and Albanian militia in Kosovo. René Lemarchand has called this *counter-genocide*.[78]

Domestic and international

Recognizing the central relationship to war has another fundamental implication for the sociological framework for explaining genocide. Too much social science has understood 'society' in exclusively national terms, and so *domesticated* social understanding. As Mann pointed out, 'Most theorists prefer abstract notions of social structure, so they ignore geographical and sociospatial aspects of societies. If we keep in mind that "societies" are *networks*, with definite spatial contours, we can remedy this.'[79] In reality modern power networks have always been simultaneously *national and international*, and are now increasingly *global* as well.[80] Yet many genocide scholars have reproduced the domestic fallacy. For example, Robert Melson refers to '[t]otal domestic genocides like the Armenian Genocide and the Holocaust, including the extermination of the Gypsies, . . . the destruction of the Kulaks and the Cambodian "autogenocide"'.[81] Yet the Holocaust did not target only German Jews (a mere twentieth of all Jewish victims), but the Jews of an entire continent conquered through international war. International wars were central to the genesis of the Armenian and Cambodian genocides. From Melson's list only the destruction of the *kulaks* could be considered domestic in both scope and genesis – but even here a full explanation would need to include the origins of Stalinism and militarization in internationalized civil war, and how international rivalry and threat shaped Stalinist ideology. Nor were these cases exceptional. As Mann argued, 'political *and geopolitical* crises'[82] are the contexts in which elites radicalize towards murderous solutions. *Generally it is a particular combination of national and international circumstances that provides the contexts for genocidal escalation.* It follows that, when locating genocide in a general sociological framework, power sources need to be grasped in global, including international, as well as national terms. When one thinks of the origins of the concept of genocide, in *world* wars and *international* law, this should be obvious. Yet the deep-rootedness of the domestic fallacy means that genocide studies will not escape from it without a conscious commitment to global and international understanding.

Conclusion

10

The Relevance of Conceptual Analysis

Genocide in twenty-first-century politics

Unlike most books about genocide, this has been an exploration of ideas, leading through the debate to clearer concepts. Our journey has involved both a return to Raphael Lemkin's original framework and an expansion in new directions informed by sociological understanding. Although I have certainly not denied the need for specific investigations of varied historical experiences, the thrust of the argument has been *integrative*, emphasizing the limitations and even artificiality of some conceptual distinctions between forms of political violence against civilians. 'Ethnic cleansing', 'gendercide', 'politicide' and the like are not, I have contended, fundamentally different from genocide. In some cases, we do not even need new terms; genocide offers us a viable framework for understanding what they aim to describe. Whether populations are violently expelled, terrorized *in situ* or murdered; whether they are attacked for their ethnic, class, political, religious or any other kind of affiliations; whether they themselves accept their attackers' labelling of them, or not; whether they are particularly victimized as men or women, young or old, or as gays – in all these cases, the intentional destruction of social groups constitutes genocidal action. Since the many methods, targets, subjective identities and victimizations are often – indeed usually – combined in various ways, genocide gives us a framework for *bringing together* the varied phenomena of anti-civilian violence and understanding the *relationships* among them. Genocide therefore describes, and genocide theory should explain, the full range of organized violence that is specifically targeted at civilian populations. And since genocide is an illegitimate variety of the generally legitimate social activity of war, understanding genocide in this way enables us to see the *connections* – as well as the difference – between this kind of anti-civilian violence and the more common kind perpetrated both intentionally and unintentionally in warfare.

A new definition

It seems obligatory for genocide scholars to offer their own definitions. Obeying this imperative, here I summarize the arguments of this book in definitional form. While what follows is based on Lemkin's idea and derives elements of understanding from the Convention and later authorities, it places genocide within the sociological framework that I have explored in the last few chapters. Indeed, it is presented not in the spirit of 'laying down the law', *à la* Convention, but of setting out a model or ideal type that will be useful in understanding genocide. As Burger put it, 'properly interpreted, what seems to be a definition in truth is a description of the model.'[1] The most general theoretical purpose of these models 'is to serve as substitutes for some sector of empirical reality . . . [and be] used for imaginary experiments . . . [or] as fixed points of reference in comparative studies.'[2]

Thus my approach leads to the conclusion that *genocide* is

> *a form of violent social conflict, or war, between armed power organizations that aim to destroy civilian social groups and those groups and other actors who resist this destruction.*

The nature of genocide as conflict depends, therefore, on the type of action carried out by armed power organizations against civilians. Thus we also need the concept of *genocidal action* (or genocide *as action*, a sense closer to previous understandings), which can be defined as

> *action in which armed power organizations treat civilian social groups as enemies and aim to destroy their real or putative social power, by means of killing, violence and coercion against individuals whom they regard as members of the groups.*

Thus genocide is a type of unequal social *conflict* between two sets of actors, which is defined primarily by the type of *action* carried out by the more powerful side.

Clearly in specifying genocide as conflict, my definition differs from others that we have considered. This is a radical break with the ideas of 'one-sidedness' and 'helplessness'. Acknowledging the fundamental power inequality between armed collective actors and civilian social groups, the definition nevertheless refuses to treat this inequality as total (and thus incapable of remedy). It defines genocide in a way that recognizes victim groups and other actors' possibilities of resistance and countervailing power. In defining genocide as conflict, I also break with the idea that genocide is simply exceptional, outside the normal range of social phenomena, and push back towards considering how it is linked to more normal phenomena of conflict and war. The definition is also novel in specifying that genocide – as organized, violent conflict – *constitutes* war: even genocide in 'peacetime' is a form of war against social groups. However, this definition leaves open, as a secondary historical question, whether or not genocide takes place in the context of more general war.

My definition also involves a number of other important changes compared with previous definitions:

1 It restores Lemkin's original aim, increasingly abandoned, of establishing a *generic* concept that covers many distinct kinds of action. Although genocidal action has been defined by the 'intention' to destroy, my definition differs from most that have been proposed, in that genocide is neither merely certain kinds of 'acts' (as is assumed by those who focus simply on killing) nor a certain kind of outcome (as in much discussion of what constitutes 'a genocide'), but involves *a general type of social action*, characterized by the *combination of social-destructive aims and violent and coercive modalities*, which sets up *a special type of violent social conflict*. In this way the definition aims to restore the concept of genocide as a general category, capable of serving as a *framework* for understanding violent action against civilian populations.

2 Perpetrator centres are designated as *armed power organizations*, a term that suggests the combination of general political power ambitions and organized armed power capable of producing violence; these together characterize the various states, quasi-states, parties, militaries and armed settler and paramilitary movements that commit genocide. Although unarmed individuals – both officials of political institutions and 'ordinary' civilians – participate in genocide, the generally organized and armed characters of genocidal action distinguish it from improvised and less armed actions of civilians, such as the pogrom or 'deadly ethnic riot'.[3]

3 Targets are specified as *civilian social groups*, so that their common defining feature is not a particular social characteristic (race, class, nation, ethnicity, religion) but their largely unarmed character. Although the 'civilian' character of the target group and individual victims has been implicit in the genocide debate, this is the first time it has been highlighted as an element of definition. This phrasing consolidates the recent consensus that *all* social groups threatened with destruction should be seen as within the scope of genocide. It also leaves open the question of whether the groups as attacked are already constituted as self-conscious groups.

4 The definition deliberately employs the *plurals* of both 'armed power organization' and 'social group'. It does not simply assume, as have most previous definitions – despite much evidence to the contrary – the singularity of either perpetrator centres or target groups, an assumption that leads to the artificial idea of regarding simultaneous, interlinked genocidal campaigns by the same perpetrators as a series of different 'genocides'. Instead it recognizes that a genocidal episode may have *multiple* perpetrators and/or targets.

5 The aim of 'destroying' social groups is not reduced to killing their individual members, but is understood as destroying groups' *social power* in economic, political and cultural senses. It leaves open the question of whether this power, as targeted for destruction, is *real* or *putative*, since the nature of the process is fundamentally the same regardless of the answers. Clearly perpetrators' definitions matter, but since genocide is not simply one-sided so too do victims' – and others'. In this sense also this is a 'generic' definition.

6 It is emphasized that the individuals against whom genocidal acts are committed are those whom armed power organizations and their agents *regard as members of those groups*. This recognizes that those attacked may or may not regard themselves as members. Thus the definition opens up the possibility both of fantastical ideological definitions, ascribing to people group memberships that they don't themselves perceive, and of arbitrary action that harms people who do not correspond to these ideological representations.

7 It is specified that a precondition of 'destroying' groups is to define them as *enemies*, indicating the fundamentally military sense of 'enemy'. Likewise, 'destroying' is understood as inherently violent, but it is also recognized as encompassing a range of power modalities, summarized as *killing, violence and coercion* against individuals. The order of these terms suggests a hierarchy of harm, but their equal listing leaves open – as an empirical question – their specific combinations in particular cases.

New historic conditions for genocide?

This approach gives genocide a broader scope than is often allowed. It is not only about killing and is not restricted to a very few big, successful mass murders. Genocide is a type of social action and conflict, identifiable regardless of its scale or success. It is, lamentably, more common than those preoccupied with the peculiarities of the Holocaust imagine. Likewise, the problem of genocide has not passed away with the era of total war that gave birth to it, or with the last of the totalitarian regimes that were its archetypal practitioners. Yet there are real issues about historical trends in genocide. Although I have embraced Lemkin's classical concept, born of this very era, and sought to give it a more adequate foundation, one sort of variation I have not addressed is that which takes place over time. How important is the changed context of political violence in the twenty-first century? Is the problem of genocide posed differently today compared with the period when the concept was developed?

Interestingly, none of the proponents of new concepts to replace genocide has made a consistent case for historical change. Although the widespread use of 'ethnic cleansing', for example, originated in the 1990s Yugoslav wars and was linked to the idea that their atrocities were of a different order from the Holocaust, scholarly users rapidly read it back into episodes hitherto described as genocide, including the Holocaust. Conversely it seemed easy, to all but the most determined 'uniqueness' advocates, to perceive the essence of the Holocaust in Rwanda. Nevertheless the questions remain: Are the forms of genocide changing? Are there significant patterns in these changes at the beginning of our new century? And has the conceptual proliferation represented attempts, confused perhaps, to register historical transformation?

My discussion has given us some pointers in this direction. Clearly the context in which Lemkin originally described genocide – military occupation by a totalitarian, ideologically racist empire – has not been widespread in recent decades. The Convention's concern with policies affecting the reproduction of groups – in its specification of means such as 'imposing measures intended to prevent births within the group' and 'forcibly transferring children of the group to another group' – seems redolent of fading totalitarianism and has not resonated in recent episodes. On the other hand, forced migration has been an almost universal theme of these cases. And issues of rape, sexual and other gendered violence have risen on the agenda.

Of course, to mention these concerns is to recognize that changes of *discourse* reflect alterations in observers' *perceptions* quite as much as in genocidal practice. Forced migration was actually a gigantic issue in the mid-twentieth century and a key means of social destruction by totalitarian regimes. It was a deficiency of Lemkin's account and of the Convention that this was not emphasized. Sexual violence was always endemic and sometimes systematized in earlier genocides. Again, it was a weakness that this was not clearly recognized from the beginning of the genocide debate. On both these issues, perceptions are obviously key. And although military occupation by major states is now less salient – or, at least, new US-led occupations are not genocidal – every armed conflict over territory still raises the spectre of conquest, and harm to 'enemy' civilians is commonplace. Again, changed perception seems critical: we do not think of contemporary genocidal conquests by local armed movements as 'occupations', although they may well be experienced as such by conquered populations.

How then should we pose the issue of historical transformation? Do changing tendencies in the patterns of genocide have implications for the understanding that we have just summarized? Mann is a rare recent author who has considered historical trends in 'ethnic cleansing' and genocide.[4] He argued that there had been a decline in the global North, largely as a result of the success of earlier waves in creating mono-ethnic states. In the remaining multi-ethnic states, politics is defined largely by class, region and gender, while continuing ethnic politics, both historic and new, is largely non-violent. In the South, in contrast, the diffusion of the 'ideal of the nation-state' and the confusion of *demos* and *ethnos* are creating new threats of 'cleansing', reinforced by the decline of class politics, the weakening of liberalism and socialism, and the rise of fundamentalism (including 'theo-democracy', which Mann suggested could represent a third variant of his perversion of democracy thesis). Settler 'cleansing' continues against indigenous peoples, especially in Latin America; 'middlemen ethnicities' such as the Chinese in Southeast Asia remain vulnerable. Yet there are few cases in which rival bi-ethnic claims were capable of fuelling the most murderous 'cleansing' that occurred in Yugoslavia and in Rwanda and Burundi. The most dangerous ethnopolitical conflicts today, Mann argued, 'mostly exist around the fringes of the bigger imperial countries', India, Indonesia, Russia and China, as well as in the peripheral territories of states such as Turkey, Iran, Iraq, Burma and the Philippines.[5] However '[m]ost of these conflicts occur in some of the poorest, most isolated parts of the world, and so they become only local black holes.'[6] In general, Mann's account downplayed specifically *murderous* developments: 'I can think of no other closely analogous case to Rwanda/Burundi elsewhere in the world. Perhaps this was the last of the world's genocides.'[7] In line with his belief in the possibility of more or less peaceful cleansing, Mann even recommended that '[i]n some cases it may be better to deflect hatreds onto milder stages of cleansing achieved by mutual negotiation through agreed-upon population and property exchanges, border alterations and so on than to risk further cleansing by force.'[8] Perhaps, he implied, we are entering an era in which 'cleansing' can be managed so as to avoid genocide.

These suggestive arguments pushed the framing of contemporary genocide firmly back into inter-ethnic relations. Yet behind the high-lighted changes lay changes in state power and warfare, which are at least as important for the threat of genocide. Ethnic conflicts are rarely very violent within the West not only because democracy has been nor-malized, but also because state power has been internationalized and interstate wars abolished. Geopolitical pacification has deepened social pacification, increasingly squeezing violence even out of intractable eth-nopolitical conflicts such as that in Northern Ireland. Western warfare, meanwhile, has mutated far from the total war model. The new Western way emphasizes quick-fix, media-centred management of political risks, so that Southern war-zone civilians are seen not as part of the enemy, but as victims (of violent local rulers and armed actors) who will benefit from Western action – even if, in reality, life-risks are transferred to them.[9]

In contrast, deep, institutionalized, internationalized pacification has hardly developed in non-Western regions: major 'nation-states' are quasi-imperial and this is why their 'imperial fringes' are dangerous.[10] The way of war envisaged by major non-Western states remains much closer to total war, with governments and militaries less concerned for soldiers' or civilians' lives and less subject to media-electoral surveil-lance. However, despite continuing rivalries and border disputes, states are increasingly inhibited from *interstate* war by the surveillance mech-anisms of Western global dominance, market and production integra-tion, international law and mass media. The trend towards fewer major wars reduces the likelihood that these will harbour genocidal policies. The most common conditions for genocide are now in relatively local-ized wars where armed power organizations – both recognized states and insurgent movements – are closely tied to ethnic bases and armed rivalries are ethnopoliticized; and in religiously politicized campaigns identifying non-believing populations as targets. So while genocide remains a widespread danger, Mann was probably right to suggest that the *scale* of murderous attacks on civilian populations may often be more limited than before. The repeated genocidal massacres in Central Africa before and after 1994 (in Burundi and the Congo as well as in Rwanda) are more typical of what we may expect than the big Rwandan genocide. And yet we should be cautious in signalling change: very large-scale, intensely murderous campaigns like that of 1994 have always been exceptional. Before the genocide, even those who foresaw a violent crisis failed to anticipate the appalling scale and speed of the slaughter. Hopes that this could be the last event of its size are not strongly founded: the Darfur crisis since 2003 has certainly claimed hundreds of thousands of lives, including many killed directly by the genocidists. Democratizing processes may continue to destabilize authoritarian regimes and unleash violent ethnonationalisms; while the pattern of more localized wars, with a greater number of smaller-scale armed power organizations, may contain the potential for ongoing genocidal war.

Therefore shifts in scale, style and ideology are significant, but they still leave a major, probably intractable problem. We can conclude that *structural changes in global politics have not deeply inhibited genocide.* Internationalized Western-global state power is densest precisely in Northern regions where genocide is now less likely; it penetrates little into the largest, most imperial non-Western states, and although its impact is greater on smaller, weaker states, it rarely prevents escalation towards genocide or proves decisive when violence is manifest. The twenty-first-century context of war is one of global surveillance, by Western states, the United Nations system, non-governmental organizations and social movements, all working through and reflected in global networks of media coverage.[11] Every sizeable conflict achieves a significant degree of surveillance, and armed power organizations are universally aware of it. However, rarely do local actors feel fundamentally inhibited by surveillance. Instead it affects the *form* that genocidal policies take. For example, the normalization of electoral democracy provides an incentive for ethnonationalist parties violently to homogenize their electorates, simultaneously expelling members of 'other' groups and disciplining their 'own' group into supporting them. Likewise, surveillance affects the *presentation* of these policies in national and international fora. Genocidists invariably invoke abuses (actual or invented) suffered by 'their' group, pre-empting their own indictment by accusing their enemies of genocide too. Thus human rights norms are twisted to fit genocidal purposes. Even where international intervention is substantial, it may often become part of the conditions for genocide. Proto-genocidists may see international pressure for power-sharing as a threat, prompting drastic action against 'enemy' groups, as in Rwanda. Inadequately protected UN 'safe areas' may create vulnerable civilian concentrations, ripe for massacre, as at Srebrenica. Humanitarian aid represents resources that genocidal forces may tax or seize to fuel their campaigns. Even trials by international tribunals may have limited effect in deterring future genocidists: they simply do not expect it to happen to them. And the threat of indictment may be an incentive to murder witnesses.

In all these ways, genocide may adapt to global surveillance: new ways of genocide may internalize its demands. It would be wrong to overstate the transformation: modern genocidists have always been aware of international surveillance. The Ottoman Turks tried to sanitize their campaign against the Armenians for the benefit of their German allies and neutral American observers; the Nazis were aware of the damage that information about the extermination camps could do in the hands of the Allies or the neutral papacy, if either chose to make a major issue of their knowledge. Yet in the era of world wars, the concentration of informational and media power in the hands of a few all-powerful, often closed states meant that surveillance was limited. In the twenty-first century, the proliferation of state, international, legal and civil society institutions, as well as the transformations of media, media outlets and means of communication, have created networks of comprehensive global surveillance. The ability of genocidal regimes or organizations to monopolize or manage information, even locally, is less than in the totalitarian era. Globally, they must compete with major states, international organizations, human rights campaigners and others who are also trying to influence media coverage.

The demise of totalitarianisms and the rise of global surveillance affect the ideological content and targeting of genocides. Totalitarian regimes and movements developed total, systematic ideologies within which 'enemies' were multiplied and repression strategized. Their statism was autarkic and their enemies more likely to include class and gender groups that did not fit classically narrow definitions of genocide targets. In contrast, genocidal regimes and movements today – partly because they have adapted to global surveillance – are more likely to rely on simple ethnonationalism, their enemies restricted to 'other' ethnicities together with cosmopolitans who defend threatened groups and stand in the way of their supremacy. In contemporary cases, the contextually determined, incremental contingency of genocidal policy is likely to be more obvious: leaders adapt to threats and opportunities in shifting political and military conflicts. Nationalism is still ideology, of course, and genocidal policies still require fantastical constructions of 'enemies'. But these constructions are conditioned by the world in which genocidists live. They mostly use murderous means to do what many political movements do in other ways, i.e. claim their place in a world of nations. Only extreme Islamism now seems to have a total ideological framework reminiscent of mid-century totalitarianism, within which multiple enemies (Americans, Westerners, Christians, Jews, and rival Muslims) are comprehensively categorized and attacked. If its organizations remain underground terror networks, however, their capacity may remain limited to genocidal massacres rather than large-scale social destruction.

Contemporary challenge: the case of Darfur

In a world where genocidal politics are disturbingly common, but few episodes approach the scale of murder in Rwanda – let alone the archetypal Holocaust – there are many opportunities for the conceptual confusion that I have criticized. In order to explore the practical significance of the conceptual debate, I conclude with discussion of a particular case. In 2003, while I was beginning my research, a crisis erupted in the Darfur region of western Sudan, an area of a quarter of a million square miles in which 6 million people lived. After months of mounting atrocities, there was widespread international agreement on most of the pertinent facts, summed up in this mid-2004 description by Human Rights Watch (HRW), whose observers had spent time in the region:

> The Sudanese government and the Arab 'Janjaweed' militias it arms and supports have committed numerous attacks on the civilian populations of the African[12] Fur, Masalit and Zaghawa ethnic groups. Government forces oversaw and directly participated in massacres, summary executions of civilians – including women and children – burnings of towns and villages, and the forcible depopulation of wide swathes of land long inhabited by the Fur, Masalit and Zaghawa. The Janjaweed militias, Muslim like the African groups they attack, have destroyed mosques, killed Muslim religious leaders, and desecrated Qorans belonging to their enemies. The government and its Janjaweed allies have killed thousands of Fur, Masalit, and Zaghawa – often in cold blood – raped women, and destroyed villages, food stocks and other supplies essential to the civilian population. They have driven more than one million civilians, mostly farmers, into camps and settlements in Darfur where they live on the very edge of survival, hostage to Janjaweed abuses. More than 110,000 others have fled to neighbouring Chad but the vast majority of war victims remain trapped in Darfur.
>
> This conflict has historical roots but escalated in February 2003, when two rebel groups, the Sudan Liberation Army/Movement (SLA/M) and the Justice and Equality Movement (JEM) drawn from members of the Fur, Masalit, and Zaghawa ethnic groups, demanded an end to chronic economic marginalization and sought power-sharing within the Arab-ruled

Sudanese state. They also sought government action to end the abuses of their rivals, Arab pastoralists who were driven onto African farmlands by drought and desertification – and who had a nomadic tradition of armed militias.

The government has responded to this armed and political threat by targeting the civilian populations from which the rebels were drawn. It brazenly engaged in ethnic manipulation by organizing a military and political partnership with some Arab nomads comprising the Janjaweed; armed, trained, and organized them; and provided effective impunity for all crimes committed. The government–Janjaweed partnership is characterized by joint attacks on civilians rather than on the rebel forces. These attacks are carried out by members of the Sudanese military and by Janjaweed wearing uniforms that are virtually indistinguishable from those of the army.

Although Janjaweed always outnumber regular soldiers, during attacks the government forces usually arrive first and leave last. In the words of one displaced villager, 'They [the soldiers] see everything' that the Janjaweed are doing. 'They come with them, they fight with them and they leave with them.' The government–Janjaweed attacks are frequently supported by the Sudanese air force. Many assaults have decimated small farming communities, with death tolls sometimes approaching one hundred people. Most are unrecorded.

Human Rights Watch spent twenty-five days in and on the edges of West Darfur, documenting abuses in rural areas that were previously well-populated with Masalit and Fur farmers. Since August 2003, wide swathes of their homelands, among the most fertile in the region, have been burned and depopulated. With rare exceptions, the countryside is now emptied of its original Masalit and Fur inhabitants. Everything that can sustain and succour life – livestock, food stores, wells and pumps, blankets and clothing – has been looted or destroyed. Villages have been torched not randomly, but systematically – often not once, but twice. The uncontrolled presence of Janjaweed in the burned countryside, and in burned and abandoned villages, has driven civilians into camps and settlements outside the larger towns, where the Janjaweed kill, rape, and pillage – even stealing emergency relief items – with impunity.

Despite international calls for investigations into allegations of gross human rights abuses, the government has responded by denying any abuses while attempting to manipulate and stem information leaks. It has limited reports from Darfur in the national press, restricted international media access, and has tried to obstruct the flow of refugees into Chad. Only after significant delays and international pressure, were two high-level UN assessment teams permitted to enter Darfur. The government has promised unhindered humanitarian access, but has failed to deliver. Instead, recent reports of government tampering with mass graves and other evidence suggest the government is fully aware of the immensity of its crimes and is now attempting to cover up any record.[13]

Most of this detail is uncontroversial (save to the Sudanese government and its international supporters) and has been confirmed by the International Commission of Inquiry's comprehensive account.[14] By early 2005, estimates of mortality ranged from at least 180,000 victims of illness and malnutrition, excluding direct conflict deaths, according to the UN emergency relief head,[15] to a figure of 380,000 deaths from all causes.[16] The crisis was widely recognized, so that Hugo Slim could argue that 'the international community has not denied', even if 'it has delayed and dithered.'[17] But this was only true as to *factual* denial; when it came to *interpretative* and *implicatory* denial, there was much more to criticize. There was little agreement on the concepts applicable to the situation or the appropriate political response. HRW described what was happening as 'ethnic cleansing', others called it 'genocide', and many who professed concern avoided any general characterization, preferring to emphasize that atrocities were committed in the 'civil war'. Indeed some expressed impatience with the argument about whether what was happening constituted ethnic cleansing or genocide. Thus one aid worker commented: 'Since my return, my heart has sunk as arguments intensified about whether the Darfur situation should be defined as genocide or ethnic cleansing, and whether sanctions should be applied. What's happening in Darfur is the wholesale slaughter and rape of unimaginable numbers of human beings. . . . Definitions should be left to the dictionary – now is the time for action.'[18] Likewise a commentator argued: 'The humanitarian crisis is now so great in western Sudan that what you call it may be immaterial.'[19] The first academic study, by Gérard Prunier, reflected this confusion, calling Darfur 'the ambiguous genocide'.[20] He argued: 'If we use the December 1948 definition it is obvious that Darfur is a genocide, but if we use [a definition based on total obliteration] it is not.'[21]

Nevertheless both those who advocated particular labels and those who avoided them saw a clear bearing on the prospects for action to help the victims. HRW argued: 'The United Nations has repeatedly characterized the practice of ethnic cleansing as a violation of international humanitarian law, and has demanded that perpetrators of ethnic cleansing be brought to justice.'[22] Thus documenting a pattern of ethnic cleansing in West Darfur reinforced HRW's legal case for bringing the perpetrators to international justice. It was notable that most *official* responses, in contrast, had fallen short even of using the term 'ethnic cleansing'. UN Secretary-General Kofi Annan declared that he had seen no report that suggested to him that the realities in Darfur reflected either genocide or 'cleansing'.[23] The Security Council merely expressed 'its deep concern at the continuing reports of large-scale violations of human rights and of international humanitarian law in Darfur . . . and demands that those responsible be held accountable.' However, wishing to avoid specific commitments to 'holding accountable' the perpetrator government, the UN also avoided any general label that might be seen as implying action to halt the violence. Indeed, the Security Council emphasized only 'the need for immediate humanitarian access to the vulnerable population'.[24] Many other international declarations also preferred the characterization of 'humanitarian crisis', calling only for a 'humanitarian' response rather than political, legal or military action to address directly the violence that caused hunger and displacement. Although many appeals were made to the Sudanese government to 'halt' the violence, few international actors wanted to take action themselves that might force the regime's hands, preferring to believe – against a great deal of evidence – that the prime authors of the violence could be persuaded to recognize that it was in their interests to bring it under control. When leaders *were* prepared to talk of 'ethnic cleansing' (as did the British International Development Secretary, Hilary Benn)[25] this was usually because they had been asked to apply the *other* label, 'genocide', which was generally seen by politicians as far more dangerous because it implied legal obligations to 'prevent and punish'.

In the Darfur crisis, coinciding with the tenth anniversary of Rwanda, most political leaders were clearly determined to avoid the term. In the USA especially, where policy-makers were particularly aware of the critical nature of the 'genocide' label – after criticism of President Clinton's reluctance to apply it in 1994 – there was much official squirming. 'We see indicators and elements that would start to move you toward a genocide conclusion but we're not there yet', said US Secretary of State, Colin Powell. 'We can find the right label for it later, we have got to deal with it now.'[26] Ironically a publicly stated reason was that there was no comparison between events in Darfur and those in Rwanda. Powell claimed that, examining the 'evidence that is available', events in Darfur did not 'meet the tests of the definition of genocide'. 'Why', he asked, 'would we call it genocide when the genocide definition has to meet certain legal tests? It is a legal determination. And based on what we have seen, there were some indicators but there was certainly no full accounting of all indicators, which lead to a legal definition of genocide, in accordance with the terms of the genocidal treaties. That is the advice of my lawyers.'[27] Even the US Holocaust Museum, attempting to cut through the 'hand wringing about what is and is not genocide', argued that 'such discussion misses the point: A key element of the Genocide Convention is prevention. It calls for action once it is apparent that genocide is threatened. There is no need for an absolute determination, which is inevitably elusive, that genocide is underway.' In this light, the museum's Committee on Conscience declared a 'genocide emergency', saying that genocide was imminent or was actually happening in the Darfur region of Sudan. 'We don't use the term [genocide] lightly', said Jerry Fowler, the committee's staff director, 'but the situation clearly has reached the point now where that term is appropriate.'[28] While the point about prevention was well taken, it was not clear how one could prevent something that could not be determined. In what sense did determination need to be 'absolute' and why was that 'inevitably elusive'? The most plausible explanation for these statements was that the committee was thinking of *legal* standards of proof necessary to convict people of genocide in a court of law. However, to make a political judgement that it was imminent – or indeed actually taking place – it was clearly not necessary to 'determine' genocide in the same way as for a criminal conviction. The avoidance of an unequivocal statement that genocide *was happening* seemed unnecessarily cautious. As Eric Reeves pointed out, 'It is impossible to avoid the conclusion that Khartoum's actions – in Darfur and in the "systematic" obstruction of humanitarian aid – deliberately threaten a "substantial part" of the African groups, and that this will "have an impact on these groups as a whole".'[29] The Sudanese regime and its militia allies were destroying the 'African' peoples in a way that far exceeded 'collateral damage' from the counter-insurgency war, and the evidence cited by HRW in support of 'ethnic cleansing' could equally justify the charge of genocide.

This, of course, was what the US administration eventually decided. Appearing before the US Senate Foreign Relations Committee on 9 September 2004, Powell changed US policy with the announcement: 'We concluded that genocide has been committed in Darfur and that the government of Sudan and the Janjaweed bear responsibility and genocide may still be occurring.'[30] Yet Powell's statement did *not* signal a new determination to stop the genocide – he baldly acknowledged: 'In fact, no new action is dictated by this determination.'[31] After two months in which the Sudanese government had continued to sponsor violence and had not met key demands, the USA was proposing to allow it another thirty days. Certainly, as Reeves pointed out, in making his declaration,

Powell made history of a grim sort: this is the first time that a sovereign nation has accused another sovereign nation of active genocide under the 1948 UN Convention on the Prevention and Punishment of the Crime of Genocide. But as important as this determination is, and as profoundly as it works to force the rest of the international community to consider more deeply the nature of human destruction in Darfur, it is not by itself enough. Indeed, by arguing . . . that the obligation to 'prevent' genocide entails so very little, Powell has done what his State Department spokesmen have done for months: he has made it less likely that the Genocide Convention will ever be used as a tool to serve the primary purpose for which it was created.[32]

As John Prendergast of the International Crisis Group put it, 'the finding of genocide will only be meaningful if it's backed up by more assertive action at the UN Security Council.'[33] Yet, as Reeves predicted, quite the opposite happened. When Powell's month was up, there was still no action. 'Relentlessly grim news from Darfur' prompted Reeves to pose the question: 'Are there no circumstances that must compel an international humanitarian intervention that is both adequate to protect all vulnerable civilian populations and capable of providing the transport and logistical capacity that is presently far beyond the UN and other humanitarian organizations operating in Darfur?' Answering negatively, he concluded that the international community was 'acquiescing in genocide by attrition'.[34] Later still, this persistent defender of the threatened people of Darfur felt obliged to claim: 'Any global assessment of recent commentary and developments must discern a pattern of disturbing disingenuousness, an expedient reaching for the lowest common denominator of international agreement, and a profound moral failure to value, as fully human, Darfuri lives.'[35]

Despite this comprehensive failure in *action* – the only intervention was by a small, lightly armed African Union force with a limited mandate, which could not seriously protect threatened people – the Report of the International Commission of Inquiry, established by the Security Council, produced an authoritative *account* of the Darfur violence that even Reeves admitted was 'of immense importance'.[36] Indeed the report led to the Security Council's referral of Darfur to the International Criminal Court, with the likelihood that Sudanese officials would be prosecuted for crimes against humanity and war crimes. Yet, Reeves argued, the report was 'badly compromised in its tendentious and poorly reasoned conclusion about the absence of evidence of "genocidal intent" on the part of Khartoum in Darfur. Indeed, so egregiously poor are the legal and factual arguments about the issue of "genocidal intent" that we must conclude this Commission did not feel politically free to make a determination of genocide.'[37] The USA was alone among the permanent members of the Security Council in having endorsed this finding; Sudan's ally, China, and other members were unlikely to accept it. Nevertheless, the report established the Sudanese government's initiative in calling 'Arab' tribes in Darfur to arms against two rebel armed movements based mainly on 'African' tribes.[38] It recognized the conflict as far more than a normal war between state and insurgents: 'the most significant element of the conflict has been the attacks on civilians.'[39] It followed the Rwanda Tribunal's updating of the understanding of victim groups in genocide, to argue that the non-Arab or African tribal groups of Darfur 'who were victims of attacks and killings subjectively make up a protected group.' It established state responsibility for the violence: 'the Commission is confident that the large majority of the attacks on villages conducted by militia have been carried out with the acquiescence of state officials.'[40] Indeed: 'It can safely be said that the magnitude and large-scale nature of some crimes against humanity, indiscriminate attacks in [sic] civilians, forced transfer of civilians, as well as their consistency over a long period of time (February 2003 to the present), necessarily imply that these crimes result from a central planning operation.'[41] Thus the report even acknowledged: 'Some elements emerging from the facts, including the scale of atrocities and the systematic nature of the attacks, killing, displacement and rape, as well as racially motivated statements by perpetrators that have targeted members of the African tribes only, could be indicative of the genocidal intent.' And yet it argued that

> there are other more indicative elements that show the lack of genocidal intent. The fact that in a number of villages attacked or burned by both militia and Government forces, the attackers refrained from exterminating the whole population that had not fled, but instead selectively killed groups of young men, is an important element. . . . the intent of the attackers was not to destroy an ethnic group as such, or part of the group. Instead the intention was to murder all those young men they considered as rebels, as well as to forcibly expel the whole population so as to vacate the villages and prevent the rebels from hiding among, or getting support from, the local population.
>
> Another element that shows the Sudanese government's lack of genocidal intent can be seen from the fact that persons forcibly dislodged from their villages are collected in IDP camps. In other words, the persons surviving attacks on villages are not killed outright, so as to eradicate the group: they are rather forced to abandon their homes and live together in areas selected by the Government.[42]

So the commission concluded: 'One crucial element appears to be missing, at least as far as the central Government authorities are concerned: genocidal intent. Generally speaking the policy of attacking, killing and forcibly displacing members of some tribes does not evince a specific intent to annihilate, in whole or in part, a group distinguished on racial, ethnic, national or religious grounds. Rather, it would seem that those who planned and organized attacks on villages pursued the intent to drive the victims from their homes, primarily for purposes of counter-insurgency warfare.' This was true even if some individuals may have had genocidal intent, or even committed 'extermination as a crime against humanity'.[43]

Reeves entered some powerful factual objections to these arguments.[44] Even if in *some* villages not all the population was killed or exposed to death, 'there have been a great many "villages attacked and burned by both militias and Government forces" in which the whole population was in fact killed or forced into flight that held clear risk of death. Why is this not, by the same evidentiary logic, indication of "genocidal intent"?' Secondly, a very large percentage of the displaced population had not been 'forced to abandon their homes and live together in areas selected by the Government [of Sudan]: they have been forced to flee into inaccessible rural areas presently beyond the reach of any humanitarian relief efforts. They are dying in great numbers.' Moreover, those who had fled to Chad – well over 200,000 and rising by 2005 – were clearly not 'living together in areas selected by the Government': they were 'living in a foreign land, in harsh and forbidding conditions, where competition with indigenous Chadians for water and pasturable land has on several occasions turned violent.' The commission's 'factual misrepresentation of the conditions in the camps and the history of humanitarian access' was equally shameful: 'In fact, a number of camps have indeed been extermination sites at some point in their history.' Finally Reeves pointed out the 'conspicuous evidence of "genocidal intent" on the part of the Janjaweed', with 'language clearly referring to ethnic/racial destruction or extermination'. If such genocidal intent can be demonstrated, Khartoum and its military officials 'must incur responsibility for complicity in genocide.' Yet important as these clarifications were, Reeves also argued that, even on its own assumptions and assessment, the commission had got its non-determination of genocide wrong:

> we must recall that the language of the Genocide Convention twice refers to destruction of a protected group 'in whole or in part.' The selective sparing of life, in some circumstances, hardly diminishes the obvious fact that the ethnically-targeted destruction of the non-Arab/African tribal populations of Darfur has been achieved in very substantial part – certainly meeting all the 'substantiality' criteria for what constitutes a 'part' in the Genocide Convention.

The commission's factual distortions and logical failures could only be evidence, Reeves concluded, of the political constraints under which they were working. In this light, of course, merely correcting these errors would not change things: politics is about interests as well as ideas. As the US case showed, a mere 'determination' of genocide does not guarantee effective action. In the end, however convincing this book, it will not by itself change political realities. Nevertheless intellectual clarification provides pointers for political action. Genocide denial – of the interpretative and practical kinds at work in international responses to Darfur – involves false assertions of complexity. This can be effectively attacked at the intellectual level, by analytical critique such as Reeves's and by general conceptual clarification such as I have attempted. The commission's denial rested not only on factual distortions and logical failures, but on the general errors of genocide theory that have been central to my critique. The report assumed the identity of genocide with 'physical destruction', i.e. the killing of the members of the threatened groups. Although in this respect the report necessarily adhered to the Convention definition of genocide, it interpreted it through the maximal, Holocaust standard of physical extermination, interpreting evidence of 'mere' displacement (or 'ethnic cleansing') as evidence of sub-genocidal 'crimes against humanity'.[45] It avoided using some of the flexibility that the Convention itself allowed, notably in its neglect of the 'in part' provision.

Yet although, following the Convention, the commission should have concluded that genocide was taking place, *its task would have been enormously simpler, and opportunities for obfuscation less, if genocide had been understood (as proposed in this book) as social and not simply physical destruction.* For there could be no doubting the intention of the Janjaweed and Sudanese government to achieve widespread destruction of Fur, Masalit and Zaghawa society and ways of life, through extensive (if variable) violence. Clearly legal decisions will always have to be made on the basis of the Convention and its case law, but political decisions, at national and international levels, must respond to the ideas of genocide that are held within world society. *If a broader, more sociologically coherent conception becomes accepted not just in academia, but in public debate, then decisions about intervention (political and humanitarian as well as legal and military) in genocidal crises will be less easily avoided by confusing legal references.* Welcome as the reference of Sudanese suspects to the International Criminal Court was, legal action should not have replaced political and military action to protect threatened civilians when they could still be helped. Nor should legal definitions generally restrict political debate. Ultimately law must respond to politics, and politics must be informed by the best social understanding. This experience reinforces the case for genocide to be considered less in narrowly legal terms, and more as a general socio-political phenomenon.

The other main assumption that the commission relied on was the categorical separation of genocide from war which I have criticized. It argued that, if what was happening was 'counter-insurgency warfare', then it could not be genocide. Given the intimate associations between genocide and war, *the standard form of genocide denial by perpetrators is to represent genocidal action as conventional military struggle – and the standard form of denial by bystanders is to collude in this representation.* Analytically, the Darfur Commission gave plenty of acknowledgement that Janjaweed and government atrocities were often 'reported to have occurred without any military justification in relation to any specific activity of the rebel forces. This has strengthened the general perception amongst observers that the civilian population has been knowingly and deliberately targeted.'[46] But their fallback intellectual position was that these were 'crimes against humanity' committed during 'counter-insurgency war'. Their failure to follow through the genocidal logic of targeting civilian groups would not have been so easy had it been acknowledged that, *while genocide and warfare may be distinguished as ideal types, empirically they are commonly intertwined, so that much genocide and warfare correspond to the combined type of genocidal war.* Counter-insurgency war often becomes genocidal, when targeting civilians as a means of defeating the armed enemy leads to targeting civilians as a distinct end of policy in itself. Once we recognize the genocide–war relationship then we are able to defeat war-based denial of the kind all too evident in the Darfur Commission's report.

To conclude: this discussion has tried to demonstrate the relevance of the arguments in this book to understanding a particular case, and to the political arguments surrounding it. Although social scientific conceptualization is different from political advocacy, the arguments I have pursued, necessarily abstract at times, should be returned not only to empirical analysis but to political discourse – to where decisions of life-and-death importance are made.

Notes

1 The Sociological Crime

1 Quoted by John K. Roth, 'The Ethics of Uniqueness', p. 29.
2 Ibid., p. 23.
3 Tone Bringa, 'Averted Gaze: Genocide in Bosnia-Herzegovina, 1992–1995', p. 202.
4 Israel W. Charny, 'Foreword', p. x.
5 Stanley Cohen, *States of Denial: Knowing about Atrocities and Suffering*, p. 7.
6 Ibid., p. 8.
7 Vahakn N. Dadrian, 'The Comparative Aspects of the Armenian and Jewish Cases of Genocide: A Sociohistorical Perspective'.
8 Richard Evans, *Lying About Hitler: History, the Holocaust and the David Irving Trial.*
9 William Schabas, *Genocide in International Law*, p. 10.
10 Gretchen E. Schafft, 'Scientific Racism in the Third Reich: German Anthropologists in the Nazi Era', p. 119.
11 Ibid., pp. 127–30.
12 Ibid., p. 128.
13 Ibid., p. 126.
14 Ibid., p. 124.
15 Alexander Laban Hinton, 'The Dark Side of Modernity: Toward an Anthropology of Genocide', p. 14.

16 Thomas Cushman, 'Anthropology and Genocide in the Balkans: An Analysis of Conceptual Practices of Power'.

17 Max Weber, *The Theory of Social and Economic Organization*, p. 138.

18 Wolfgang Glatzer, 'German Sociological Association'.

19 William L. Shirer, *Berlin Diary: The Journal of a Foreign Correspondent 1934–1941*.

20 Samantha Power, *'A Problem from Hell': America and the Age of Genocide*, p. 21.

21 Helen Fein, 'Genocide: A Sociological Perspective', p. 5.

22 Irving Louis Horowitz, quoted ibid., p. 6.

23 Michael Mann, *The Dark Side of Democracy: Explaining Ethnic Cleansing*, p. ix.

24 Zygmunt Bauman, *Modernity and the Holocaust*, pp. 9–10.

25 Ibid., p. 3.

26 Ibid., p. 29. Emphasis in original.

27 Ibid., p. xii.

28 Ibid., p. viii.

29 Herbert Hirsch, *Genocide and the Politics of Memory: Studying Death to Preserve Life*, p. 81.

30 Bauman, *Modernity and the Holocaust*, p. xiii.

31 Mann, *The Dark Side*.

32 Weber, *The Theory of Social and Economic Organization*, p. 140.

33 Nigel Eltringham, *Accounting for Horror*, p. 7.

2 Neglected Foundations

1 See particularly Power, *'A Problem from Hell'*, pp. 17–78.

2 Presented to the Fifth Conference for the Unification of Penal Law, held in Madrid; ibid., p. 21.

3 Raphael Lemkin, *Acts Constituting a General (Transnational) Danger Considered as Offences Against the Law of Nations*, 1933.

4 Ibid., but I have altered James Fussell's translation of *danger interétatic* as 'transnational danger'. This makes contemporary sense, but the word 'transnational' was not available in Lemkin's day. *Interétatic* means literally 'interstate' but is more comprehensibly rendered as 'international'.

5 Quoted by Power, *'A Problem from Hell'*, p. 29.

6 Ibid.

7 Raphael Lemkin, *Axis Rule in Occupied Europe: Laws of Occupation, Analysis of Government, Proposals for Redress*, p. 79.
8 Ibid., p. 79n. Interestingly, this term now describes a dimension or variant of genocide: see chapter 5.
9 Ibid., p. 79.
10 Ibid., pp. xi–xii
11 In this sense, it went beyond the 'brutality and exploitation' that had marked the earlier German occupations in the First World War, even if, as Isabel V. Hull concluded, these 'certainly provided a foundation for later developments' (*Absolute Destruction: Military Culture and Practices of War in Imperial Germany*, p. 248).
12 Schabas, *Genocide*, p. 25.
13 Steven T. Katz, *The Holocaust in Historical Context*, Vol. 1, pp. 127–9. Emphases in original.
14 Ibid., p. 129n.
15 Ibid.,
16 Ibid., pp. 129–30n.
17 Lemkin, *Axis Rule*, p. 79.
18 Ibid., p. 81.
19 Ibid., pp. 81–2.
20 Ibid., p. 82.
21 Power, *'A Problem from Hell'*, p. 43.
22 *France et al. v. Goering et al.* (1946), cited by Schabas, *Genocide*, pp. 37–8.
23 Witness the aim 'to physically destroy an *entire* group' seen as essential by Katz, *The Holocaust*.
24 *Convention on the Prevention and Punishment of the Crime of Genocide*.
25 See Paul Q. Hirst, 'The International Origins of National Sovereignty', pp. 216–22.
26 Lemkin, *Axis Rule*, p. 91.
27 Ibid., pp. 90–1.
28 Ibid., p. 91n.
29 During the Cold War, minority rights issues faded in international (especially European) politics, being seen more as domestic issues. They resurfaced after 1989: see Jennifer Jackson Preece, *National Minorities and the European Nation-States System*.
30 Ibid., p. 91.
31 Lemkin, *Axis Rule*, p. 93.
32 Ibid., p. 92.
33 Ibid., p. 93.
34 Lemkin, quoted by Power, *'A Problem from Hell'*, p. 51.

35 So named after the restatement by the early nineteenth-century jurist Jean-Étienne-Marie Portalis of the ideas of Jean-Jacques Rousseau.

36 Lemkin, *Axis Rule*, p. 80.

37 Mark Levene, *Genocide in the Age of the Nation State*, Vol. 1: *The Meaning of Genocide*, p. 51. See also my *War and Genocide*, chapter 2.

38 Lemkin, *Axis Rule*, p. 94.

39 Schabas, *Genocide*, p. 29.

40 Ibid., p. 31.

41 Ibid., p. 34.

42 Quoted ibid., p. 35.

43 *France et al. v. Goering et al.* (1946), cited in ibid., pp. 37–8.

44 Ibid., p. 45.

45 Ibid., p. 46.

46 Ibid., pp. 51–81.

47 Leo Kuper, *Genocide*.

48 Schabas, *Genocide*, p. 73.

49 Ibid., p. 73.

50 Ibid., p. 87. Moreover 'some sources suggest that the prohibition on genocide under customary international law is even broader than under the Convention.' Steven Ratner and Jason Abrams, *Accountability for Human Rights Atrocities in International Law: Beyond the Nuremberg Legacy*, p. 42.

51 Schabas, *Genocide*, p. 78.

52 Shaw, *War and Genocide*, table 2.1, pp. 42–3.

53 Ibid., pp. 41–9.

54 Fein, 'Genocide', p. 24.

55 Ibid.

56 Frank Chalk and Kurt Jonassohn, *The History and Sociology of Genocide: Analyses and Case Studies*, p. 23.

57 Fein, 'Genocide', p. 13.

58 Fein criticizes this aspect of Chalk and Jonassohn's definition (ibid.).

59 I. W. Charny, 'Toward a Generic Definition of Genocide', p. 75.

60 Lucy Davidowicz, *The War Against the Jews*. The idea of the Nazi genocide as a 'war on the Jews' was current much earlier: Lemkin (*Axis Rule*, p. 88n.) cites the Institute of Jewish Affairs of the American Jewish Congress and World Jewish Congress, *Hitler's Ten-Year War on the Jews*, 1943.

61 Charny, 'Toward a Generic Definition', p. 88.

62 Ibid., p. 81.

63 Israel W. Charny, 'Foreword', p. x.

64 Sociological readers will recognize my deployment of Weber's distinction between explanation and understanding. I return to this in chapter 6.
65 Carl von Clausewitz, *On War*.
66 Shaw, *War and Genocide*, p. 37.

3 The Maximal Standard

1 Charny, 'Foreword', p. x. Emphasis in original.
2 A. Dirk Moses, 'Conceptual Blockages and Definitional Dilemmas in the "Racial Century"', p. 10.
3 Katz, *The Holocaust in Historical context*, p. 130.
4 See, for example, D. E. Stannard, 'Uniqueness as Denial', and Ian Hancock, 'Responses to the Porrajmos'.
5 Christopher Browning, *The Path to Genocide*, chapter 1.
6 Ibid., p. ix.
7 Stannard, 'Uniqueness', p. 272. Emphasis in original. In Katz's case, this tautology is to be pursued through three volumes!
8 Daniel Goldhagen, *Hitler's Willing Executioners*, p. 414. Emphasis in original.
9 Phillip Lopate, 'Resistance to the Holocaust', p. 287.
10 Ibid., pp. 287–8.
11 Quoted, ibid., p. 289.
12 G. D. Rosenfeld, 'The Politics of Uniqueness', p. 30. Emphasis in original.
13 Ibid., pp. 47–8.
14 Charney, 'Foreword', p. xi.
15 Rosenfeld, 'The Politics', p. 30. I leave aside, for the moment, Rosenfeld's understandable concern about certain forms of politicization – concern that can also be extended, as he acknowledges, to 'instrumental usages' of 'uniqueness' itself (p. 44).
16 Ibid., p. 30.
17 Ibid., p. 32.
18 Ibid.
19 Ibid., pp. 32–3.
20 Alan S. Rosenbaum, ed., *Is the Holocaust Unique?*
21 Robert F. Melson, 'The Armenian Genocide as Precursor and Prototype', p. 129.
22 Ibid., p. 130.
23 Vahakn Dadrian, 'The Comparative Aspects of the Armenian and Jewish Cases of Genocide', p. 135.

24 Yehuda Bauer, *A History of the Holocaust*, p. 332.
25 Bauer, cited in Rosenbaum, *Is the Holocaust Unique?*, p. xxi.
26 Stannard, 'Uniqueness', p. 273.
27 David E. Stannard, *American Holocaust: The Conquest of the New World*.
28 Lopate, 'Resistance', p. 292.
29 Levene, *Genocide*, vol. 1, pp. 50, 36.
30 Barbara Harff and Ted Robert Gurr, *Ethnic Conflict in World Politics*, p. 222.
31 Mann, *The Dark Side of Democracy*, table 1.1, 'The extent of cleansing and violence in intergroup relations', p. 12. Curiously he later refers to 'systematic genocide' (p. 149), which seems (in his terms) an oxymoron, although it does raise the interesting possibility that some genocide may after all not be 'systematic'.
32 Ibid., p. 188.
33 Ibid., p. 185.
34 Ibid., p. 186.

4 The Minimal Euphemism

1 Drazen Petrovic, 'Ethnic Cleansing – An Attempt at Methodology' (page references are not given in the online version). See also the account in Schabas, *Genocide*, pp. 189–92.
2 Mann, *The Dark Side of Democracy.*
3 M. Banks and M. Wolfe, 'Ethnicity and Reports of the 1992–95 Bosnian Conflict', p. 152.
4 Petrovic, 'Ethnic Cleansing'.
5 Philip J. Cohen, cited by Klejda Mulaj, 'Ethnic Cleansing in Yugoslavia in the 1990s', p. 696.
6 Banks and Wolfe, 'Ethnicity', pp. 152–3.
7 Petrovic, 'Ethnic Cleansing'.
8 Ibid. The summary that follows uses the quotations collected by Petrovic, ibid.
9 Andrew Bell-Fialkoff, 'A Brief History of Ethnic Cleansing', quoted by Petrovic, ibid.
10 Petrovic, 'Ethnic Cleansing'.
11 Andrew Bell-Fialkoff, *Ethnic Cleansing*, pp. 3–4.
12 'The Situation in Bosnia and Herzegovina', UN Doc. A/RES/47/121. UN Doc A/47/PV.91, p. 99, quoted by Schabas, *Genocide*, p. 192. As Schabas makes clear, this reference was 'reaffirmed in a number of subsequent resolutions'.

13 Power, 'A Problem from Hell', p. 483.

14 Quoted by Schabas, Genocide, p. 194.

15 Prosecutor v. Karadžić and Mladić (Case No. IT-95–18-I), confirmation of Indictment, cited by Schabas, Genocide, pp. 197–8.

16 Ibid., p. 199.

17 Bell-Fialkoff, Ethnic Cleansing, p. 1.

18 Norman Naimark, Fires of Hatred, p. 3.

19 Ibid., p. 186.

20 Ibid., pp. 3–4.

21 Bell-Fialkoff, Ethnic Cleansing, p. 2.

22 Naimark, Fires of Hatred, p. 193.

23 Schabas, Genocide, p. 194.

24 A. Honwana, 'Children of War: Understanding War and War Cleansing in Mozambique and Angola'.

25 Jocelyn Alexander, JoAnn McGregor and Terence Ranger, Violence and Memory: One Hundred Years in the Dark Forests of Matabeleland, pp. 269–70.

26 Bell-Fialkoff, Ethnic Cleansing, p. 1.

27 Naimark, Fires of Hatred, pp. 3–4.

28 Schabas, Genocide, p. 196.

29 UN Doc. E/447, p. 24, quoted ibid.

30 Ibid., p. 195. According to Stephen B. Vardy and T. Hunt Tooley, Ethnic Cleansing in Twentieth-Century Europe, p. 6, 16.5 million Germans may have been victims.

31 Melchior Palyi, review, p. 497.

32 Hull highlighted the precedents for these deportations in the First World War, when Imperial Russian armies began 'the deportations of ethnic Germans (Russian subjects)' in 1914, a deportation which 'swiftly widened its scope until whole provinces were "empty" of German speakers' (Absolute Destruction, p. 234).

33 The sinking of the Wilhelm Gustloff was fictionalized by Günther Grass, in Crabwalk.

34 Alfred de Zayas, Nemesis at Potsdam: The Anglo-Americans and the Expulsion of the Germans, p. 60.

35 Daily Mail, 6 August 1945, quoted ibid., p. 106.

36 Bertrand Russell, The Times, 19 October 1945, quoted ibid., p. 108.

37 Daily Mail, 6 August 1945, quoted ibid., p. 106.

38 De Zayas, Nemesis, p. 125.

39 F. A. Voigt, quoted ibid., p. 107.

40 Bertrand Russell, New Leader, 8 December 1945, quoted ibid., p. 109.

41 Robert Murphy quoted ibid., p. 115.

42 Naimark, *Fires of Hatred*, p. 115.
43 De Zayas, *Nemesis*, p. 104.
44 Ibid., p. 89.
45 Ibid., p. 81.
46 Ibid., p. 104n.
47 Ibid., p. 103.
48 Ibid., p. 90.
49 Lemkin, *Axis Rule*, p. 79.
50 Adolf Hitler, statement to Hermann Rauschning, cited ibid., p. 86n. Emphasis in original.
51 Michael Mann, *Fascists*, p. 184.
52 Stannard, 'Uniqueness', p. 264, quoting Yehuda Bauer on Nazism.
53 Wehrmacht handbook (1939) quoted by Hamburg Institute for Social Research, *The German Army and Genocide: Crimes Against War Prisoners, Jews and Other Civilians in the East, 1939–1944*, p. 22.
54 Adolf Hitler, *Mein Kampf*, quoted ibid., p. 28.
55 Banks and Wolfe, 'Ethnicity', p. 153.
56 Goetz Aly, 'Medicine', in G. Aly, P. Chroust and C. Pross, *Cleansing the Fatherland: Nazi Medicine and Racial Hygiene*, p. 82.
57 Hamburg Institute, *The German Army*, p. 23.
58 Ibid., p. 66.
59 Regional Commissar Erren in Slonim, 25 January 1943, quoted ibid, p. 128.
60 The Hamburg Institute, which recorded these usages, used 1990s terminology to describe the whole process as 'ethnic cleansing': *The German Army*, p. 168.
61 Quoted by Benny Morris, *The Birth of the Palestinian Refugee Problem Revisited*, p. 41.
62 Ibid., p. 43. Morris, who in the original edition of his book simply described and explained this process, has himself embraced this logic in his new edition.
63 Ibid., p. 44.
64 Ibid., p. 60.
65 Nur Masalha, *A Land without a People: Israel, Transfer and the Palestinians 1949–96*, p. x.
66 Charles Glass, ' "It Was Necessary to Uproot Them" ', p. 23, citing Nur Masalha.
67 'There has never been a truly voluntary transfer of populations.' Report to the Institut de Droit International, 1952, quoted in Schabas, *Genocide*, pp. 195–6.
68 Ibid., p. 196.
69 De Zayas, *Nemesis*, p. 130.

70 Ibid., p. 60.
71 Browning, *The Path to Genocide*, chapter 1.

5 Conceptual Proliferation

 1 Lemkin, *Axis Rule*, p. 80.
 2 Mann, *The Dark Side of Democracy*, table 1, p. 12.
 3 Rudy Rummel, *Death by Government*, p. 36.
 4 Lemkin, *Axis Rule*, p. 79n. Emphases in original.
 5 Stuart D. Stein, 'Ethnocide'. Emphases in original.
 6 René Lemarchand, *Burundi: Ethnic Conflict and Genocide*, p. xxvi.
 7 Ibid.
 8 UNESCO Latin American Conference, Declaration of San José, 11 December 1981, UNESCO Doc. FS 82/WF.32, reproduced in Crawford, *The Rights of Peoples*.
 9 Israel W. Charny, 'Toward a Generic Definition of Genocide'.
10 Moses, 'Conceptual Blockages', p. 26.
11 Mann, *The Dark Side*, p. 12.
12 Mike Davis, *Late Victorian Holocausts*.
13 Robert Conquest, *The Harvest of Sorrow: Soviet Collectivization and the Terror Famine*; Jasper Becker, *Hungry Ghosts: China's Secret Famine*.
14 Stein, 'Ethnocide'.
15 Mary Anne Warren, *Gendercide: The Implications of Sex Selection*, p. 22.
16 Adam Jones, 'Gendercide and Genocide', pp. 185–6.
17 Ibid., p. 185.
18 Ibid., p. 186.
19 Richard Plant, *The Pink Triangle: The Nazi War Against Homosexuals*.
20 Jones, 'Gendercide and Genocide', p. 186.
21 Schabas, *Genocide*, pp. 134–45.
22 Ibid., p. 140, quoting Beth van Schaack.
23 For this distinction, see the discussion of Michael Mann's work in chapter 4.
24 Schabas, *Genocide*, p. 134.
25 Bauman, *Modernity and the Holocaust*, p. 119. Thus, as he points out, the Nazis' reliance on Jewish elites to police ghetto communities was paradoxically unique, but rational: 'Deploying the rationality of the victims was a much more rational solution' than wholesale murder (p. 139).

26 Harff and Gurr, *Ethnic Conflict*; Mann, *The Dark Side*, table 1, p. 12.
27 Karl Marx, *Capital*, Vol. 1, Pt VIII, 'The So-called Primitive Accumulation'.
28 Hence his attention to violent dispossession of the peasantry in the development of capitalism.
29 Conquest, *The Harvest of Sorrow*.
30 Becker, *Hungry Ghosts*.
31 Kiernan, *The Pol Pot Regime*, passim.
32 Mann, *The Dark Side*, pp. 17, 320.
33 Hannah Arendt, *The Origins of Totalitarianism*.
34 Robert Conquest, *The Great Terror: A Reassessment*.
35 Helen Fein, 'Genocide', p. 14.
36 As Magnorella argued, 'the Tutsi–Hutu distinction in Rwanda does not fit into any of the . . . categories [national, ethnic, racial or religious groups]. . . . Consequently, had the ICTR justices stopped there, they would have been forced to conclude that genocide, as legally defined in the convention and statute, had not occurred in Rwanda. Fortunately, the justices did not stop there' ('Recent Developments', p. 318).
37 See the discussion in Steven Graham, ed., *Cities, War and Terrorism*.
38 Martin Coward, 'Urbicide in Bosnia', p. 166.
39 Schabas, *Genocide*, p. 118.
40 Ibid., p. 119.
41 Ibid., p. 118.
42 Kiernan, *The Pol Pot Regime*, pp. 460–3.
43 Schabas, *Genocide*, pp. 119–20.
44 Lemkin, *Axis Rule*, p. 80.

6 From Intentionality to a Structural Concept

1 Thomas W. Burger, *Max Weber's Theory of Concept Formation*, p. 160. Emphasis in original.
2 Schabas, *Genocide*, p. 207.
3 Ibid., p. 208.
4 Ibid., p. 207.
5 *Kayishema and Ruzindana*, quoted in ibid., p. 209.
6 Schabas, *Genocide*, pp. 213–14.
7 Ibid., p. 214.
8 Quoted ibid., p. 218.
9 Ibid., p. 222.

10 Magnorella, 'Recent Developments', p. 319.
11 Guénaël Mettraux, *International Crimes and the* ad hoc *Tribunals*, pp. 210–15.
12 Ibid., p. 211.
13 Schabas, *Genocide*, pp. 254–5.
14 See Browning, *The Path to Genocide*, chapter 1.
15 Mann, *The Dark Side of Democracy,* p. 112.
16 Ibid., p. 7. Emphasis in original.
17 Ibid., p. 8.
18 Ibid., p. 17. Although I question Mann's assumption that genocide exists only when the intention is physically to 'wipe out' a group, it is significant that (he showed) even the movement over *this* threshold is the outcome of incremental decision-making in response to situational dynamics.
19 Ibid., p. 26.
20 Kenneth Rizer, 'Bombing Dual-Use Targets: Legal, Ethical, and Doctrinal Perspectives'. Emphasis in original. Instead this manner of killing is described by the infamous euphemism 'collateral damage'.
21 Ibid.
22 Fein, 'Genocide', p. 15.
23 Tony Barta, quoted ibid., p. 16. Emphasis in original.
24 Fein, 'Genocide', p. 19.
25 Ibid., p. 20.
26 Weber, *The Theory of Social and Economic Organization*, p. 101.
27 Ibid., p. 88.
28 Ibid., p. 89. Emphasis in the original.
29 Ibid., p. 110.
30 Ibid.
31 Ibid.
32 Ibid., p. 92.
33 Ibid., p. 107.
34 Ibid., p. 115. The two types of rational action were, of course, part of a fourfold classification of action that also included 'traditional' and 'charismatic' action. I have omitted these two types from my discussion, as they are less relevant to genocide.
35 Talcott Parsons, editorial comment, ibid., p. 115n.
36 Bauman, *Modernity and the Holocaust*, p. 91.
37 Mann, *The Dark Side*, p. 26.
38 This paradox – first elaborated in critiques of nuclear war-preparation – has been fully explored in Bauman's critique of the 'modern' character of the Holocaust, to which I return.

39 Ibid., p. 74.
40 Mann, *The Dark Side*, p. 26.
41 Ringer, *Max Weber's Methodology*, p. 160. Emphasis in original. Indeed for Weber, he reminds us, most 'action takes place in dull semiconsciousness or unconsciousness'.
42 Weber accepted 'Rickert's distinction between history on the one hand and all sciences, natural and social on the other'. Rex, 'Typology and Objectivity', p. 18; see also Burger, *Max Weber's Theory, passim*.
43 Ibid., p. 161. Thus many argue that history and sociology need to be combined in a 'sociological history' or a 'historical sociology'. See C. Wright Mills, *The Sociological Imagination*; Philip Abrams, *Historical Sociology*.
44 Burger, *Max Weber's Theory*, p. 138. Emphasis added.
45 Ibid., p. 220.
46 Weber, quoted ibid., p. 136.
47 Burger, *Max Weber's Theory*, p. 136.
48 Carlo Antoni, *From History to Sociology*, p. 177.
49 Weber, *The Theory of Social and Economic Organization*, p. 99.
50 Weber, quoted in Burger, *Max Weber's Theory*, p. 124. Emphasis in original.
51 Ibid., p. 114.
52 Ibid., p. 106.
53 Ibid., p. x. Emphasis added.
54 Ibid., p. 116. As Burger explained: 'although their form is general, i.e. although they refer to many phenomena, their contents do not contain elements which all these phenomena have *strictly* in common. Rather, some of the definitional characteristics are present *in different degrees* in different instances.'
55 Ibid., p. 125. Emphasis in original.
56 Alexander von Schelting quoted in ibid., p. 121.
57 Ibid., p. 123: 'This utopian world is so constructed that what are "characteristic" and "significant" elements, existing in gradations in the empirical world, become common elements in the imaginary one. These are shared by all relevant phenomena to the same degree.'
58 Ibid., p. 177. Emphasis in original.
59 Such a concept will of course be an ideal type. Rex ('Typology and Objectivity', pp. 34–5) argued that 'the use of the term "ideal types" to refer to Weber's structural concepts' was 'not helpful'. However, as Burger demonstrated (*Max Weber's Theory*, pp. 133–4), Weber did indeed understand his structural concepts in an ideal-typical sense.

60 Rex, 'Typology and Objectivity', pp. 29–30. Weber went on to develop more general concepts, 'to give system to the concepts which had previously developed *ad hoc* in his historical studies. . . . The types of action that lie behind the process of *Verstehen* are not designed simply to interpret the social or other action of particular actors. They are the building blocks from which the whole edifice of Weber's theory is constructed' (p. 31).

61 Ibid., p. 34.

62 Ibid., p. 33.

63 Burger, *Max Weber's Theory*, p. 125.

64 Ibid., p. 219. This criterion is therefore different from causal significance, as Burger explains.

65 Weber, quoted ibid., p. 122. Emphasis in original.

66 Jeffrey Alexander, 'On the Social Construction of Moral Universals: The "Holocaust" from War Crime to Trauma Drama'.

67 Rex, 'Typology and Objectivity', p. 33.

68 Ibid.

69 Vahakn Dadrian, quoted in Fein, 'Genocide', p. 13. Emphasis added..

70 Rex, 'Typology and Objectivity', p. 31.

71 Weber, *The Theory of Social and Economic Organization*, p. 118.

72 Ibid., p. 119.

73 Raul Hilberg, quoted in Bauman, *Modernity and the Holocaust*, p. 117.

74 Levene, *Genocide*, vol. 1, p. 49.

75 Bauman, *Modernity and the Holocaust*, p. 139.

76 Ibid., 149.

77 Alan J. Kuperman, in 'Provoking Genocide: A Revised History of the Rwandan Patriotic Front', argues that armed resisters actually *sought* this outcome in order to create pressure for international intervention.

78 Anthony Giddens, *The Constitution of Society*, p. 376.

7 Elements of Genocidal Conflict

1 Schabas, *Genocide*, p. 106.

2 Ibid., p. 105.

3 Ibid., p. 107.

4 Ibid., p. 108.

5 Ibid., pp. 103–4.

6 Ibid., p. 113.

7   Fein, 'Genocide', p. 14. Emphasis added.
8   Raphael Lemkin, quoted in Schabas, *Genocide*, p. 134.
9   Schabas, *Genocide*, p. 113.
10 Ibid., p. 110.
11 Ibid., pp. 132–3.
12 Max Weber, quoted ibid., p. 125.
13 Ibid., pp. 132–3. He takes this position despite recognizing that 'the term "racial group" ', although unproblematic in 1948, may now be 'increasingly antiquated' (ibid., p. 120).
14 Weber, *The Theory of Social and Economic Organization*, p. 138.
15 Fein, 'Genocide', p. 23.
16 Ibid., pp. 23–4.
17 Quoted in Schabas, *Genocide*, pp. 131–2. Emphasis added.
18 Fein, 'Genocide', p. 24. Emphasis added.
19 For a classic work, see George C. Homans, *The Human Group*, and a recent study, Charles Stangor, *Social Groups in Action and Interaction*.
20 'A social relationship will be called "communal" if and so far as the orientation of social action . . . is based on a subjective feeling of the parties, whether affectual or traditional, that they belong together. A social relationship will, on the other hand, be called "associative" if and in so far as the orientation for social action within it rests on a rationally motivated adjustment of interests or a similarly motivated agreement' (*The Theory of Social and Economic Organization*, p. 136). As Parsons points out his 'usage here is an adaptation of the well-known terms of [Ferdinand] Tönnies, *Gemeinschaft* and *Gesellschaft*': editorial comment, p. 136n.
21 Ibid., p. 139. 'Whether a relationship is open or closed may be determined traditionally, affectually, or rationally in terms of values or expediency.'
22 Ibid., pp. 145–6.
23 'The development of the modern form of the organization of corporate groups in all fields is nothing less than identical with the development and continual spread of bureaucratic administration.' Ibid., p. 337.
24 Nearer to this concept is his other term, *Stand*, explained by Parsons: 'The term *Stand* with its derivatives is perhaps the most troublesome single term in Weber's text. It refers to a social group the members of which occupy a relatively well-defined common status, particularly with reference to social stratification, although this reference is not always important. In addition to common status, there is a further criterion that the members of a *Stand* have a common mode of life and usually more or less well-defined code of behaviour.'

Interestingly, *Ständische Herrschaft* – the type of authority – was translated by Parsons as 'decentralized authority', a description that might fit some of the looser collectivities referred to in genocide studies. (Parsons, editorial comment, ibid., pp. 347–8n.). However, *Stände* were groups within national societies, not nations.

25 Levene, *Genocide*, vol. 1, p. 36.
26 Weber, *The Theory of Social and Economic Organization*, p. 424.
27 Ibid., pp. 428–9.
28 Benedict Anderson, *Imagined Communities*.
29 Mann, *The Dark Side of Democracy*, p. 11.
30 Ibid., p. 25.
31 Schabas, *Genocide*, p. 109.
32 Ibid., p. 110. Emphasis added.
33 Mettraux, *International Crimes*, p. 225.
34 Nigel Eltringham, *Accounting for Horror*, p. 6.
35 Ibid., p. 7.
36 Ibid., p. 8.
37 Ibid., p. 10.
38 UN General Assembly Resolution 96(I), 11 December 1946, quoted in Schabas, *Genocide*, p. 45. Emphasis added.
39 Weber, *The Theory of Social and Economic Organization*, p. 101. Of course, Weber added, 'concepts of collective entities which are found both in common sense and in juristic and other technical forms of thought, have a meaning in the minds of individual persons . . . . Actors thus in part orient their action to them, and in this role such ideas have a powerful, often a decisive, causal influence on the course of action of real individuals.' Thus sociology 'keeps this non-sociological language' (p. 102).
40 Schabas, *Genocide*, p. 228.
41 Cited in Eugen Weber, *Peasants into Frenchmen*, p. 113.
42 Ibid.
43 Ibid.
44 Mark Levene, *Genocide in the Age of the Nation-State*, vol. II: *The Rise of the West and the Coming of Genocide*, p. 158.
45 Ibid., p. 215.
46 Fein, 'Genocide', p. 17.
47 Lemkin, *Axis Rule*, p. 79.
48 Bauman, *Modernity and the Holocaust*, p. 119.
49 Here I differ fundamentally from Mann's use of 'extent of violence', along with 'extent of cleansing', as defining different forms of political violence in his table 'The extent of cleansing and violence in inter-group relations', *The Dark Side*, p. 12.

50 Moses, 'Conceptual Blockages'.
51 Weber, *The Theory of Social and Economic Organization*, pp. 132–3. The term translated as 'conflict' is *Kampf*, which of course can also be rendered 'struggle' or 'fight'. Conflict is the widely used sociological term.
52 Ibid.
53 Dadrian, 'The Comparative Aspects', p. 143.
54 Ibid., p. 145.
55 Jefremovas, *Brickyards to Graveyards*, p. 119.
56 Harff and Gurr, *Ethnic Conflict*, p. 19.
57 Ibid., p. 5.
58 Hence the title of his table 'The extent of cleansing and violence in inter-group relations': Mann, *The Dark Side*, p. 12.
59 Ibid., p. 5. Emphases in original.
60 Jocelyn Alexander, Jo Ann McGregor and Terence Ranger, 'Ethnicity and the Politics of Conflict: The Case of Matabeleland', p. 307.
61 K. Fukui and J. Markakis quoted ibid.
62 Ibid., p. 311.
63 Ibid., p. 305. Or, 'how wars which are not ethnic in their causation can come to be experienced as (at least in part) ethnic by those involved' (p. 314).
64 Mann, *The Dark Side*, p. 21. Indeed he is absolutely clear that 'whole nations or ethnic groups *never* act collectively' (p. 20).
65 Shaw, *War and Genocide*, especially chapter 2, table 1.
66 Carl von Clausewitz, *On War*, p. 236.
67 See my *War and Genocide*, pp. 23–6.
68 James J. Reid, 'Total War, the Annihilation Ethic, and the Armenian Genocide, 1870–1918'.
69 Hull, *Absolute Destruction*.
70 This distinction between instrumental and substantive rationality is developed, in relation to nuclear war, in Herbert Marcuse's critique of Weber ('Industrialization and Capitalism'). See also E. P. Thompson, 'Exterminism: The Last Stage of Civilization'.

8 The Missing Concept

1 I am aware that there may be differences of meaning between *civilians* and *non-combatants*, but I argue below that the core meanings of these terms are interchangeable.
2 R. Headland, cited in Mann, *The Dark Side of Denocracy*, p. 187.

3 Ibid. In most cases, a minority of the victims take up arms to defend the civilian population that is attacked, although they thereby abandon their own civilian status.

4 Karma Nabulsi, 'Evolving Conceptions of Civilians and Belligerents', p. 9. Nabulsi uses the acronym IHL for international humanitarian law in some of the further quotations below.

5 Hugo Slim, 'Why Protect Civilians?', p. 495.

6 Nabulsi, 'Evolving Conceptions', p. 9.

7 Ibid., p. 10.

8 Geoffrey Best, *Civilians in Contemporary Wars* (no page numbers can be given for this online publication).

9 Nabulsi, 'Evolving Conceptions', p. 12.

10 Ibid., p. 15.

11 Ibid., p. 16.

12 Ibid., p. 19.

13 Ibid.

14 Ibid., p. 18.

15 Slim, 'Why Protect Civilians?', p. 495.

16 Ibid., p. 499.

17 Ibid., p. 486.

18 Ibid., p. 483.

19 Ibid., p. 497.

20 Walzer, *Just and Unjust Wars*, p. 136.

21 Best, *Civilians*.

22 Ibid.

23 Ibid. Emphasis added.

24 Ibid.

25 Ted Honderich, 'Terrorism for Humanity' (since this online paper is not paginated, I have not repeated the reference for the following quotations from the same source).

26 See Honderich, 'Terrorism for Humanity'; Barry Buzan, 'Who May We Bomb?'

27 Slim, 'Why Protect Civilians?', p. 496.

28 Ibid., p. 497.

29 Ibid., p. 498.

30 Best, *Civilians*.

31 For the definition of militarism, see my *Post-Military Society*, chapter 1.

32 See Mary Kaldor, *New & Old Wars*.

33 We know that in any case it is formally acknowledged by states involved in more conventional wars.

34 Jacques Semelin, *Unarmed Against Hitler*, p. 1. Emphasis in original.

35 Ibid., p. 27.
36 Ibid., p. 29.
37 Ibid., p. 2.
38 Ibid., p. 30.
39 Ibid., p. 2.
40 Ibid.
41 Ibid., p. 3.
42 Ibid., p. 27.
43 Ibid., p. 28.
44 Ibid., p. 64.
45 Ibid., p. 65.
46 Ibid., p. 77.
47 Ibid., p. 3.
48 Adam Roberts, 'Civilian Defence Strategy', p. 216.
49 Semelin, *Unarmed Against Hitler*, p. 30.
50 Ibid.
51 H. R. Kedward, *In Search of the Maquis: Rural Resistance in Southern France, 1942–1944*, p. vi.
52 Jean-Pierre Azéma, quoted in Semelin, *Unarmed Against Hitler*, p. 23.
53 Ibid.
54 Ibid., p. 24.
55 Kedward, *In Search*, p. 88.
56 Ibid., p. 87.
57 Ibid.
58 Ibid., p. 93.
59 Ibid., p. 114.
60 Ibid., p. 112.
61 Ibid., p. 158.
62 Ibid., pp. 190–1.
63 Ibid., p. 219.
64 Weber, *Peasants into Frenchmen*, p. 297.
65 Richard Cobb, *The People's Armies*, p. 2.
66 Joanna K. M. Hanson, *The Civilian Population and the Warsaw Uprising of 1944*, p. 3.
67 Semelin, *Unarmed Against Hitler,* p. 111.
68 Studies I have found useful include Jocelyn Alexander, Jo Ann McGregor and Terence Ranger, *Violence and Memory*; Howard Clark, *Civil Resistance in Kosovo*; and Andrew Rigby, *Living the Intifada.*
69 Ulrich Beck, *Risk Society.*
70 Beck, 'Risk Society Revisited', p. 224.

71 For an exploration of the significance of this distinction in the context of contemporary warfare, see my *The New Western Way of War*.
72 Quoted by Alan Scott, 'Risk Society or Angst Society?', p. 38.
73 Hanson, *The Civilian Population*, p. 178.
74 Ibid.
75 See Clark, *Civil Resistance*.

9 Explanations

1 Burger, *Max Weber's Theory*, pp. 133–4.
2 Ibid., pp. 154–5.
3 Ibid., p. 140. Emphasis in original.
4 Weber, *The Theory of Social and Economic Organization*, pp. 110–11.
5 Ibid., pp. 110–11.
6 Ibid., p. 110.
7 Chalk and Jonassohn, *The History and Sociology of Genocide*, p. 29.
8 Israel W. Charny, 'Toward a Generic Definition', pp. 76–7.
9 Alison Palmer, *Colonial Genocide*.
10 Samuel Totten, William S. Parsons and Robert H. Hitchcock, 'Confronting Genocide and Ethnocide of Indigenous Peoples', pp. 68–74.
11 For the most part I leave this last issue to one side. Mann's interesting discussion identifies no fewer than nine major sets of perpetrator motives: *The Dark Side of Democracy*, pp. 27–9.
12 Chalk and Jonassohn, *The History and Sociology of Genocide*, pp. 58–65.
13 Mann, *The Dark Side*, p. 54.
14 Foucault, *The Will to Knowledge*, pp. 136–7.
15 Ibid., p. 136.
16 Ibid., p. 143.
17 Ibid., p. 138.
18 Ibid., p. 137.
19 Ibid., pp. 136–7.
20 For this aspect see Dan Stone, 'Genocide as Transgression'.
21 Bauman, *Modernity and the Holocaust*, p. xiii.
22 Ibid., p. 12.
23 Ibid., p. 8.
24 Raul Hilberg, quoted ibid.
25 Ibid., p. 149.
26 Ibid., p. 14.

27 Ibid., p. 17. Emphasis in original.
28 Ibid., p. 26.
29 Ibid., p. 82. Emphasis in original.
30 Ibid., p. 89.
31 Scheper-Hughes, 'Coming to our Senses', p. 366. See also David Maybury-Lewis, 'Genocide against Indigenous Peoples'.
32 Moses, 'Conceptual Blockages', p. 10.
33 Donald Bloxham, 'Bureaucracy and Mass Murder: A Comparative Historical Analysis'.
34 Scheper-Hughes, 'Coming to our Senses', p. 369.
35 Ibid., pp. 374–5.
36 Mann, *The Dark Side*, p. 6. Likewise, ethnic groups involved in 'cleansing' are 'macro-ethnicities formed by social relations other than biology or kinship. None of the ethnic conflicts considered here are natural or primordial. They and their conflicts are socially created' (p. 10).
37 Christopher C. Taylor, 'The Cultural Face of Terror in the Rwandan Genocide of 1994', p. 139.
38 Liisa Malkki, *Purity and Exile*.
39 Taylor, 'The Cultural Face', p. 141.
40 See Christopher Browning's discussion in *Ordinary Men: Reserve Police Battalion 101 and the Final Solution in Poland*.
41 Ervin Staub, *The Roots of Evil: The Origins of Genocide and Other Group Violence*.
42 Mann, *The Dark Side*, p. 109.
43 Mark Levene, 'A Dissenting Voice', p. 165.
44 Mark Levene, 'The Chittagong Hill Tracts', p. 339.
45 Villia Jefremovas, *Brickyards to Graveyards*, p. 119.
46 Ibid.
47 Hinton, 'The Dark Side of Modernity', p. 29.
48 Mahmood Mamdani, *When Victims Become Killers*, cited by Elisa von Joeden-Forgey, review.
49 Dadrian, 'The Comparative Aspects', p. 155.
50 Mann, *The Dark Side*, p. 2.
51 Ibid.
52 Ibid., p. 3. Mann adds to this general thesis that 'demos' has also been entwined with class and, recently, with religion, so that this thesis has class and religious as well as the basic ethnic variants: for further discussion, see below.
53 Ibid., p. 4.
54 Ibid.
55 Ibid., p. 8.

56 Ibid., p. 5. Whole sentence emphasized in original.
57 Ibid.
58 Ibid.
59 Ibid., p. 7.
60 Ibid., p. 6.
61 Ibid., p. 7.
62 Ibid.
63 Ibid., p. 9.
64 Ibid., p. ix.
65 Ibid., p. 4.
66 Bauman, *Modernity and the Holocaust*, p. 52.
67 Ibid., p. 53.
68 Mann, *The Dark Side*, pp. 3–4.
69 Ibid., p. 9.
70 Ibid., p. 7. Emphasis added.
71 See my *Dialectics of War* for a critique of this tendency in sociology.
72 Mann, *The Dark Side*, p. 32. Likewise Norman Naimark: 'Ethnic cleansing is very often closely related to war. The cases examined in this book all have taken place during war or during the chaotic transition from war to peace. War provides cover for rulers . . . the opportunity to deal with a troublesome minority by suspending civil law in the name of military exigency. . . . War habituates its participants to killing and obeying orders. No one ever totally acclimatizes to bloodshed and rotting corpses, but the soldier adapts more readily than others. Regular armies are almost always involved in ethnic cleansing. . . . But war also breeds paramilitary groups that more often than not do most of the damage in ethnic cleansing. . . . War provides governments and politicians with strategic arguments for ethnic cleansing' (*Fires of Hatred*, pp. 187, 188).
73 Mann, *The Sources of Social Power*, vol. 1, pp. 10–11.
74 Mann, *Fascists*, p. 206.
75 Ibid., p. 69.
76 See my discussion in *War and Genocide*.
77 I explored these connections more fully in *War and Genocide*.
78 René Lemarchand, 'Genocide in the Great Lakes: Which Genocide? Whose Genocide?'
79 Mann, *The Sources*, vol. 1, p. 9. Emphasis in original.
80 The corollary of this, of course, is that international relations as a field has often assumed a total separation of international from domestic power relations. I have explored these questions further in my *Theory of the Global State*.

81 Melson, *Revolution and Genocide*, p. 18.
82 Mann, *The Dark side*, p. 7. Emphasis added.

10 The Relevance of Conceptual Analysis

1 Burger, *Max Weber's Theory*, p. 178.
2 Ibid., pp. 165–6.
3 In contrast to genocide, Donald L. Horowitz's study *The Deadly Ethnic Riot* (p. 1) defines it as a 'lethal attack by civilian members of one ethnic group on civilian members of another ethnic group' that is 'intense, sudden, though not necessarily unplanned'.
4 The following summarizes Mann, *The Dark Side of Democracy*, pp. 506–18.
5 Ibid., p. 517.
6 Ibid., p. 518.
7 Ibid., p. 517.
8 Ibid., p. 525.
9 See my *The New Western Way of War: Risk-Transfer War and its Crisis in Iraq*.
10 For a systematic contrast between the internationalized Western and quasi-imperial non-Western states, see my *Theory of the Global State: Globality as Unfinished Revolution*, pp. 208–10 and 233–7, especially table 1, pp. 206–7.
11 For further discussion of the 'global surveillance' mode of warfare, see my *The New Western Way of War*, chapter 3.
12 'African' is meant in an essentially (and therefore problematic) racial sense: these peoples are 'blacks', distinguished by race rather than religion from the 'Arabs' who attacked them.
13 Human Rights Watch, *Darfur Destroyed: Ethnic Cleansing by Government and Militia Forces in Western Sudan*.
14 International Commission of Inquiry on Darfur, *Report of the International Commission of Inquiry on Darfur*.
15 Jan Egeland, quoted, http://news.bbc.co.uk/2/hi/africa/4349063.stm [13 April 2005].
16 Eric Reeves, 'Darfur Mortality Update', *H-Genocide*, 11 March 2005. Gérard Prunier came to 'a casualty figure ranging between 280,000 and 310,000 at the beginning of 2005' (*Darfur: The Ambiguous Genocide*, p. 152).
17 Hugo Slim, 'Dithering over Darfur? A Preliminary Review of the International Response', p. 811.

18 Bob MacPherson, 'Stop the Slaughter', *Washington Post*, 8 August 2004, p. B07.
19 James Smith, ' "Cleansing" in Sudan May Soon Become Genocide', *The Times*, 18 May 2004.
20 Prunier, *Darfur*, p. 164.
21 Ibid., p. 156. Prunier had proposed the latter definition in his *The Rwanda Crisis: History of a Genocide*.
22 Human Rights Watch, *Darfur Destroyed*.
23 Kofi Annan, 17 June 2004, quoted by Eric Reeves, 'Unmistakable Evidence of Genocidal Intent: A Legal Analysis of Khartoum's Continuing Obstruction of Humanitarian Access to Darfur'. *H-Genocide*, 16 June 2004.
24 Presidential statement S/PRST/2004/18, 1 June 2004.
25 Interviewed by Jonathan Dimbleby, ITV, 20 June 2004.
26 http://news.bbc.co.uk/1/hi/world/africa/3849593.stm [4 July 2004].
27 Colin Powell, 30 June 2004, interview with National Public Radio, http://www.sudanvisiondaily.com/modules.php?name=News&file=article&sid=1970 [17 August 2004].
28 http://www.ushmm.org/conscience/staring_genocide_in_the_face/index.php [17 August 2004].
29 Eric Reeves, 'Unmistakable Evidence of Genocidal Intent', *H-Genocide*, 16 June 2004.
30 Colin Powell, quoted BBC News, 9 September 2004, http://news.bbc.co.uk/go/pr/fr/-/1/hi/world/africa/3641820.stm [12 April 2005].
31 Quoted, ibid.
32 Eric Reeves, 'Secretary of State Colin Powell's Genocide Determination: What it Does, and Doesn't, Mean for Darfur', *H-Genocide*, 10 September 2004.
33 Quoted, ibid.
34 Eric Reeves, 'Is There No Threshold for Humanitarian Intervention in Darfur?', *H-Genocide*, 18 October 2004.
35 Eric Reeves, 'A "Perfect Storm" of Indifference and Disingenuousness', *H-Genocide*, 18 February 2005.
36 Eric Reeves, 'The Report of the International Commission of Inquiry on Darfur: A Critical Analysis (Part I)', *H-Genocide*, 2 February 2005.
37 Ibid.
38 International Commission, *Report*, p. 24.
39 Ibid., p. 25.
40 Ibid., p. 37.
41 Ibid., p. 140.
42 Ibid., pp. 130–1.

43 Ibid., p. 132.
44 The following is summarized, with quotes, from Reeves, 'The Report . . .: (Part I)'.
45 Although the commission formally denied the existence of a 'hierarchy' of international crimes, its argument that atrocities constituted 'crimes against humanity', even of 'extermination', rather than genocide in reality assumed a hierarchy in which genocide is the maximum offence.
46 International Commission, *Report*, p. 55.

References and Bibliography

Abrams, P. (1982) *Historical Sociology*. Shepton Mallet: Open Books.

Akçam, T. (2004) *From Empire to Republic: Turkish Nationalism and the Armenian Genocide*. London: Zed.

Alexander, J., J. McGregor and T. Ranger (2000) *Violence and Memory: One Hundred Years in the Dark Forests of Matabeleland*. London: James Currey.

—— (2000) 'Ethnicity and the Politics of Conflict: The Case of Matabeleland', in E. W. Nafziger, F. Stewart and R. Värynen, eds, *War, Hunger and Displacement: The Origins of Humanitarian Emergencies*, vol. 1. Oxford: Oxford University Press, 305–32.

Alexander, J. C. (2002) 'On the Social Construction of Moral Universals: The "Holocaust" from War Crime to Trauma Drama', *European Journal of Social Theory*, 5, 1, 5–85.

Alvarez, A. (2001) *Governments, Citizens, and Genocide: A Comparative and Interdisciplinary Approach*. Bloomington: Indiana University Press.

Aly, G., P. Chroust and C. Pross (1994) *Cleansing the Fatherland: Nazi Medicine and Racial Hygiene*. Baltimore: Johns Hopkins University Press.

Anderson, B. (1983) *Imagined Communities: Reflections on the Origin and Spread of Nationalism*. London: Verso.

Andreopoulous, G. A., ed. (1994), *Genocide: Conceptual and Historical Dimensions*. Philadelphia: University of Pennsylvania Press.

Antoni, C. (1959) *From History to Sociology*. Detroit: Wayne State University Press.

Apsel, J., and H. Fein (2002) *Teaching About Genocide: An Interdisciplinary Guidebook with Syllabi for College and University Teachers*. Washington, DC: American Sociological Association, for the Institute for the Study of Genocide.

Arendt, H. (1967) *The Origins of Totalitarianism*. London: Allen & Unwin.

Banks, M., and M. Wolfe (1999) 'Ethnicity and Reports of the 1992–95 Bosnian Conflict', in T. Allen and J. Seaton, eds, *The Media of Conflict: War Reporting and Representations of Ethnic Violence*. London: Zed, 147–61.

Barnett, M. (2002) *Eyewitness to a Genocide: The United Nations and Rwanda*. Ithaca, NY: Cornell University Press.

Bartov, O. (2000) *Mirrors of Destruction: War, Genocide and Modern Identity*. Oxford: Oxford University Press.

Bauer, Y. (1982) *A History of the Holocaust*. New York: F. Watts.

Bauman, Z. (1989) *Modernity and the Holocaust*. Cambridge: Polity.

Beck, U. (1992) *Risk Society*. London: Sage.

—— (2000) 'Risk Society Revisited', in B. Adam, U. Beck and J. van Loon, eds, *Risk Society and Beyond*. London: Sage: 211–29.

Becker, J. (1996) *Hungry Ghosts: China's Secret Famine*. London: John Murray.

Bell-Fialkoff, A. (1993) 'A Brief History of Ethnic Cleansing', *Foreign Affairs*, 72, 3.

—— (1996) *Ethnic Cleansing*. Basingstoke: Macmillan.

Best, G. (1984) *Civilians in Contemporary Wars: A Problem in Ethics, Law, and Fact*. London: King's College Department of War Studies, <http://www.airpower.maxwell.af.mil/airchronicles/aureview/1984/mar-apr/best.html>.

Bloxham, D. (2005) *The Great Game of Genocide*. Oxford: Oxford University Press.

—— (forthcoming) 'Bureaucracy and Mass Murder: A Comparative Historical Analysis'.

Bringa, T. (2002) ' "Averted Gaze": Genocide in Bosnia-Herzegovina 1992–1995', in A. L. Hinton, ed., *Annihilating Difference: The Anthropology of Genocide*. Berkeley: University of California Press, 194–228.

Browning, C. R. (1992) *The Path to Genocide*. Cambridge: Cambridge University Press.

—— (1992) *Ordinary Men: Reserve Police Battalion 101 and the Final Solution in Poland*. New York: Harper Collins.

Browning, C. R. (2000) *Nazi Policy, Jewish Workers, German Killers.* Cambridge: Cambridge University Press.

Bucaille, L. (2004) *Growing Up Palestinian: Israeli Occupation and the Intifada Generation.* Princeton, NJ: Princeton University Press.

Burger, T. (1987) *Max Weber's Theory of Concept Formation: History, Laws and Ideal Types.* Durham, NC: Duke University Press.

Buzan, B. (2002) 'Who May We Bomb?' in K. Booth and T. Dunne, eds, *Worlds in Collision: Terror and the Future of Global Order.* London: Palgrave, 85–94.

Chalk, F. (1994) 'Redefining Genocide', in G. A. Andreopoulous, ed., *Genocide: Conceptual and Historical Dimensions.* Philadelphia: University of Pennsylvania Press, 47–63.

Chalk, F., and K. Jonassohn (1990) *The History and Sociology of Genocide: Analyses and Case Studies.* New Haven, CT: Yale University Press.

Charny, I. W. (1991) 'The Psychology of Denial of Known Genocides', in Charny, ed., *Genocide: A Critical Bibliographical Review*, vol. 2. London: Mansell, 3–37.

—— (1994) 'Toward a Generic Definition of Genocide', in G. A. Andreopoulous, ed., *Genocide: Conceptual and Historical Dimensions.* Philadelphia: University of Pennsylvania Press, 64–94.

—— (2001) 'Foreword', in A. S. Rosenbaum, ed., *Is the Holocaust Unique? Perspectives on Comparative Genocide.* Boulder, CO: Westview, ix–xvi.

Chesterman, S., ed. (2001) *Civilians in War.* Boulder, CO: Lynne Rienner.

Clark, H. (2000) *Civil Resistance in Kosovo.* London: Pluto.

Clausewitz, C. von (1976) *On War*, ed. M. Howard and P. Paret. Princeton, NJ: Princeton University Press.

Cobb, R. (1987) *The People's Armies: The* Armées Révolutionnaires, *Instrument of the Terror in the Departments April 1793 to Floréal Year II*, trans. M. Elliott. New Haven, CT: Yale University Press.

Cohen, S. (2001) *States of Denial: Knowing about Atrocities and Suffering.* Cambridge: Polity.

Conquest, R. (1986) *The Harvest of Sorrow: Soviet Collectivization and the Terror Famine.* London: Hutchinson.

—— (1990) *The Great Terror: A Reassessment.* London: Hutchinson.

Coward, M. (2004) 'Urbicide in Bosnia', in S. Graham, ed., *Cities, War and Terrorism.* Oxford: Blackwell, 154–71.

Crawford, J. (1988) *The Rights of Peoples.* Oxford: Clarendon Press.

Cushman, T. (2004) 'Anthropology and Genocide in the Balkans: An Analysis of Conceptual Practices of Power', *Anthropological Theory*, 4, 1, 5–28.

Dadrian, V. N. (2001) 'The Comparative Aspects of the Armenian and Jewish Cases of Genocide: A Sociohistorical Perspective', in A. S. Rosenbaum, ed., *Is the Holocaust Unique? Perspectives on Comparative Genocide*. Boulder, CO: Westview, 133–68.

Davidowicz, L. (1985) *The War Against the Jews*. London: Penguin.

Davis, M. (2000) *Late Victorian Holocausts*. London: Verso.

Delbo, C. (1995) *Auschwitz and After*, trans. R. C. Lamont. New Haven, CT: Yale University Press.

Durkheim, E. (1982) *The Rules of Sociological Method, and Selected Texts on Sociology and its Method*, trans. W. D. Halls. London: Macmillan.

—— (1984) *The Division of Labour in Society*, trans. W. D. Halls, London: Macmillan.

Eltringham, N. (2004) *Accounting for Horror: Post-Genocide Debates in Rwanda*. London: Pluto.

Evans, R. (2001) *Lying About Hitler: History, the Holocaust and the David Irving Trial*. Harmondsworth: Penguin.

Fein, H. (1990) 'Genocide: A Sociological Perspective', *Current Sociology*, 38, 1.

—— (1994) 'Genocide, Terror, Life Integrity and War Crimes', in G. A. Andreopoulous, ed., *Genocide: Conceptual and Historical Dimensions*. Philadelphia: University of Pennsylvania Press, 95–108.

Finkelstein, N. (2000) *The Holocaust Industry*. London: Verso.

Foucault, M. (1998) *The Will to Knowledge: The History of Sexuality*, vol. 1, trans. R. Hurley. Harmondsworth: Penguin.

—— (2003) *Society Must Be Defended: Lectures at the Collège de France, 1975–76*, trans. D. Macey. New York: Picador.

Gellately, R. (2001) *Backing Hitler: Consent and Coercion in Nazi Germany*. New York and Oxford: Oxford University Press.

Geras, N. (1998) *The Contract of Mutual Indifference: Political Philosophy after the Holocaust*. London: Verso.

Giddens, A. (1984) *The Constitution of Society: Outline of the Theory of Structuration*. Cambridge: Polity.

—— (1985) *The Nation-State and Violence*. Cambridge: Polity.

Glass, C. (2004) ' "It Was Necessary to Uproot Them" ', *London Review of Books*, 24 June, 4–6.

Glatzer, W. (n.d.) 'German Sociological Association', <http://www.soziologie.de/dgs/history.htm#3.%20Die%20DGS%20und%20der%20NS>.

Goldhagen, D. J. (1996) *Hitler's Willing Executioners: Ordinary Germans and the Holocaust*. New York: Little, Brown.

Gordon, S. (1984) *Hitler, Germans and the 'Jewish Question'*. Princeton, NJ: Princeton University Press.

Gourevich, P. (2000) *We Wish to Inform You that Tomorrow We Will be Killed with our Families: Stories from Rwanda*. London: Picador.

Graham, S., ed. (2004) *Cities, War and Terrorism: Towards an Urban Geopolitics*. Oxford: Blackwell.

Grass, G. (2002) *Crabwalk*. London: Faber & Faber.

Gray, C. (2000) *International Law and the Use of Force*. Oxford: Oxford University Press.

Green, B. B. (2001) 'Stalinist Terror and the Question of Genocide: The Great Famine', in A. S. Rosenbaum, ed., *Is the Holocaust Unique?* Boulder, CO: Westview, 169–89.

H-Genocide (discussion network) <http://www.h-net.org/~genocide>.

Hamburg Institute for Social Research (1999) *The German Army and Genocide: Crimes Against War Prisoners, Jews and Other Civilians in the East, 1939–1944*. New York: New Press.

Hancock, I. (2001) 'Responses to the Porrajmos: The Romani Holocaust', in A. S. Rosenbaum, ed., *Is the Holocaust Unique?* Boulder, CO: Westview, 69–95.

Hanson, J. K. M. (1992) *The Civilian Population and the Warsaw Uprising of 1944*. Cambridge: Cambridge University Press.

Harff, B., and T. R. Gurr (2002) *Ethnic Conflict in World Politics*, 2nd edn. Boulder, CO: Westview.

Hilberg, R. (1993) *Perpetrators, Victims, Bystanders : The Jewish Catastrophe 1933–1945*. London: Lime Tree.

Hinton, A. L., ed. (2002) *Annihilating Difference: The Anthropology of Genocide*. Berkeley: University of California Press.

—— (2002) 'The Dark Side of Modernity: Toward an Anthropology of Genocide', in Hinton, ed., *Annihilating Difference*. Berkeley: University of California Press, 1–42.

Hirsch, H. (1995) *Genocide and the Politics of Memory: Studying Death to Preserve Life*. Chapel Hill: University of North Carolina Press.

Hirsh, D. (2003) *Law Against Genocide: Cosmopolitan Trials*. London: Glasshouse.

Hirst, P. Q. (1997) 'The International Origins of National Sovereignty', in *From Statism to Pluralism: Democracy, Civil Society and Global Politics*. London: Routledge, 216–35.

Homans, G. C. (1951) *The Human Group*. London: Routledge.

Honderich, T. (2004) 'Terrorism for Humanity', lecture to the International Social Philosophy Conference, Boston, <http://www.ucl.ac.uk/~uctytho/terrforhum.html>.

Honwana, A. (2001) 'Children of War: Understanding War and War Cleansing in Mozambique and Angola', in S. Chesterman, ed., *Civilians in War*. Boulder, CO: Lynne Rienner, 123–44.

Horowitz, D. L. (2001) *The Deadly Ethnic Riot*. Berkeley: University of California Press.

Hull, I. (2004) *Absolute Destruction: Military Culture and Practices of War in Imperial Germany*. Ithaca, NJ: Cornell University Press.

Human Rights Watch (1996) *Shattered Lives: Sexual Violence during the Rwandan Genocide and its Aftermath*. New York: Human Rights Watch.

—— (2004) *Darfur Destroyed: Ethnic Cleansing by Government and Militia Forces in Western Sudan*. New York: Human Rights Watch.

Huttenbach, H. (2002) 'From the Editor: Towards a Conceptual Definition of Genocide', *Journal of Genocide Research*, 4, 167–75.

Ignatieff, M. (2001) 'The Legacy of Raphael Lemkin', Washington, DC: United States Holocaust Memorial Museum, <http://www.ushmm.org/conscience/analysis/index.php?content=details.php%3Fcontent%3D2000–12–13%26menupage%3DHistory%2B%2526%2BConcept>.

International Commission of Inquiry on Darfur (2005) *Report of the International Commission of Inquiry on Darfur*, <http://www.un.org/News/dh/sudan/com_inq_darfur.pdf>.

International Tribunal for Violations of International Law in the Former Yugoslavia, Appeals Chamber (2004) review of 'Prosecutor v. Radislav Krstic', Case No. IT-98-33-T, <http://www.un.org/icty/krstic/Appeal/judgement/index.htm>.

Jackson Preece, J. (1998) *National Minorities and the European Nation-States System*. Oxford: Clarendon Press.

Jacobs, S. L., ed. (1992), *Raphael Lemkin's Thoughts on Genocide: Not Guilty*. Lewiston, NY: Edwin Mellen Press.

Jefremovas, V. (2002) *Brickyards to Graveyards: From Production to Genocide in Rwanda*. Albany: State University of New York Press.

Joas, H. (2003) *War and Modernity*. Cambridge: Polity.

Joeden-Forgey, E. von (2005) Review of V. Jefremovas, *Brickyards to Graveyards*, http://www.h-net.org/reviews/showrev.cgi?path=80031109089734.

Jorgensen, N. H. (2001) 'The Definition of Genocide: Joining the Dots in the Light of Recent Practice', *International Criminal Law Review*, 1, 285–313.

Jones, A. (2000) 'Gendercide and Genocide', *Journal of Genocide Research*, 2, 2, 185–211.

Jones, A. (2004) *Gendercide and Genocide*. Nashville: Vanderbilt University Press.

——, ed. (2004) *Genocide, War Crimes and the West*. London: Zed.

Judah, T. (2000) *Kosovo: War and Revenge*. New Haven, CT: Yale University Press.

Kaldor, M. (1999) *New & Old Wars*. Cambridge: Polity.

Kansteiner, W. (2001) 'The Rise and Fall of Metaphor: German Historians and the Uniqueness of the Holocaust', in A. S. Rosenbaum, ed., *Is the Holocaust Unique?* Boulder, CO: Westview, 221–44.

Katz, S. T. (1994) *The Holocaust in Historical Context*, vol. 1. New York: Oxford University Press.

Kedward, H. R. (1993) *In Search of the Maquis: Rural Resistance in Southern France, 1942–1944*. Oxford: Clarendon Press.

Kiernan, B., ed. (1993) *Genocide and Democracy in Cambodia: The Khmer Rouge, the United Nations and the International Community*. New Haven, CT: Yale University Southeast Asia Studies.

—— (1996) *The Pol Pot Regime: Race, Power and Genocide in Cambodia under the Khmer Rouge, 1975–79*. New Haven, CT: Yale University Press.

—— (2002) 'Cover-up and Denial of Genocide: Australia, the USA, East Timor, and the Aborigines', *Critical Asian Studies*, 34, 2, 163–92.

Klinghoffer, A. J. (1998) *The International Dimension of Genocide in Rwanda*. Basingstoke: Macmillan.

Korrey, W. (2001) *Epitaph for Raphael Lemkin*. New York: Jacob Blaustein Institute for the Advancement of Human Rights.

Kuper, L. (1981) *Genocide*. Harmondsworth: Penguin.

Kuperman, A. J. (2001) *The Limits of Humanitarian Intervention: Genocide in Rwanda*. Washington, DC: Brookings Institution Press.

—— (2004) 'Provoking Genocide: A Revised History of the Rwandan Patriotic Front', *Journal of Genocide Research*, 6, 1, 61–84.

Lemarchand, R. (1996) *Burundi: Ethnic Conflict and Genocide*. Cambridge: Cambridge University Press.

—— (1998) 'Genocide in the Great Lakes: Which Genocide? Whose Genocide?' New Haven, CT: Yale University Genocide Studies Program Working Papers.

Lemkin, R. (1933) *Acts Constituting a General (Transnational) Danger Considered as Offences Against the Law of Nations*, trans. James Fussell, <http://www.preventgenocide.org/lemkin/madrid1933-english.htm>.

Lemkin, R. (1944) *Axis Rule in Occupied Europe: Laws of Occupation, Analysis of Government, Proposals for Redress.* New York: Carnegie Endowment for International Peace.

Levene, M. (1999) 'The Chittagong Hill Tracts: A Case Study in the Political Economy of "Creeping" Genocide', *Third World Quarterly*, 20, 2, 339 – 69.

—— (2004) 'A Dissenting Voice', Parts I and II, *Journal of Genocide Research*, 6, 2, 153–66, and 6, 3, 431–46.

—— (2005) *Genocide in the Age of the Nation State*, 2 vols. London: I. B. Tauris.

Lipstadt, D. (1996) *Denying the Holocaust: The Growing Assault on Truth and Memory.* Harmondsworth: Penguin.

Lopate, P. (1989) 'Resistance to the Holocaust', in D. Rosenberg, ed., *Testimony: Contemporary Writers Make the Holocaust Personal.* New York: Random House, 285–308.

Macmillan, M. (2003) *Paris 1919.* New York: Random House.

Magnorella, P. J. (2002) 'Recent Developments in the International Law of Genocide: An Anthropological Perspective on the International Criminal Tribunal for Rwanda', in A. L. Hinton, ed., *Annihilating Difference.* Berkeley: University of California Press, 310–24.

Malkki, L. H. (1995) *Purity and Exile: Violence, Memory, and National Cosmology among Hutu Refugees in Tanzania.* Chicago and London: University of Chicago Press.

Mamdani, M. (2001) *When Victims Become Killers: Colonialism, Nativism and the Genocide in Rwanda.* Princeton, NJ: Princeton University Press.

Mann, M. (1986, 1993) *The Sources of Social Power,* vols I and II. Cambridge: Cambridge University Press.

—— (2004) *Fascists.* Cambridge: Cambridge University Press.

—— (2005) *The Dark Side of Democracy: Explaining Ethnic Cleansing.* Cambridge: Cambridge University Press.

Marcuse, H. (1965) 'Industrialization and Capitalism', *New Left Review*, 30, March–April, 3–17.

Marx, K. (1992) *Capital*, vol. I. Harmondsworth: Penguin.

Masalha, N. (1997) *A Land without a People: Israel, Transfer and the Palestinians 1949–96.* London: Faber.

Maybury-Lewis, D. (2002) 'Genocide against Indigenous Peoples', in A. L. Hinton, ed., *Annihilating Difference.* Berkeley: University of California Press, 43–53.

Melson, R. F. (1996) *Revolution and Genocide: On the Origins of the Armenian Genocide and the Holocaust.* Chicago: University of Chicago Press.

Melson, R. F. (2001) 'The Armenian Genocide as Precursor and Prototype', in A. S. Rosenbaum, ed., *Is the Holocaust Unique?* Boulder, CO: Westview, 119–32.

Melvern, L. R. (2000) *A People Betrayed: The Role of the West in Rwanda's Genocide.* London: Zed.

Mettraux, G. (2005) *International Crimes and the* ad hoc *Tribunals,* Oxford: Oxford University Press.

Mills, C. W. (1959) *The Sociological Imagination.* London: Oxford University Press.

Morris, B. (2004) *The Birth of the Palestinian Refugee Problem Revisited.* Cambridge: Cambridge University Press.

Moses, A. D. (2002) 'Conceptual Blockages and Definitional Dilemmas in the "Racial Century"', *Patterns of Prejudice,* 36, 4, 7–36.

Mulaj, K. (2003) 'Ethnic Cleansing in Yugoslavia in the 1990s', in S. B. Vardy and T. H. Tooley, eds, *Ethnic Cleansing in Twentieth-Century Europe.* Boulder, CO: Social Science Monographs, 693–711.

Nabulsi, K. (2001) 'Evolving Conceptions of Civilians and Belligerents: One Hundred Years after the Hague Peace Conferences', in S. Chesterman, ed., *Civilians in War.* Boulder, CO: Lynne Rienner.

Naimark, N. M. (2001) *Fires of Hatred: Ethnic Cleansing in Twentieth-Century Europe.* Cambridge, MA: Harvard University Press.

Natsios, A. S. (2001) *The Great North Korean Famine: Famine, Politics, and Foreign Policy.* Washington, DC: US Institute of Peace Press.

Neu, D., and R. Therrien (2003) *Accounting for Genocide: Canada's Bureaucratic Assault on Indigenous People.* London: Zed.

Novick, P. (2000) *The Holocaust and Collective Memory: The American Experience.* London: Bloomsbury.

Omaar, R., and A. de Waal (1994) *Rwanda: Death, Despair and Defiance.* London: Africa Rights.

O'Neill, B. E. (1991) 'The Intifada in the Context of Armed Struggle', in R. O. Freedman, ed., *The Intifada: Its Impact on Israel, the Arab World, and the Superpowers.* Miami: Florida International University Press, 37–69.

Osiel, M. (2000) *Mass Atrocity, Collective Memory, and the Law.* New Brunswick, NJ: Transaction.

Palmer, A. (1998) 'Colonial and Modern Genocide: Explanations and Categories', *Ethnic and Racial Studies,* 21, 1, 89–115.

—— (2000) *Colonial Genocide.* Adelaide: Crawford House.

Palyi, M. (1946) Review of R. Lemkin, *Axis Rule in Occupied Europe, American Journal of Sociology,* 51, 5, 496–7.

Parsons, T. (1972) *The Social System.* London: Tavistock.

Petrovic, D. (1994) 'Ethnic Cleansing – An Attempt at Methodology', *European Journal of International Law*, 5, 3, 1–19, <http://www.ejil.org/journal/Vol5/No3/art3.html>.

Plant, R. (1987) *The Pink Triangle: The Nazi War Against Homosexuals*. Edinburgh: Mainstream.

Porteous, J. D., and S. E. Smith (2001) *Domicide: The Global Destruction of Home*. Montreal: McGill–Queen's University Press.

Power, S. (2003) *'A Problem from Hell': America and the Age of Genocide*. London: Flamingo.

Prunier, G. (1995) *The Rwanda Crisis: History of a Genocide*. London: Hurst.

—— (2005) *Darfur: The Ambiguous Genocide*. London: Hurst.

—— (2006) *From Genocide to Continental War: The Congolese Conflict and the Crisis of Contemporary Africa*. London: Hurst.

Ratner, S. R., and J. S. Abrams (2001) *Accountability for Human Rights Atrocities in International Law: Beyond the Nuremberg Legacy*. Oxford: Oxford University Press.

Reid, J. J. (1992) 'Total War, the Annihilation Ethic, and the Armenian Genocide, 1870–1918', in R. G. Hovanissian, ed., *The Armenian Genocide: History, Politics, Ethics*. Basingstoke: Macmillan, 21–52.

Reuter, C. (2004) *My Life is a Weapon: A Modern History of Suicide Bombing*. Princeton, NJ: Princeton University Press.

Rex, J. (1971) 'Typology and Objectivity: A Comment on Weber's Four Sociological Methods', in A. Sahay, ed., *Max Weber and Modern Sociology*. London: Routledge & Kegan Paul, 17–35.

Rigby, A. (1994) *Living the Intifada*. London: Zed.

Ringer, F. (1997) *Max Weber's Methodology: The Unification of the Social and Cultural Sciences*. Cambridge, MA: Harvard University Press.

Rittner, Carol (2004) 'Educating about Genocide, Yes: But What Kind of Education?', in S. Totten, ed., *Teaching About Genocide*. Greenwich, CT: Information Age, 1–5.

Rizer, K. (2001) 'Bombing Dual-Use Targets: Legal, Ethical, and Doctrinal Perspectives'. *Airpower Chronicles*, <http://www.airpower.maxwell.af.mil/airchronicles/cc/Rizer.html>.

Roberts, A. (1967) 'Civilian Defence Strategy', in Roberts, ed., *The Strategy of Civilian Defence*. London: Faber & Faber, 215–54.

Roberts, A., and R. Guelff, eds (1999) *Documents on the Laws of War*. Oxford: Oxford University Press.

Rosenbaum, A. S., ed. (2001) *Is the Holocaust Unique? Perspectives on Comparative Genocide*. Boulder, CO: Westview.

Rosenfeld, G. D. (1999) 'The Politics of Uniqueness: Reflections on the Recent Polemical Turn in Holocaust and Genocide Scholarship', *Holocaust and Genocide Studies*, 13, 1, 28–62.

Roth, J. K. (2001) 'The Ethics of Uniqueness', in A. S. Rosenbaum, ed., *Is the Holocaust Unique?* Boulder, CO: Westview, 21–32.

Rummel, R. J. (1997) *Death by Government*. New Brunswick, NJ: Transaction.

Sayigh, Y. (1997) *Armed Struggle and the Search for State: The Palestinian National Movement, 1949–1993*. Oxford: Oxford University Press.

Schabas, W. A. (2000) *Genocide in International Law*. Cambridge: Cambridge University Press.

Schafft, G. E. (2002) 'Scientific Racism in the Third Reich: German Anthropologists in the Nazi Era', in A. L. Hinton, ed., *Annihilating Difference*. Berkeley: University of California Press, 117–34.

—— (2004) *From Racism to Genocide: Anthropology in the Third Reich*. Urbana: University of Illinois Press.

Scheper-Hughes, N. (2002) 'Coming to our Senses: Anthropology and Genocide', in A. L. Hinton, ed., *Annihilating Difference*. Berkeley: University of California Press, 348–81.

Scott, A. (2000) 'Risk Society or Angst Society?', in B. Adam, U. Beck and J. van Loon, eds, *Risk Society and Beyond*. London: Sage, 33–45.

Semelin, J. (1993) *Unarmed Against Hitler: Civilian Resistance in Europe, 1939–1943*. Westport, CT: Praeger.

Shaw, M. (1988) *Dialectics of War: An Essay in the Social Theory of War and Peace*. London: Pluto.

—— (1991) *Post-Military Society: War, Militarization and Demilitarization at the End of the Twentieth Century*. Cambridge: Polity.

—— (2000) *Theory of the Global State: Globality as Unfinished Revolution*. Cambridge: Cambridge University Press.

—— (2003) *War and Genocide: Organized Killing in Modern Society*. Cambridge: Polity.

—— (2004) 'New Wars of the City: "Urbicide" and "Genocide"', in S. Graham, ed., *Cities, War and Terrorism*. Oxford: Blackwell, 141–53.

—— (2005) *The New Western Way of War: Risk-Transfer War and its Crisis in Iraq*. Cambridge: Polity.

Shaw, M. N. (1997) *International Law*. Cambridge: Cambridge University Press.

Shirer, W. L. (1941) *Berlin Diary: The Journal of a Foreign Correspondent 1934–1941*. London: Hamish Hamilton.

Slim, H. (2003) 'Why Protect Civilians? Innocence, Immunity and Enmity in War', *International Affairs*, 79, 3, 481–501.

—— (2004) 'Dithering over Darfur? A Preliminary Review of the International Response', *International Affairs*, 80, 5, 811–28.

Sofsky, W. (1997) *The Order of Terror: The Concentration Camp.* Princeton, NJ: Princeton University Press.

Stangor, C. (2004) *Social Groups in Action and Interaction.* Hove: Psychology Press.

Stannard, D. E. (1992) *American Holocaust: The Conquest of the New World.* Oxford: Oxford University Press.

—— (2001) 'Uniqueness as Denial: The Politics of Genocide Scholarship', in A. S. Rosenbaum, ed., *Is the Holocaust Unique?* Boulder, CO: Westview, 245–90.

Stanton, G. H. (1993) 'The Cambodian Genocide and International Law', in B. Kiernan, ed., *Genocide and Democracy in Cambodia.* New Haven, CT: Yale University Southeast Asia Studies.

Staub, E. (1989) *The Roots of Evil: The Origins of Genocide and Other Group Violence.* New York: Cambridge University Press.

Stein, S. D. (2002) 'Geno and Other Cides: A Cautionary Note on the Accumulation of Knowledge', *Journal of Genocide Research*, 4, 1, 39–63.

—— (2003) 'Ethnocide', in E. Cashmore, ed., *Encyclopedia of Race and Ethnic Studies.* London: Routledge.

Stone, D. (2004) 'Genocide as Transgression', *European Journal of Social Theory*, 7, 1, 45–65.

Tatz, C. (2003) *With Intent to Destroy: Reflecting on Genocide.* London: Verso.

Taylor, C. C. (2002) 'The Cultural Face of Terror in the Rwandan Genocide of 1994', in A. L. Hinton, ed., *Annihilating Difference.* Berkeley: University of California Press, 137–78.

Thompson, E. P. (1982) 'Exterminism: The Last Stage of Civilization', in New Left Review, ed., *Exterminism and Cold War.* London: Verso, 1–34.

Tönnies, F. (1998) *Community and Society*, trans. C. P. Loomis. New Brunswick, NJ: Transaction.

Totten, S., ed. (2004) *Teaching About Genocide: Issues, Approaches and Resources.* Greenwich, T: Information Age.

Totten, S., W. S. Parsons and I. W. Charny, eds (1997) *Century of Genocide: Eyewitness Accounts and Critical Views.* New York: Garland.

Totten, S., W. S. Parsons and R. H. Hitchcock (2002) 'Confronting Genocide and Ethnocide of Indigenous Peoples', in A. L. Hinton, ed., *Annihilating Difference*. Berkeley: University of California Press, 54–94.

Trotsky, L. D. (1965) *History of the Russian Revolution*. London: Gollancz.

United Nations (1948) *Convention on the Prevention and Punishment of the Crime of Genocide*, in A. Roberts and R. Guelff, eds, *Documents on the Laws of War*. Oxford: Oxford University Press, 181–94.

United Nations Commission on Human Rights, Sub-Commission on Prevention of Discrimination and Protection of Minorities (1997) *Freedom of Movement: Human Rights and Population Transfer*, final report of the Special Rapporteur, A. S. Al-Khasawneh, <http://www.hri.ca/fortherecord1997/documentation/subcommission/e-cn4-sub2–1997–23.htm>.

Vardy, S. B., and T. H. Tooley, eds. (2003) *Ethnic Cleansing in Twentieth-Century Europe*. Boulder, CO: Social Science Monographs.

Walzer, M. (1992) *Just and Unjust Wars*, 2nd edn. New York: Basic Books.

Warren, M. A. (1985) *Gendercide: The Implications of Sex Selection*. Totowa, NJ: Rowman & Allanheld.

Weber, E. (1977) *Peasants into Frenchmen: The Modernization of Rural France 1870–1914*. London: Chatto & Windus.

Weber, M. (1964) *The Theory of Social and Economic Organization*, ed. T. Parsons. New York: Free Press of Glencoe.

Weitz, E. (2003) *A Century of Genocide: Utopias of Race and Nation*. Princeton, NJ: Princeton University Press.

Zayas, A. M. de (1979) *Nemesis at Potsdam: The Anglo-Americans and the Expulsion of the Germans*, 2nd edn. London: Routledge & Kegan Paul.

Zunes, S., L. R. Kurtz, and S. B. Asher, eds (1999) *Non-Violent Social Movements*. Oxford: Blackwell.

Index